12g

D1520619

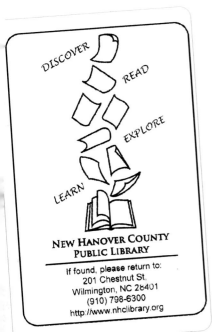

The Atlantic Coast Conference
1953–1978

The Atlantic Coast Conference
1953–1978

Silver Anniversary

Bruce A. Corrie

Carolina Academic Press
Durham, North Carolina

© 1978 Carolina Academic Press
All Rights Reserved
ISBN Number: 0-089089-025-0
Library of Congress Card Number: 78-67832

Carolina Academic Press
P.O. Box 8791
Durham, North Carolina 27707

Printed in the United States of America

To my wife, Jane, my daughters, Linda and Bonnie, and my mother and father for their love and support.

Contents

List of Illustrations
(with full captions)

The pictures selected for this book were coordinated by the author with the Sports Information Directors of each of the member institutions. Only those athletes and coaches who were outstanding in college during the 25 year period, 1953–1978, were considered. Unfortunately, there was not room to include everyone, nor was consideration given to those who excelled before 1953 or did not reach acclaim until their professional career.

55 **Dickie Hemric,** Wake Forest, All-American 1954 and 1955, ACC Basketball Player of the Year in 1954 and 1955, ACC Athete of the Year 1955, All-ACC Basketball 1954 and 1955, ACC All-time leading scorer with 2587 points (4 years). **Buzz Wilkinson,** Virginia, All-American 1955, All-ACC Basketball 1954 and 1955, Highest scoring average in ACC with 32.1 points per game in 1955, Leading scorer career (2233 points) and season (898 points) at Virginia. **Grady Wallace,** South Carolina, All-American 1957, All-ACC Basketball 1957, Nation's leading scorer in 1957 with a 31.2 average.

56 **Reynolds Coliseum,** Raleigh, N.C., Site of ACC Championships 1954–1966, Site of Dixie Classic 1949–1960. **Ronnie Shavlik,** North Carolina State, All-American 1955 and 1956, ACC Basketball Player of the Year 1956, All-ACC Basketball 1955 and 1956, Leading rebounder for North Carolina State for single game (35), season (58l), and career (1598). **Everett Case,** North Carolina State, Head Basketball Coach 1947–1964, ACC Basketball Coach of the Year 1954, 1955, and 1958, ACC Champions 1954, 1955, 1956, 1959.

60 **Dave Sime,** Duke, All-American in track, World record holder in 1956 in 220 yard dash and 220 yard low hurdles, Silver Medal in 100 meter dash in 1960 Olympics. **Dick Christy,** North Carolina State, All-American 1957, ACC Football Player of the Year 1957, ACC Athlete of the Year 1958, All-ACC Football 1957. **Bob Pellegrini,** Maryland, All-American 1955, ACC Football Player of the Year 1955, All-ACC Football 1955.

65 **University of North Carolina NCAA Basketball Champions,** 1957, Pre-game line-up in finals against Kansas, Coach Frank McGuire, Joe Quigg (41), Tommy Kearns (40), Pete Brennan (35), Bob Cunningham (32), and Lennie Rosenbluth (10). **Lennie Rosenbluth,** North Carolina, All-American 1955, 1956, and 1957, ACC Basketball Player of the Year 1957, ACC Athlete of the Year 1957, National Player of the Year 1957, Second leading career scorer at North Carolina (2045 points), All-ACC Basketball 1955, 1956, and 1957.

68 **Bud Millikan,** Maryland, Head Basketball Coach 1951–1967, ACC Basketball Championship 1958, and **Gene Shue,** Maryland, All-American 1954, All-ACC Basketball 1954, Second leading season scorer (654 points) and third leading career scorer (1397 points) at Maryland. **William W. (Bill) Cobey,** Maryland, Athletic Director 1956–1968.

71 **1953 Football National Champions,** University of Maryland, Athletic Director Bill Cobey and Head Coach Jim Tatum with coaching staff. **University of North Carolina,** Dixie Classic Champions 1956, ACC Champions 1957, Eastern Regional Champions 1957, NCAA Basketball Champions 1957, Undefeated in 32 games.

81 **Vic Bubas,** Duke, Head Basketball Coach 1960–1969, ACC Coach of the Year 1963, 1964, and 1966, 2nd in NCAA 1964, 3rd in NCAA 1963 and 1966, Commissioner of the Sun Belt Conference 1976 to present. **Jeff Mullins,** Duke, All-American 1964, ACC Basketball Player of the Year 1964, ACC Athlete of the Year 1964, All-ACC Basketball 1962, 1963, and 1964. **Art Heyman,** Duke, All-American 1961, 1962, and 1963, National Player of the Year 1963, ACC Basketball Player of the Year 1963, All-ACC Basketball 1961, 1962, and 1963, All-time leading scorer at Duke (1,984 points). **Bob Verga,** Duke, All-American 1967, All-ACC Basketball 1965, 1966, and 1967, Highest season average at Duke with 26.1 points per game in 1967.

91   **Greensboro Coliseum,** Greensboro, N.C., Site of ACC Championships 1967, 1971–1975, 1977–1978. **Charlotte Coliseum,** Charlotte, N.C., Site of ACC Championships 1968–1970.

94   **Billy Cunningham,** North Carolina, All-American 1964 and 1965, ACC Basketball Player of the Year 1965, All-ACC Basketball 1963, 1964, and 1965, Leading career rebounder at North Carolina (1062). **Charlie Scott,** North Carolina, All-American 1969 and 1970, ACC Athlete of the Year 1970, All-ACC Basketball 1968, 1969, and 1970, Third leading career scorer at North Carolina (2007 points).

98   **Roman Gabriel,** North Carolina State, All-American 1960 and 1961, ACC Football Player of the Year 1960 and 1961, ACC Athlete of the Year 1961, All-ACC Football 1960 and 1961. **Brian Piccolo,** Wake Forest, All-American 1964, ACC Football Player of the Year 1964, All-ACC Football 1964, ACC Athlete of the Year 1965, Led nation in rushing (1044 yards) and scoring (111 points) in 1964.

99   **Len Chappell,** Wake Forest, All-American, ACC Basketball Player of the Year 1961 and 1962, ACC Athlete of the Year 1962, All-ACC Basketball 1960, 1961, and 1962, and **Horace (Bones) McKinney,** Wake Forest, Head Basketball Coach 1958–1965, ACC Coach of the Year 1960 and 1961, 3rd in NCAA in 1962. **Randy Mahaffey,** Clemson, All-ACC Basketball 1967, Third leading rebounder at Clemson (705), One of four brothers to play basketball 12 consecutive years at Clemson. **Rusty Adkins,** Clemson, All-American Baseball 1965, 1966, and 1967, All-ACC Baseball 1965, 1966, and 1967, Led ACC in 7 0f 9 categories in 1967.

100   **Buddy Gore,** Clemson, ACC Football Player of the Year 1967, All-ACC Football 1967, Leading career rusher (2571 yards) and season (1045 yards) at Clemson, Gore (44) gained 117 yards in opening game win, 40–35, over Virginia in 1966. **Frank Quayle,** Virginia, ACC Football Player of the Year 1968, ACC Athlete of the Year 1969, All-ACC Football 1967 and 1968, Varsity lacrosse, Second leading career (2695 yards), season (1213 yards), and game (221 yards) rusher at Virginia.

105   **Tom McMillen,** Maryland, All-American 1972, 1973, and 1974, All-ACC Basketball 1972 and 1973, Rhodes Scholar, Single season scoring leader (667 points) and second leading career scorer (1807 points) at Maryland.

116   **Emmett Voelkel** of Virginia (#29 white) scores against goalie **Gary Niels** of Maryland in Scott Stadium in 1975, when Virginia beat Maryland 14–13. **1972 NCAA Lacrosse Champions,** University of Virginia, Head Coach Glenn Thiel and Jay Connor receive trophy from Bruce Allison and Maryland Lt. Governor Blair Lee at College Park, Md. **Pete Eldridge,** Virginia, All-American Lacrosse 1971 and 1972, Career record goals (94) and goals in a season (36) at Virginia, National Player of the Year 1972, MVP in Hero's Tournament 1972 and North-South Game 1972. **1973 NCAA Lacrosse Champions,** University of Maryland, Head Coach Bud Beardmore receives trophy from Fred Shabel, Athletic Director at Pennsylvania, site of Championship game, Doug Schreiber (#26) Player of the Year.

125   **North Carolina State,** Big Four Champions 1974, ACC Champions 1974, Eastern Regional Champions 1974, NCAA Basketball Champions 1974, Record

30–1. **David Thompson** scores two of his 21 points in leading North Carolina State to a 76–64 victory over Marquette in the 1974 NCAA Championship game in the Greensboro Coliseum. Tom Burleson watches in the background.

135 **Capital Centre,** Landover, Md., Site of the 1976 ACC Championship. **Greensboro Coliseum,** N.C. State vs. Wake Forest, Big 4 Action.

137 **1976 USA Olympic Team,** First row (left to right): **Head Coach Dean Smith** (North Carolina); **Assistant Coach Bill Guthridge** (North Carolina); Manager Joe Vancisin (NABC); **Walter Davis** (North Carolina); Adrian Dantley (Notre Dame); Ernie Grunfeld (Tennessee); **Steve Sheppard** (Maryland); **Tate Armstrong** (Duke); Quinn Buckner (Indiana); **Phil Ford** (North Carolina); Second row (left to right): Assistant Coach John Thompson (Georgetown); Trainer Bob Beeten (Idaho State); **Mitch Kupchak** (North Carolina); **Tom LaGarde** (North Carolina); Phil Hubbard (Michigan); **Kenny Carr** (North Carolina State); Scott May (Indiana). **Wake Forest,** Repeated in 1975 as NCAA Champions with Jay Haas as Individual Champion succeeding Curtis Strange.

151 **Jim Spanarkel,** Duke, ACC Basketball Rookie of the Year 1976, MVP ACC Tournament and Eastern Regionals 1978, All-ACC Basketball 1978. **Rod Griffin,** Wake Forest, All-American 1977, ACC Basketball Player of the Year 1977, All-ACC Basketball 1977 and 1978. **Phil Ford,** North Carolina, All-American 1976, 1977, and 1978, ACC Basketball Player of the Year 1978, ACC Athlete of the Year 1977 and 1978, National Player of the Year 1978, Leading career scorer at North Carolina (2290 points), All-ACC Basketball 1976, 1977, and 1978.

156 **Billy Packer and Dick Enberg,** Broadcasters for the 1978 NCAA Basketball Championships, Packer was All-ACC Basketball in 1961 at Wake Forest. **Bill Foster,** Duke, ACC Champions and Eastern Regional Champions 1978, 2nd in NCAA Championship 1978, ACC Coach of the Year 1978, National Co-Coach of the Year 1978.

163 **Robert C. (Bob) James,** ACC Commissioner 1971 to present, Mid-American Conference Commissioner 1964–1971. **Bill Dooley,** North Carolina, Head Football Coach 1967–1978, ACC Football Coach of the Year 1971, ACC Football Championship 1971, 1972, 1977, Six bowl games, Won most games (69) at North Carolina. **Dean Smith,** North Carolina, Head Basketball Coach 1962 to present, ACC Basketball Coach of the Year 1967, 1968, 1971, 1976, and 1977, National Coach of the Year 1977, U.S. Olympic Team Head Coach 1976, NIT Champions 1971, 2nd in NCAA Championship in 1968 and 1977. **Lou Holtz,** North Carolina State, Head Football Coach 1972–1975, ACC Football Coach of the Year 1972, ACC Football Champions 1973, Ranked 10th in the nation in 1974, Went to 4 bowl games in 4 years. **Norm Sloan,** North Carolina State, Head Basketball Coach 1967 to present, ACC Basketball Coach of the Year 1970, 1973, and 1974, National Coach of the Year 1974, Team in 1973 was 27–0, Team in 1974 won the NCAA Championship.

164 **Wayne (Tree) Rollins,** Clemson, All-ACC Basketball second team 1975, 1976, and 1977, Leading career rebounder (1311) and third leading career scorer (1463 points) at Clemson, Only athlete at Clemson to have his uniform retired (#30). **John Lucas,** Maryland, All-American 1974, 1975, and 1976, All-ACC Basketball 1974, 1975, and 1976, ACC Athlete of the Year 1976, Career scoring leader (2015 points) at Maryland. **John Roche,** South Carolina, All-American

1969 and 1970, ACC Basketball Player of the Year 1969 and 1970, All-ACC Basketball 1969, 1970, and 1971. **Tony Waldrop,** North Carolina, All-American track, ACC Athlete of the Year 1974, 9 consecutive sub-four minute miles in 1974, Set the world indoor record in the mile of 3:55 in 1974 (since broken). **Wally Walker,** Virginia, MVP ACC Tournament 1976, 2nd leading Virginia career scorer (1849 points). **Steve Fuller,** Clemson, ACC Football Player of the Year 1977, All-ACC Football 1977, 1977 ACC total offense leader (1900 yards).

165 **Damon Ogunsuyi,** Clemson, soccer star. **Godwin Ogbueze,** Clemson, ACC Soccer Player of the Year 1975 and 1976, All-ACC Soccer 1975 and 1976. **Dave Buckey,** North Carolina State, All-ACC Football 1975, Single game total offense leader (314 yards), career total offense leader (4787 yards), and career passing leader (4286 yards) at State.

171 **Clyde Brown,** Clemson, ACC Soccer Player of the Year 1972, 1973, 1974, and 1975, All-South team 1972, 1973, 1974, and 1975, Honorable Mention All-American 1973 and 1974. **Craig White,** Clemson, All-ACC Baseball in 1971 and 1973, ACC Baseball Player of the Year 1973, Holds Clemson career records for hits (184), home runs (27), total bases (325), and runs batted in (127). **Joel Wells,** Clemson, All-ACC Football 1955 and 1956, Led team in rushing three consecutive seasons.

172 **Harry Olszewski,** Clemson, All-American 1967, All-ACC Football 1966 and 1967. **George (Butch) Zatezalo,** Clemson, 2nd team All-ACC Basketball 1968, 1969, and 1970, Leading career scorer (1761 points) amd average (23.5 points) at Clemson. **Bennie Cunningham,** Clemson, All-American 1974 and 1975, All-ACC Football 1974 and 1975.

177 **Bill Murray,** Duke, Head Football Coach 1951–1965, ACC Coach of the Year 1954, 1960, and 1962, Executive Secretary of the American Football Coaches Association 1965 to present, and **Mike McGee,** Duke, All-American 1959, ACC Football Player of the Year 1959, ACC Athlete of the Year 1960, All-ACC Football 1958 and 1959, Outland Trophy 1959, Head Football Coach at Duke 1971 to present. **Ernie Jackson,** Duke, All-American 1971, ACC Football Player of the Year 1971, All-ACC Football 1971. **Jack Marin,** Duke, All-ACC Basketball 1965 and 1966, and **Mike Lewis,** Duke, All-ACC Basketball 1968, against Wake Forest's Paul Crinkley (#20) in ACC Tournament in 1966.

178 **Leo Hart,** Duke, All-ACC Football 1968, 1969, 1970, All-time ACC total offense leader (2340 yards in 1968). **Jay Wilkinson,** Duke, All-American 1963, ACC Football Player of the Year 1963, All-ACC Football 1963. **Steve Jones,** Duke, ACC Football Player of the Year 1972, All-ACC Football 1972.

185 **Jim Kehoe,** Maryland, Athletic Director 1969–1978, Head Track Coach 1946–1968, and **Chris Weller,** Maryland, Assistant Athletic Director for Women's Sports 1976 to present and Head Basketball Coach 1975 to present. **Charles (Lefty) Drisell,** Maryland, Head Basketball Coach 1970 to present, ACC Coach of the Year 1975, NIT Champions 1972. **Deane Beman,** Maryland, U.S. Amateur Champion 1960 and 1963, British Amateur Champion 1959, Walker Cup team 1959, 1961, 1963, and 1965, Commissioner U.S. Professional Golf Association 1974 to present.

186 **Gary Collins,** Maryland, All-American 1961, All-ACC Football 1960 and 1961. **Frank Urso,** Maryland, All-American Lacrosse 1973, 1974, 1975, and 1976,

National Player of the Year 1975. **Randy White,** Maryland, All-American 1973 and 1974, ACC Football Player of the Year 1974, All-ACC Football 1973 and 1974, Outland Trophy 1974, and **Jerry Claiborne,** Maryland, Head Football Coach 1972 to present, ACC Coach of the Year 1973, 1975 and 1976, National Coach of the Year 1974.

191   **Thompson Mann** (right), North Carolina, All-American swimming, Set world record in 100 yard backstroke in 1964 (since broken), Olympic Gold Medal in 400 medley relay in 1964. **Jim Beatty,** North Carolina, All-American track, Three-time ACC cross-country, mile, and two mile champion and ex-world record holder in the indoor mile and outdoor two mile.

192   **Mike Voight,** North Carolina, All-American 1976, ACC Football Player of the Year 1975 and 1976, All-ACC Football 1975 and 1976, ACC career rushing record (3971 yards), gains 169 yards against Notre Dame in 21–14 loss in 1975. **Larry Miller,** North Carolina, All-American 1967 and 1968, ACC Basketball Player of the Year 1967 and 1968, ACC Athlete of the Year 1968, All-ACC Basketball 1967 and 1968. **Don McCauley,** North Carolina, All-American 1970, ACC Football Player of the Year 1969 and 1970, ACC Athlete of the Year 1971, All-ACC Football 1969 and 1970, ACC single game rushing record (279 yards) and season rushing record (1720 yards).

196   **Willis R. Casey,** North Carolina State, Athletic Director 1969 to present, Head Swimming Coach 1947–1957 and 1960–1970, Won 9 ACC Swimming Championships, In 1973–1974 State won ACC Championships in football, basketball, and baseball, The 1974–1975 overall sports program ranked 10th in the nation. **Earle Edwards,** North Carolina State, Head Football Coach 1954–1970, ACC Football Coach of the Year 1957, 1963 (tie), 1965, 1967, ACC Football Champions 1957, 1963 (tie), 1964, 1965, and 1968. **David Thompson,** North Carolina State, All-American 1973, 1974, and 1975, ACC Basketball Player of the Year 1973, 1974, and 1975, ACC Athlete of the Year 1973 and 1975, National Player of the Year 1974 and 1975, Second leading career scorer in ACC (2309 points-3 years), All-ACC Basketball 1973, 1974, and 1975. **Steve Rerych,** North Carolina State, All-American swimming 1966, 1967, and 1968, Gold medal winner in 400 meter and 800 meter free style relay in 1968 Olympics.

197   **Ted Brown,** North Carolina State, ACC Rookie of the Year 1975, Single game rushing leader (227 yards) and season rushing leader (1251 yards) at State. **Willie Burden,** North Carolina State, ACC Football Player of the Year 1973, All-ACC Football 1972 and 1973.

201   **Jim Bakhtier,** Virginia, All-American 1957, All-ACC Football 1956 and 1957, Third leading career rusher (2434 yards) at Virginia. **Bob Davis,** Virginia, ACC Football Player of the Year 1966, All-ACC Football 1964 and 1966, Single game passing (312 yards) and total offense leader (376 yards) at Virginia. **Keith Witherspoon,** Virginia, All-American track, ACC Meet record holder in triple jump, Varsity football.

202   **Jay Connor,** Virginia, All-American Lacrosse 1971 and 1972, Career record for points (204) and assists (129) at Virginia, All-South Soccer 1971. **Evan J. (Bus) Male,** Virginia, Director of Facilities and Finance 1956 to present, Head Basketball Coach 1952–1957, Head Baseball Coach 1955–1958. **Barry Parkhill,** Virginia, All-American 1972, ACC Basketball Player of the Year 1972, ACC Athlete of the Year 1972, All-ACC Basketball 1972, Single game high scorer (51

points) at Virginia.

207 **Bill Armstrong,** Wake Forest, All-American 1976, All-ACC Football 1975 and 1976. **Lanny Wadkins,** Wake Forest, All-American 1969, Individual ACC Golf Co-Champion 1969, Walker Cup Team 1971. **Jesse Haddock,** Wake Forest, Head Golf Coach 1960 to present, NCAA Coach of the Year 1974 and 1975, NCAA Golf Champions 1974 and 1975. **Norm Snead,** Wake Forest, All-American 1960, All-ACC Football 1959 and 1960, Leading career passer (4040 yards) and total offense (3986 yards) at Wake Forest.

208 **Charlie Davis,** Wake Forest, All-American 1971, ACC Basketball Player of the Year 1971, All-ACC Basketball 1969, 1970, and 1971, Leading career scoring average (24.9 points) at Wake Forest. **Skip Brown,** Wake Forest, All-ACC Basketball 1975 and 1977, Single game (12), season (187), and career (579) leader in assists at Wake Forest. **Murray Greason,** Wake Forest, Head Basketball Coach 1934–1957, ACC Coach of the Year 1956, Most career victories (285) at Wake Forest.

212 **Frank McGuire,** South Carolina, Associate Director of Athletics and Head Basketball Coach 1965 to present, Head Basketball Coach at North Carolina 1953–1961, ACC Basketball Coach of the Year 1957 and 1969, National Coach of the Year 1957. **Bobby Bryant,** South Carolina, All-American 1966, ACC Athlete of the Year 1967, All-ACC in Football in 1966 and Baseball in 1967. **Billy Gambrell,** South Carolina, ACC Football Player of the Year 1962, All-ACC Football 1961 and 1962. **Paul Dietzel,** South Carolina, Athletic Director and Head Football Coach 1966–1974, ACC Football Coach of the Year 1969.

213 **Alex Hawkins,** South Carolina, ACC Football Player of the Year 1958, All-ACC Football 1958.

217 **Norvall Neve,** Administrative Assistant and Supervisor of Officials 1969 to present, Acting Commissioner 1970–1971. **Marvin (Skeeter) Francis,** Administrative Assistant and Service Bureau Director 1969 to present. **Mrs. Nancy Thompson,** Administrative Assistant and Secretary 1954 to present. **Mrs. Jean Patton,** Secretary 1968 to present. **Smith Barrier,** Service Bureau Director 1954–1967. **Irwin Smallwood,** Assistant Director of Service Bureau 1954–1966. **Eugene (Gene) Corrigan,** Administrative Assistant and Director of Service Bureau 1967–1969; Athletic Director at Virginia 1971 to present.

218 **H.C. (Joby) Hawn,** Supervisor of Football Officials 1956–1968. **Lou Bello,** ACC Basketball Official 1953–1971, ACC Football Official. **Merrill P. (Footsie) Knight,** Supervisor of Basketball Officials 1957–1968.

Photo Credits:

Thanks go to these sources who have photographs appearing on the following pages: ABS/USA p. 137; Atlantic Coast Conference pp. 37, 56, 135, 163, 196, 212, 217; Smith Barrier pp. 47, 317, 218; Lou Bello p. 218; Charlotte Coliseum p. 91; Clemson University pp. 36, 99, 100, 164, 165, 171, 172; Duke University pp. 36, 37, 60, 81, 151, 156, 177, 178; Greensboro Coliseum p. 91; Herald-Sun Papers pp. 71, 125, 218; NBC p. 156; North Carolina State University p. 56, 60, 98, 125, 163, 165, 196, 197; University of Maryland pp. 37, 60, 68, 71, 105, 116, 164, 185, 186; University of North Carolina pp. 36, 65, 94, 151, 163, 164, 191, 192; University of South Carolina pp. 36, 37, 55, 164, 212, 213; University of Virginia pp. 36, 55, 100, 116, 164, 201, 202; Wake Forest University pp. 55, 98, 99, 137, 151, 207, 208.

ACKNOWLEDGMENT

The author wishes to acknowledge those people who have assisted and cooperated in the writing of this book. Although, it is not possible to mention the names of all who have contributed, particular, thanks is given to the following people: Robert C. James, Commissioner, of the Atlantic Coast Conference, his staff, Marvin (Skeeter) Frances and Norvall Neve, his secretaries, and the late Commissioner, James H. Weaver, for their cooperation and assistance in research at the Conference office; Edmund M. Cameron, retired Athletic Director at Duke University, for his counsel in discussing Conference affairs; and to the late Dr. Oliver K. Cornwell, Faculty Chairman of Athletics and Chairman of the Physical Education Department at the University of North Carolina, for his guidance and assistance throughout the study, as well as the use of his files and records.

The time and effort spent by Wallace Wade, (retired Athletic Director at Duke and Commissioner of the Southern Conference), Charles P. Erickson, (the late Athletic Director at North Carolina), Merrill P. Knight, (retired Supervisor of ACC Basketball Officals), Hugo Germino, (retired Sports Editor of the *Durham Sun*), and Lloyd Jordan (retired Commissioner of the Southern Conference) in personal interviews was very beneficial.

The cooperation and assistance received from the Athletic Directors, Faculty Chairmen, Sports Information Directors, and Educational Foundation Directors of each of the member institutions was also appreciated. They include: Clemson - Bill McClellan, Dr. Kenneth Vickery, Bob Bradley and George Bennett; Duke - Tom Butters, Dr. Ed Cady and Tom Mickle; Maryland - Jim Kehoe, Dr. John Faber, Jack Zane, and Colonel Tom Fields; North Carolina - Bill Cobey, Dr. Benson Wilcox, Rick Brewer, and Ernie Williamson; North Carolina State - Willis Casey, Dr. Robert Bryan, Ed Seamon, and Charlie Bryant; Virginia - Gene Corrigan, Dr. Alan Williams, Barney Cooke, and Tom Davenport; Wake Forest - Dr. Gene Hooks, Dr. John Sawayer, Bruce Herman, and Bob Bartholomew; Georgia Tech - Doug Weaver, Jim Schultz, and Jack Thompson, South Carolina - Tom Price and Ed Pitts.

A special word of gratitude is also given to Ted Saros, Linda and Keith Sipe and Richard Simpson for their help in publishing this book; thanks also goes to Linda Huff and Georgann Eubanks who were responsible for the cover design and picture layout respectively.

The deepest appreciation is reserved for Robbie Williams not only for her typing of the manuscript, but for her assistance and loyalty as the author's secretary for nine years.

Part I

The Development of Athletics and Athletic Conferences in the South

1

The Heritage of Competitive Athletics

The formation of intercollegiate athletic conferences in the past eighty years has played an important part in the standardization and stabilization of competitive athletics in the colleges and universities of the United States. This is the story of the events leading up to the formation and the development of one of these athletic conferences, the Atlantic Coast Conference.

Progress was slow in the development of competitive sports in the schools and colleges during the period between the Declaration of Independence and the Civil War. In the early American college brains and brawn were considered to be opposed to each other and were developed separately. Much of this attitude was based on the fact that a large proportion of the undergraduates of those days were intending to enter the Christian ministry. Howard J. Savage, writing for the Carnegie Foundation, observed that, "It was more than half a century before the discovery was made that Christianity could be muscular."

Competitive athletics on the college campus in the first half of the nineteenth century manifested itself in the form of unorganized and impromptu sports. Later, intramural contests and matches were held between classes and campus clubs. Although these inter-class rivalries often became intense, they were usually informal and comparatively disorganized affairs, conducted primarily for the amusement of the students. The attitude of the college faculties at this time was fairly tolerant of the undergraduate pastimes, except when they became rowdy and dangerous to life and property.

As the number of colleges increased and the students became more proficient in sports, their interest began to spread to competition against neighboring schools. The first recorded intercollegiate contest in the United States was a race between the boat clubs of Harvard and Yale in 1852. The second sport to be played on an intercollegiate basis was a baseball game between Amherst and Williams in 1859. In 1869, Rutgers beat Princeton in what is considered to be the first intercollegiate football game, although the game was actually more like soccer.

The college faculties at this time adhered to a classical philosophy rather than a social, educational one. Athletics were considered to be

3

a nuisance and waste of time rather than an educational experience. This indifference on the part of the faculty left the management of athletics to the students. Due to the instability of student bodies, and their preoccupation with more academic affairs, rules and regulations of athletic events were irregular or nonexistent. Out of this chaotic situation, student athletic associations were organized and financed independent of the universities. In some instances alumni took over the control of athletics and perpetuated the intense rivalry of their undergraduate days. To cope with these confused conditions, various sports associations formed with the hope of solving the existing problems. Of primary concern was a uniform set of rules that would help equalize competition between teams.

At this same time athletic clubs, promoting primarily track and field activities, were developing. The Olympic Club of San Francisco, organized in 1860, is considered to be the first athletic club in the United States. The New York Athletic Club, one of the oldest and most prestigious athletic clubs, was officially organized on September 8, 1868, and two months later it held the first track and field meet indoors.

The mushrooming growth of the universities and the expansion of intercollegiate sports after 1870, with the *laissez-faire* attitude of the faculties, formed an ideal climate for all the ills and irregularities of competitive athletics. Professionalism, proselyting, "tramp" athletes and "ringers", gambling, irregular eligibility requirements, poor playing conditions, and lack of standardized rules were all problems that manifested themselves at this time.

The problems relating to intercollegiate football attracted the most attention. The increase of abuses and injuries became so great that in 1894 the Harvard faculty formally voted to abolish football. Other colleges made similar attempts to control the game. Two years later Harvard renewed football, and the "central committee plan" was inaugurated whereby alumni, undergraduates, and faculty undertook as a group the regulation of athletics. President Eliot of Harvard, in his annual report for 1892–93, set forth the advantages and disadvantages of college athletics. Immediately, a general controversy arose between the proponents and detractors of competitive athletics.

In a speech to a Phi Beta Kappa Society meeting in 1893, Francis A. Walker discussed the importance of college athletics and its implications. He opened his speech with these words: "No theme is today of greater consequence to the colleges and universities of our land, whether as influencing school discipline or as affecting the standard over scholarship. Alike those who applaud and those who deprecate the growth of athletics must admit the importance of the

4

subject."

Although the college faculties were in the middle of the tumult and many of them were well acquainted with the problems, for the most part they did very little except abolish football at a number of institutions.

Casper Whitney, Sports Editor for *Harper's Weekly* in the 1890s, had some astute observations on college athletics and football during that period. Whitney, one of the most respected sports writers of his day, did much to raise the standard of college athletics. His widely read column on "Amateur Sport" extolled the virtues of amateur sport and vigorously condemned professionalism. In 1889, Whitney, along with Walter Camp, conceived the idea of an All-American football team, and thereafter the selections were announced in *Harper's Weekly*.

That Whitney was a devoted sportsman, and deeply concerned with the controversy over football and its outcome, there can be no doubt. An article written in December of 1894 bore this out, and his feelings were eloquently expressed in the following two excerpted paragraphs.

We have as a basis, first of all, that football is a rough, vigorous game; one that demands courage, physical and mental activity, endurance, and judgment. Is it desirable to cultivate these qualities in Young America? Obviously it is. Is there any other game in which they are so essential to success or which develops them to such a degree as football? I am quite sure that if the complete catalogue of games be gone over carefully, none will be found to so entirely fill the requirements as football. Only two approach it in all-round qualifications, viz., lacrosse and polo, and the first, for some reason or other, seems to fail of the popularity it merits, while the second could never attain wide popularity by reason of its comparative expensiveness. Hence we come in natural sequence to the question, is it desirable, is it wise to abolish a game that has so much to commend it as football? I am very much mistaken in the intelligence of the American people if such a query put to vote would not call forth a universal and emphatic negative.

There remains only one more point for me to take up in my line of argument for a rightful consideration of football. Only one, but the most important of them all—viz., the influence of the game for the moral and physical betterment of the American youth. No one will dispute the truth of *mens sano in corpore sano*, nor that the surest way to attain the first is by giving the body the exercise needful to its healthful nourishment . . . Any faculty member or any Eastern *alumnus* thirty-five years of age, who has made a study of this matter, will bear me out when I assert that the general morale of the undergraduate body has been materially elevated since athletics became a recognized part of college life. Dissipation is neither of so frequent occurrence nor so general as it was fifteen to twenty years ago; the animal spirits that then found bent in orgies of greater or less degree are now more often exploded on the football or baseball field or the running track. A large share of the tribute once paid to Bacchus now goes to Hercules. These are facts that may be had for asking by any interested reader. Has football no claim on our consideration after this evidence?

A year later, however, Whitney felt that the promises of temperance in football were still not being fulfilled. Since the alumni and undergraduates were ignoring the unwholesome tendencies of the game, he advocated that action should be taken by the faculties. He urged the meeting of faculty representatives from competing universities, the adoption of faculty control, and agreement upon uniform rules as the best way to ensure "the spirit of sport for sport's sake."

2

Athletic Associations and Conferences

Foremost among the early sports associations that were formed for competition under a uniform set of rules was the Intercollegiate Association of Amateur Athletics of America (IC4-A). Founded in 1875, the purpose of this organization was to "foster and maintain competition among its members in track and field athletics on a high plain of true amateurism, sportsmanship, and friendly relations." A year later, at a meeting in New York, college representatives met to establish rules for intercollegiate football competition. This association was the forerunner of the Football Rules Committee of today.

The biggest problem at this time, however, was "amateurism." Betting and gambling were widespread and challenges for a stake race were even advertised in the newspapers. Many athletes were openly competing for money. Consequently, the New York Athletic Club instigated a series of meetings with other prominent athletic clubs in the New York City area to discuss the problems of control and supervision over athletes, and the definition of an "amateur athlete." As a result, seven athletic clubs organized the National Association of Amateur Athletes of America in 1879. As the Association grew, problems developed, and in 1888 the Amateur Athletic Union (AAU) of the United States was founded by fourteen of these dissatisfied clubs. A year later the remaining clubs in the National Association joined the AAU giving it a significant degree of stability and respectability.

The IC4-A became affiliated with the National Association in the early 1880s, but resigned from this organization in 1889 when it was absorbed by the AAU. The IC4-A was offered membership in the AAU but decided to remain independent. One of the major problems of this period was the proselyting of college athletes by the athletic clubs. Some of the clubs offered free membership, training tables, and after-season jobs to the college athletes. The AAU disapproved of these practices and sought an alliance with the IC4-A to correct these abuses and insure further cooperation. In 1896 the alliance was ratified, and it was hailed by the press as a milestone for amateur athletics.

By the early 1900s, three other organizations were founded by the colleges and universities that fostered mutual interests in intercollegiate athletics. These organizations played a major role in the development of athletic associations and conferences in the United States. The first of these organization was the Southern Intercollegiate Athletic Association, founded in 1894. A year later, in 1895, the Western Intercollegiate Conference was founded, and in 1905, the Intercollegiate Athletic Association. The latter differed from the first two which were essentially regional, in that it was an association national in scope with a national representative body.

On January 11, 1895, the presidents of seven Midwestern universities met in Chicago to cope with the corrupt athletic policies of that time. The problems and control of intercollegiate athletics were discussed, and an organization of faculty representatives, one from each institution, was formulated. The seven institutions represented were: Purdue, Chicago, Northwestern, Illinois, Wisconsin, Minnesota, and Michigan. This Western Intercollegiate Conference (formally referred to as the Intercollegiate Conference of Faculty Representatives) became popularly known as the "Big Ten." Iowa and Indiana were admitted in 1899, and Ohio State in 1912. The University of Chicago withdrew in 1946, and Michigan State was admitted in 1949. The "Big Ten" Conference was influential in the development of many other athletic conferences in the Middle West and West, particularly the Ohio Conference and the Missouri Valley Conference. It continues today as one of the biggest and most influential of all athletic conferences and associations.

At the turn of the century football was typified by mass formations, the flying wedge, and gang trackling. In 1905, the rugged nature of the game and the abuses of the rules accounted for 18 deaths and 149 serious injuries. Many colleges either discontinued the game or advocated that it be abolished from the intercollegiate program. The problem that faced educators of the day was how to handle the football situation.

The only rules-making body at this time was the Intercollegiate Football Rules Committee. This association, under the leadership of its secretary, Walter Camp, was made up primarily of representatives from Eastern colleges. Camp had played a major role in the development of the game and the formulation of its rules; consequently, his committee was reluctant to make any changes. By the fall of 1905, however, opposition was growing for rule reforms. The coaches in the Middle West wanted a more open game, as well as a bigger voice on the Rules Committee. Those who were concerned about the dangerous features in football were demanding that new rules be passed to enhance the safety of the game. The controversy grew until President Theodore Roosevelt, interested in preserving the values of fair play, invited representatives from Yale, Harvard, and Princeton to the White House on October 9, 1905. It was hoped that these schools would agree on the proper conduct of the game of football.

Meanwhile, Chancellor Henry B. McCracken of New York University, disturbed by the serious injuries and the public demand that football be changed or abolished, called a meeting for the purpose of deciding on a united course of action. Representatives from thirteen Eastern institutions attended a meeting on December 9, 1905. They decided to initiate a reform movement rather than to abolish football, and called a second meeting on December 28. Representatives from 62 institutions attended and made preliminary plans for the organization of a national body to formulate sound requirements for intercollegiate athletics. A new football rules committee was also appointed to coordinate with the Intercollegiate Football Rules Committee.

When the Rules Committee, under Camp, refused to cooperate with the new group, it was President Roosevelt who again exerted his influence on behalf of a joint committee with equal representation. Under Roosevelt's urgings, Camp and the reluctant members of the Rules Committee finally recognized the new group, and the Association gained the status it needed. Theodore Roosevelt played a significant role in the establishment of the Intercollegiate Athletic Association, as it was then called, and the game of football reached its maturity during his tenure in office.

This Association, "which was originally conceived as an educational organization with neither legislative nor executive functions," adopted a Constitution and By-Laws on March 31, 1906, and held its First Annual Convention on December 20, 1906. Captain Palmer E. Pierce of the U.S. Military Academy was elected President of the Association which had a membership of 39 colleges and universities. This Association of voluntary institutional membership was composed of faculty representatives from member institutions and conferences and was an example of the principle of faculty control of athletics. On December 29, 1910, at the Fifth Annual Convention, the name of the Intercollegiate Athletic Association was changed to the National Collegiate Athletic Association (NCAA) The membership at that time had grown to 76 colleges and universities. As stated in the constitution, the object of the NCAA was, "the regulation and supervision of college athletics throughout the United States, in order that the athletic activities in the colleges and universities of the United States may be maintained on an ethical plane in keeping with the dignity and high purpose of education."

There was also in 1905, among the larger institutions, a tendency towards uniformity of admissions requirements and granting of degrees. This was an important trend for college athletics for two reasons: first, it demonstrated the advantages of free discussion of common interests; and second, it affected the standards of eligibility for intercollegiate competition. In fact the majority of all intercollegiate rules established by athletic conferences has dealt with the problem of eligibility, and an acceptable definition, such as, "that status upon which any undergraduate in good academic standing, who is a genuine amateur athlete, may compete in intercollegiate contests as a member of an athletic organization representing his university or college."

It was therefore a logical step for colleges and universities in the same geographical area to form athletic conferences to standardize rules and regulations. The institutions were usually similar in size, curriculum, entrance requirements, and educational philosophy. Rules for intercollegiate competition were democratically agreed upon, and a means of compliance and enforcement of these rules was usually established. The governing of the conference was done by faculty representatives of the member institutions. These representatives were usually the chairmen of the faculty athletic committees at each school. Athletic directors and coaches belonged to their own organizations which made recommendations to the faculty committee of the conference. This committee was invested with the power of all decisions regarding conference policies, rules, and regulations. Each member institution had to adhere to these policies, but the control of the individual athletic programs was left up to each institution. These principles have evolved down through the years, and are the basis for most athletic conferences today.

3

Athletics in the South

The Southern colleges and universities after the Civil War were not on a very solid foundation economically. Many institutions had closed during the War, and it was a struggle for them to reopen and regain their former positions. Most of the colleges were small and attended only by the wealthy. Recovery was slow throughout the Reconstruction Era, and it wasn't until the turn of the century that any real progress was discernable.

Athletic programs were slow to develop also, and there was little intercollegiate competition. An information bulletin from the Bureau of Education in 1885 stated that, "Neither the general nor college public at the South manifests much interest in athletics or gymnastics . . . Military drill is in vogue in many places in the South, but athletic *organizations* comparable with those below noted do not exist." Those colleges noted were: Yale, Harvard, Princeton, Amherst, Bowdoin, Rutgers, Dartmouth, Columbia, Connecticut Wesleyan, and California.

Football had been played in Eastern colleges for more than ten years before it was introduced into the South by faculty members who had migrated from the north. The first "scientific" game of football played below the Mason-Dixon Line was played in Raleigh, N.C. on Thanksgiving Day, November 29, 1888. Trinity College (later known as Duke University) beat the University team from Chapel Hill 16 to 0. At that same time, Trinity College, North Carolina, and Wake Forest organized the "North Carolina Inter-Collegiate Football Association" to arrange a round robin football series. In 1891, Trinity College claimed the championship of the South by beating Furman, North Carolina, and Virginia. The influence of these colleges was so great that by 1894, football had spread to approximately thirty colleges in the South. Although there were no uniform game rules to govern contests in those days and arrangements varied between teams, progress had been made in the playing techniques of the game. This was due primarily to the employment of better coaches and to the strict rules against professionalism of the Southern Intercollegiate Athletic Association. According to Casper Whitney, "Nearly every team in the South reached a higher degree of skill hereto, rough playing was reduced to a minimum, and no complaints within the association were heard as to the playing of 'hired' men."

The formation of the Southern Intercollegiate Athletic Association (SIAA) was the first serious attempt to create a regulatory body for intercollegiate athletics in the South. On December 22, 1894, representatives from Vanderbilt, The University of the South (Sewanee), Georgia, Georgia Tech, Alabama, Auburn, and North Carolina attended an informal meeting at the Kimball Hotel in Atlanta. The meeting was called by Dr. William L. Dudley of Vanderbilt University to found an organization whose "object shall be the development, regulation, and purification of college athletics in the South." Dr. Dudley was elected the first president, and invitations to join the Association were sent to those Southern institutions not represented at that meeting. Those joining in the first year were considered to be charter members. North Carolina declined membership in the Association because of the great distance between it and the other schools.

Since all the official records of the SIAA were destroyed by fire in 1930, it is difficult to accurately determine the dates various members joined the Association during the early years. However by 1896, membership had grown to include: Tulane, Louisiana State, Mississippi State, Mississippi, Clemson, Tennessee, Cumberland University, Southwestern Presbyterian University, The University of Nashville, Mercer, Texas, and Kentucky. The Association now included most of the prominent universities in the South, with two notable exceptions—North Carolina and Virginia. Although these were two of the leading educational institutions in the South, both had been offenders of the "amateur rule" since each school had used ineligible players.

The primary concern of the SIAA at its inception was the abuses in baseball. Baseball was the most widely played of any sport in the South and was controlled by the students. The Association immediately enacted legislation which gave regulation and control of all college athletics to a faculty committee at each school. They passed the "migratory rule" which required a transfer student to be in residence for one year before he was allowed to participate, and no student athlete was allowed to play summer baseball for money. The problem with North Carolina and Virginia was that they had allowed men who had played on professional teams to play on their amateur teams. In 1895, North Carolina had proposed a tightening of the rules which would have admitted both colleges to the Association, but Virginia declined to go along. At the Nashville meeting of the SIAA in December of 1896, Tulane was suspended for the 1897 football season because they also had used an ineligible player.

Casper Whitney made an extended tour throughout the United States in 1896 observing the organization, administration, and conduct of amateur sports. His comments on conditions in the South were enthusiastic and he was complimentary towards the influence of the Southern Intercollegiate Athletic Association. However in Atlanta, on October 31, 1897, an event occurred that shook the future of Southern football: Von Gammon, the fullback for Georgia, died from injuries received in a game against Virginia. Cries of protest immediately arose, and with few exceptions, football schedules were discontinued by the Southern colleges. It was a letter by the victim's mother to the trustees of the University of Georgia, declaring that football should be allowed to continue, that saved the game. By the season of 1898, encouraged by this letter of support, the Southern colleges were ready to resume their football schedules.

Through the turn of the century there was a continuous effort to maintain the high ethical standards upon which the SIAA had been founded. This was due to the vision and unselfish contribution of many men, particularly Dr. Walter M. Riggs, President of Clemson, and the second president of the SIAA, and Dr. William L. Dudley of Vanderbilt, founder and president of the Association for twenty years and the dominating influence during this period. Dr. Dudley believed in strong athletic controls, strong regional associations, a national amateur spirit, and a national organization to promote it. He was also active in the development of the National Collegiate Athletic Association, and during its formative years, Vanderbilt was the only member of the SIAA to also belong to the NCAA. The SIAA served the purpose of an association so well that the other Southern colleges did not feel a need to join the NCAA.

Dr. Dudley extolled the role of athletics in college life and the necessity of strict faculty control. In discussing the SIAA and its purposes, he stated, "This association was not organized to institute or foster that 'will o' the wisp'; that promoter and harborer of professionalism and corruption, commonly known as 'championship.' It was organized to promote sportsmanship, honor and morals."

At its Tenth Anniversary meeting in 1904, the SIAA made a major change in its constitution by dividing its territory into four districts. Each district was presided over by an executive vice-president. This change was necessitated by the large geographical area encompassing the member institutions, and the diversity of purpose among the large universities, small colleges, state schools, private schools, and technical institutes. Similiar factors later brought about the formation of the Southeastern Conference by thirteen of these institutions in 1932, and later in 1953, the formation of the Atlantic Coast Conference by seven other institutions.

In 1909 Dr. Dudley stated in his report to the NCAA that, "The athletic conditions in the colleges of the South are, on the whole, very good. All of the institutions of any importance belong to some intercollegiate athletic association or have faculty rules which, in a measure, serve the purpose."

The SIAA had been effective in controlling athletics in the South from South Carolina to Texas, and by 1912 had a membership of twenty-five of the larger and more important colleges and universities. However, there was a need for a strong organization in the northern area of the section, as most of the colleges in North Carolina, Virginia, and Maryland did not belong to the Association. In 1911 an effort had been made to organize these colleges, and the South Atlantic Intercollegiate Athletic Association was founded. The following institutions were members: Johns Hopkins, Georgetown, Virginia Polytechnic Institute, Richmond, Washington and Lee, the University of North Carolina, and North Caroline State. However, this was solely an organization of undergraduates whose purpose was to promote track athletics and arrange meets between the members. It was not an institutional or faculty organization.

One of the major problems facing the SIAA in the early 1900s was the question of freshman eligibility. The larger institutions, in an effort to improve athletic conditions, advocated a "freshman rule" whereby students were not eligible to compete on varsity teams. However, as the majority of the membership in the Association consisted of small colleges, the "freshman rule" proposal was defeated at every meeting. The small colleges felt they needed freshmen on their teams to help equalize the competition when they faced the bigger universities. This was a frustrating problem to the large universities because they competed on an intersectional basis with colleges in the East and Midwest who played under the "freshman rule". These institutions had found it to be an effective aid in the control of questionable recruiting practices, migrant athletes, "ringers", and unauthorized subsidization. In fact, a Southern sportswriter, Fuzzy Woodruff, called the fall of 1907, "the famous ringer season in Southern football."

The inability of the SIAA to reach a satisfactory agreement on the "freshman rule" resulted in two new conferences being formed by dissident members of the Association. The Athletic Conference of Southern State Universities was the first to organize in January 1915 in Columbia, South Carolina. Its members were the state universities of Georgia, Virginia, North Carolina, South Carolina, and Tennessee. It was based on the honor system in that each institution was responsible for settling its own eligibility questions—a system North Carolina and Virginia had employed for years. The ACSSU considered itself to be "the union of the big state universities of the south for the very finest thing possible in athletics."

The other conference formed was the Southern Athletic Conference. It was tentatively organized at the annual meeting of the SIAA in New Orleans in December 1915, and formally organized at a second meeting on January 28, 1916 in Knoxville. Clemson, Auburn, Mississippi State and Kentucky were included in this group. The two new conferences met in Knoxville and agreed to jointly make the "freshman rule" effective as soon as possible. This rule was claimed to be "the only safeguard against professionalism and 'ringers' creeping into college athletics." All the institutions represented at this joint meeting were also members of the SIAA, with the exception of North Carolina and Virginia. Gambling, summer baseball, and the aforementioned "honor system" were also discussed, and the cooperation at this meeting was in contrast to the increasingly frequent debates of the SIAA meetings.

The entry of the United States into World War I had a strong effect on the competitive athletic programs of the colleges and universities. At the close of the 1917 football season, many athletes at Southern colleges left school to join the Armed Forces. Tennessee and Georgia discontinued intercollegiate football entirely with the intention of giving athletic training to all students. Other institutions curtailed or suspended their athletic programs. Existing teams were frequently composed of men from the Student Army Training Corps units which had been established at many of the institutions. During the next few years the energies and concerns of the country were focused on the successful completion of the war effort.

4

The Southern Conference

The American economy boomed during the post-World War I years. Increased income, better transportation and communication, and shorter working hours created a demand for recreational pastimes. There was a great increase in the number of male students in the colleges and universities, and the returning veterans brought with them a renewed interest in physical training and football. The athletic programs that had been curtailed were revived. College and professional sports, with high quality athletes and increased newspaper publicity, captured a greater interest among the American public. This increase in mobility and leisure time pursuits ushered in the period of American history known as the "Roaring Twenties" or the "Jazz Age." In sports it was the "Golden Era," and in this environment the Southern Conference was organized and developed.

By 1920, the Southern Intercollegiate Athletic Association had grown to a membership of twenty-nine colleges and universities. The problems of geographical distances and diversity of philosophies became more acute. As a result, Dr. S.V. Sanford of Georgia, during the annual meeting of the SIAA in Gainesville, Florida on December 13, called a special meeting of representatives from several of the larger institutions. Plans were made to hold a second meeting in Atlanta in February in order to form a new conference. The principle basis on which this conference was organized was the "freshman rule" and an effort to solve the summer baseball problem.

At the NCAA meetings in 1920, Thomas Nelson foretold the importance of the proposed conference in his Third District report when he said, "Probably the most significant event that has happened in recent years in connection with Southern institutions, and one which will influence athletics to a very marked degree, especially in the larger institutions, is the proposed Southern Conference."

In Atlanta on February 25 and 26, 1921, the new association was organized as the Southern Intercollegiate Conference (SIC). The name was later changed to the Southern Conference in 1923. Representatives from fifteen state universities, colleges, and technical schools in the South attended this meeting. The principles upon which the new Conference would operate were drawn up, a new set of rules disregarding the regulations of the SIAA were adopted, and these rules and regulations were submitted to the faculties of the institutions represented for ratification.

On August 21, 1921, it was announced that the following fourteen institutions were charter members of the Southern Intercollegiate Conference: Alabama, Auburn, Clemson, Georgia, Georgia Tech, Kentucky, Mississippi State, Tennessee, Maryland, North Carolina, North Carolina State, Virginia, Virginia Tech, and Washington and Lee. Tulane was at the original meeting but delayed commitment until 1922, when it joined along with Florida, Louisiana State, Mississippi, South Carolina, and Vanderbilt.

In the "Basic Principles for Organization" adopted by the SIC at the Atlanta meeting, membership was limited to sixteen institutions, principally the state institutions of the South. However, because of traditional ties that could not be broken, the membership soon increased beyond the original limit. Virginia Military Institute was admitted in September 1923, and the University of the South joined in December of that year. At the annual meeting on December 7 and 8, 1923, the name was changed to the Southern Conference.

The men who organized the Southern Conference did so with confidence and high expectations that it would be the solution to the control of athletic abuses. The member institutions had a similarity of purpose and were in agreement with the objectives for athletic control. During the 1920's, the leaders worked hard in developing and refining the rules and regulations of the Conference. The outstanding leader of this time was Dr. S.V. Sanford of Georgia. He was founder and president of the Conference from 1922 to 1929, as well as being a college dean, President of the University of Georgia, and later Chancellor of the Georgia State system of higher education. He was very active in the affairs of the NCAA, and his District Reports were detailed accounts of the achievements and problems of the Southern Conference. He believed in strong conferences as the avenue for advancement of college athletics, and the development of the Conference reflected his ideals and principles.

In a report to the NCAA, Sanford stated the philosophy of the new conference.

A conference composed of institutions of the same relative size, of the same entrance requirements, and operating under the same stringent and progressive regulations should be a factor of such power as to be the means of keeping athletic ideals on a high plane.

It is believed that this gentlemen's agreement will largely eliminate many of the serious or apparently serious mistakes that have been made in the past. This means that each institution must "assume full responsibility for its athletic disposition, attitude, obligation, honor, in enforcing rigidly and fearlessly all the rules and regulations of the constitution of the Conference—not in letter only, but in spirit also." Within each institution must be discovered the center of its own moral gravity.

In writing the Constitution, the Southern Conference established a Committee on Colleges to "recommend to the Conference from time to time such institutions as should be considered colleges for Conference purposes." This question of "athletic equality" of non-member institutions created some problems, since such institutions were required to abide by Conference rules when competing against Conference members. The committee would publish annually a list of those colleges that qualified. Athletic relationships with the colleges remaining in the SIAA were good, and by 1926, all members of the SIAA were included on the published list, as well as twenty other colleges.

Other problems arose during this period concerning eligibility and the definitions of "college," "freshman," "passing grade," etc., but overall, the Conference made notable progress in putting its principles into practice. Intercollegiate athletics among the member institutions showed great improvement. One of the basic principles of the Conference was faculty responsibility and control of intercollegiate athletics. The voting delegate had to be appointed by the President of his college and be a full-time member of the faculty. Those principles were an important factor in the growth and strength of the Conference. Its sound athletic policies were adopted by many other conferences and associations.

Although Fuzzy Woodruff reported that the passion for intersectional games had worn off by 1923, two years later the Southern Conference waived the rule that the football season would end the Saturday after Thanksgiving. By unanimous consent, Section I of Article VII of the Bylaws was suspended so that the University of Alabama might be allowed to play football on New Year's Day in California. Alabama won the Southern Conference Championship in 1924, and when they repeated in 1925 with an undefeated season under Wallace Wade, they were invited to the Rose Bowl. This was the first time a Southern team had been selected, and the Conference waived the rule. This new desire to promote intersectional relations set a precedent for the years to come. Alabama responded to this honor by upsetting the University of Washington in a thriller 20 to 19 for the National Championship. In 1926, Alabama won the Southern Conference Championship for the third year in a row with another undefeated season. Breaking all precedent, Alabama was invited back to the Rose Bowl for the second consecutive year. Alabama tied Pop Warner's undefeated Stanford team 7 to 7, in the last four minutes of the game on a blocked kick. The tying point-after-touchdown was kicked by Herschell Caldwell who went on to become an assistant football coach at Duke University for many years. Wallace Wade, later to become head football coach at Duke and the first Commissioner of the Southern Conference, had put Southern football on the map to stay.

In addition to the Southern Conference and the Southern Intercollegiate Athletic Association, there were other smaller athletic conferences in the South: the Louisiana Intercollegiate Conference, the South Carolina Intercollegiate Athletic Association, the Virginia Intercollegiate Athletic Conference, and the North Carolina Intercollegiate Athletic Conference, (NCIAC). The NCIAC was organized in February 1928, and it made rules and regulations regarding eligibility in intercollegiate sports for the colleges in the state, particularly the "Big Five" schools of North Carolina, North Carolina State, Wake Forest, Duke, and Davidson. Duke University was admitted to the Southern Conference at its annual meeting on December 14, 1928, in Nashville. Wake Forest and Davidson became members of the Southern Conference in September 1936, and with all the members of the "Big Five" now under the regulations of the Southern Conference, there was no longer a need for the NCIAC.

Events during the period 1929 to 1932 far surpassed those of the preceding eight years in importance and in effect on the Southern Conference. The occurance and reaction to these events shaped the course of athletics in the South for the next forty-five years. First was the report on *American College Athletics*, published in 1929 by the Carnegie Foundation for the Advancement of Teaching. One hundred and thirty institutions were visted, among them were Georgia, Georgia Tech, North Carolina, Virginia, Alabama, Tennessee, Tulane, and Vanderbilt of the Southern Conference. The study showed the nature of athletic control and the conduct of intercollegiate athletics at institutions throughout the country. It revealed that many of the athletic practices were of a dubious nature, and in opposition to sound educational principles. It became a center of controversy, as support and denial of the findings were argued in newspapers, magazine articles, and speeches throughout the country. Although the institutions of the Southern Conference seemed to fare better than most, they still did not escape unscathed.

The results of the Carnegie Foundation Report were clouded by the economic conditions in the country at the time of its publication. The depression seriously affected many colleges and their athletic programs. In 1930 there was a general loss of revenue because of a decline in attendance at football games. This forced the colleges either to economize on athletic expenses or curtail activities. The decline in attendance was also attributed to other factors which accompanied the depression. The increase in radio broadcasts of sporting events induced people to stay in the comfort of their homes rather than fight inclement weather or the pushing crowds.

There also seemed to be a change in the attitude of the undergraduate student. He no longer had the same enthusiasm and interest in intercollegiate athletics. Though the causes for this attitude were numerous, there seemed to be a new seriousness pervading the college campuses which had been unknown earlier. The "hard times" of the depression and a reappraisal of the intellectual environment by the colleges themselves helped to develop this apathy toward athletics.

Accompanying this change of attitude toward "spectatoritis" at intercollegiate games was a resurgent interest in intramural sports. With so many and varied activities to choose from, students were discovering that there truly seemed to be a "sport for all." The joy of participating for undergraduates and alumni exposed to new recreational pursuits was fast replacing the joy of sitting by and watching others perform.

The effect of external forces and events upon intercollegiate athletics was nationwide. No conference or institution escaped their influence. As the Southern Conference entered the period of the '30s, it was soon faced with a major confrontation, one that would upset the status quo that had been maintained during the first twelve years of the Conference, and one that would set a precedent for another similar confrontation twenty-one years later.

5

The Southeastern Conference

When Duke University was admitted to membership in 1928, the Southern Conference was again subjected to charges that it was too large. It was true that the member institutions were widely scattered geographically from the Gulf of Mexico and the Mississippi River, to the Atlantic Ocean and the state of Maryland; and the Conference was composed of both large state universities and small private colleges. As a result it was difficult to arrange satisfactory schedules among Conference members and hold Conference tournaments, and there was no uniform development of Conference-wide competition in all sports. Traditions and practices varied from school to school, and the problems of some schools were entirely different from those faced at other institutions.

It was felt that progress in solving the athletic problems of the Conference could not be satisfactorily made without involving the presidents of the member institutions. They were invited to attend the annual meeting in 1929, and a committee of three presidents was appointed to investigate the diverse academic standards that existed in the Conference and to make recommendations for improvement. There was a strong feeling among many of the members that the Conference had no jurisdiction over the educational policies of an institution. The debate that ensued over eligibility requirements brought the Conference closer to separation.

By 1931 it was mutually decided that in order to avoid some of these problems it would be wise to divide the Conference. In 1932, while the nation was involved with the depression, the most influential athletic conference in the South separated into two organizations. At the annual meeting held in Knoxville, Tennessee on December 8 and 9, 1932, a division was effected along geographical lines. Thirteen institutions in the Deep South, and west of the mountains, withdrew from the Southern Conference and adopted the name "Southeastern Conference."

Dr. Sanford of Georgia presented the case for the withdrawing group—Kentucky, Tennessee, Vanderbilt, University of the South, Georgia, Georgia Tech, Alabama, Auburn, Mississippi, Mississippi State, Louisiana State, Florida, and Tulane. He stated that the division "sought to bring about a closer contact and better under-

21

standing of athletic problems on the part of the executive officers of the member institutions with the hope of the possible solution of a few of the more pressing athletic problems . . . that no changes in the athletic relationships were contemplated and certainly no criticisms implied; that this was merely a statement of a proposed action, formal notification of which should be delayed in deference to our hosts."

Dr. A. W. Hobbs of North Carolina reported for the Committee of the Conference appointed to confer with the withdrawing group. He stated that "the Constitution accorded the right of withdrawal to any member institution or institutions, and the Southern Conference must make no mistake that there were now two separate organizations." Dr. J. J. Tigert, acting as a spokesman for the withdrawing group, stated that it was not pleasant to think of separation, that no comparison of institutions was involved, and he tendered the resignation of the thirteen members.

The institutions remaining in the Southern Conference were: Clemson, Duke, Maryland, North Carolina State, North Carolina, South Carolina, Virginia, Virginia Military Institute, Virginia Tech, and Washington and Lee. It was apparent at the time of the split that, speaking geographically, the names of the two conferences were anomalous. However, as time passed and traditions became even more established, the idea of changing names was not practical.

The Southeastern Conference temporarily adopted the Constitution and Bylaws of the Southern Conference, while a committee met to prepare a new set of rules and regulations. The members of the new conference were determined to avoid the difficulties experienced in the Southern Conference. They felt that the development of a geographically compact organization would eliminate many of the problems of differing interests, objectives, and lack of understanding between member institutions. As a result, they limited the membership to thirteen, and in the ensuing years, resisted all efforts to enlarge the membership. With the hope of more effective control and regulation, the Southeastern Conference also designated the president of each member institution as the voting authority in the Conference.

Meanwhile the Southern Conference, after the withdrawal of the thirteen members, reorganized within a small region and gradually expanded its membership. In December 1934 the Constitution was changed to permit a membership of not more than sixteen. At a special meeting held in Richmond, Virginia on February 7, 1936, invitations to join the Southern Conference were extended to Davidson, William and Mary, Wake Forest, Furman, The Citadel, and the University of Richmond. All accepted and became members

22

as of September 1, 1936. At the annual meeting in Richmond, December 10, 1937, the resignation of the University of Virginia, which had been tendered the previous year, was accepted with regret. This left the membership at fifteen. Four years later this vacancy was filled by the admission of George Washington University.

Ever since the Carnegie Foundation Report in 1929, the topic of recruiting and subsidizing athletes had been bandied about in public forums. Curtailed during the depression, this practice was slowly returning to plague athletic officials, particularly as public interest and attendance at athletic events was increasing. At the 1934 Convention, the NCAA, concerned over the controversy surrounding the "Amateur Rule," the purist concept of which was the cornerstone of all athletic associations and which forebade financial aid to athletes, adopted a code identifying justifiable and unjustifiable practices. It was felt by some that this code should have contained an enforcement clause. However this was an entirely new idea to the NCAA, which thought of itself as an advisory body only, and left the matter of regulating athletic practices up to its member institutions and their regional conferences.

The Southeastern Conference took an open stand in support of athletic subsidization in 1935 when it proposed the following: "That athletes may receive for their athletic services any aid, such as scholarships, work, or other financial assistance, such as any other student may receive for participation in any other activity. Such aid, however, shall not be in excess of the legitimate expenses of attending the institution as represented by tuition, fees, books, board and lodging." When this resolution which permitted athletic scholarships was adopted at the December meeting, reaction was instantaneous and critical. Many viewed this action as an open challenge to the basic principles of amateurism.

The Southern Conference soon followed with a plan in the opposite direction. Sponsored by President Frank Porter Graham of the University of North Carolina, it stated that any student who received financial aid for his athletic ability would be ineligible to represent his institution in an intercollegiate contest. Known as the "Graham Plan," it came under much discussion and criticism, and was not a popular proposal with many of the Conference members. The President of the Conference, Forrest Fletcher, recommended its abolition; while Dean R. B. House of North Carolina argued that his institution, along with North Carolina State, "anticipated no recession in its attitude."

Eventually, in 1938, the Southern Conference did adopt a regulation very similar to that of the Southeastern Conference, and immediately Southern schools were accused by the press and public of professionalizing college athletics. The Southern institutions, however, did not waiver from this position, but instead sought to strengthen their aid programs. By the end of the decade, many institutions throughout the country were slowly changing their attitude to agree with that of the Southern schools.

In 1939, the NCAA proposed and adopted amendments which "would incorporate in our constitution a definite, affirmative code of sound institutional practices in the conduct of athletics, including specifically the matter of aid to athletes, to which member institutions should be asked to subscribe and adhere, as a condition to obtaining and retaining membership in the Association." Article III of the new amendments allowed aid to athletes based on need and legitimate employment. This standard for membership and regulation was a new concept for the NCAA, and the officers moved deliberately in the application of the code to individual institutional policy.

In the year prior to the Second World War, two noteworthy events occurred on the Southern athletic scene. The first of these was a decision by the presidents of the member institutions in the Southeastern Conference to hire a commissioner to supervise the intercollegiate athletic program of the Conference. At a meeting in Atlanta on August 19, 1940, former Governor of Mississippi, Martin Sennet (Mike) Conner, was elected Commissioner.

The other major event was the first change in membership in the Southeastern Conference with the resignation of the University of the South. Sewanee was one of the original seven institutions that formed the Southern Intercollegiate Athletic Association in 1894. It had been a member in the SIAA, the Southern Conference, and the Southeastern Conference continuously until its resignation on December 13, 1940. Although the athletic traditions of Sewanee were closely associated with other conference members, since World War I it had not kept pace with the tremendous growth of the other schools. As a result, its success in Conference athletics had suffered greatly.

6

World War II and The Post–War Period

The Selective Service Act, which was passed in September 1940 and increased the strength of the Armed Forces from 425,000 to nearly 2,000,000 by December 1941, had a tremendous impact on college athletic programs. In the ensuing years, many colleges had to discontinue or severely limit their athletic programs because of the number of students being drafted. Transportation was a major problem because of gasoline and tire rationing and the military priorities of the railroads. As a result, formal schedules were not adhered to, and athletic programs struggled along on an *ad hoc* basis.

The effect on other campuses was quite different, however, as the Army, Navy, and Marines utilized hundreds of colleges and universities as training centers. Perhaps the best known of these were the V-5, V-7, and V-12 programs instigated by the Navy. While the Army concentrated primarily on physical training programs, the Navy and Marines encouraged intramural and intercollegiate competition. This was a distinct advantage to the overall athletic programs of these schoools. The Naval Aviation Physical Training Program (V-5) made competitive sports the basic program for training personnel. This program operated from June 1942 to October 1945. In the South, Pre-Flight Schools were established at the University of North Carolina and the University of Georgia.

With the bodies constantly in a state of flux as some athletes transfered to schools that hadn't dropped intercollegiate programs (thus becoming varsity athletes at more than one school), it was inevitable that the question of freshman and transfer eligibility would arise. The NCAA took this question both pro and con, the Executive Committee of the NCAA decided to leave action on the "freshman rule" to the individual institutions and conferences. A year later, Dean A. W. Hobbs of the University of North Carolina reported to the NCAA meetings that all athletic conferences in the Third District (the South) allowed freshmen to play on varsity teams. He also stated that there were vigorous dissents from this action in the Southern Conference and the Southeastern Conference.

At the Detroit Convention in 1941, the NCAA, the American College Football Coaches Association, and the College Physical Education Association adopted a joint resolution pledging their support and cooperation in providing physical training programs and athletic competition. They stated, "That throughout the present emergency the programs of health education, physical education, recreation and competitive athletics in the American colleges be maintained, and, in every manner feasible, where not inconsistent with the demands of technical courses established as emergency measures, be expanded and intensified."

The presidents and faculty chairmen of the Southeastern Conference, meeting earlier in December just five days after Pearl Harbor, had expressed similar beliefs.

The Southeastern Conference has assembled at the most critical period in American history. The day of the American Revolution was not so ominous. The conflict which resulted in the War Between the States did not constitute such a critical moment in our history. The First World War in 1917 was far less serious than the present crisis which is upon us. We have met today not merely to consider the many problems of football, basketball, and other college sports but to consider seriously how colleges and universities can meet the issue of national defense and make their contribution in the struggle for our existence.

. . . For the time being we believe that the best thing that the colleges and universities can do is to continue their athletic program—not for the purpose of winning games but for the purpose of making men fit, strong and daring. We are pointing the athletic programs of the colleges of the Southeastern Conference in the direction of national preparedness for war . . .

Dean Hobbs echoed the same sentiments for the Southern Conference in reporting on their convention in Richmond in 1942 when he stated, "I believe that the members went away from there determined to carry on the athletic programs to the fullest extent possible with the sole belief that athletics, combat athletics, are tremendously valuable to the armed forces."

The attack on Pearl Harbor caused a great deal of concern over the vulnerability of the entire Pacific Coast, and as a result the government banned large meetings, conventions, and athletic events on the West Coast. It appeared that the famous Rose Bowl football game would have to be canceled. Duke University, by virtue of its undefeated record, had been chosen by the Rose Bowl Committee to face Oregon State. The Duke administration, with the encouragement of the city of Durham, sought to bring the Rose Bowl to Durham. They were successful, and on January 1, 1942, the Rose Bowl game was moved from Pasadena, California for the first and only time in its long and memorable history. Duke's football team was not as successful, however, as they bowed to an underdog Oregon State team 20-16 before 56,000 spectators—the largest crowd ever to see a football game in the Southern Conference area at that time.

As the international conflict intensified, 1943 became one of the most difficult years in history in terms of the administration and control of intercollegiate athletics. One problem was the delayed announcement of whether or not Army and Navy teams would be permitted to participate in the college athletic programs. As stated earlier, the Navy decided affirmatively, and the Army decided otherwise. For the second year in a row, due to increasing travel demands by the military, the NCAA did not hold their annual convention. This was the first interruption since the Association was organized in 1905.

The Olympic Games were also a victim of the world dissension, as they were canceled for the second consecutive time in 1944. This marked the third time (1916 and 1940) in less than half a century that the modern Olympics were canceled because of world wars. This was in sharp contrast to the original Olympic Games which endured for 1,168 years (776 B.C. to 392 A.D.) without interruption.

In the South, the intensity of the war effort was reflected in the decline of institutions participating in an intercollegiate program. The Southern Conference had ten colleges participating out of sixteen: Duke, North Carolina, South Carolina, and Richmond with V-12 personnel; and Clemson, Maryland, Wake Forest, North Carolina State, Davidson, and Virginia Military Institute with civilian personnel. In the Southeastern Conference, four schools out of eleven participated: Tulane and Georgia Tech with V-12 personnel, and Georgia and Louisiana State with civilian personnel. Vanderbilt had an informal team.

In 1944 there were signs of increased participation in college athletics in the South because freshmen were now being used on most all of the teams. There were many excellent service teams in the area also. It is interesting to note that Dean Hobbs in his report to the NCAA that year stated, "most colleges in the area played without rules, since the Southern Conference and the Southeastern were operating under a suspension of rules for the duration . . ."

With the ending of hostilities on "V-J Day," August 14, 1945, the colleges were faced with a tremendous influx of returning veterans when the doors opened for fall semester that year. A total of 450,605 male veterans were registered in institutions of higher education in 1945–46. Two years later, in the fall of 1947, making full use of their government subsidy under the G.I. Bill, this total had jumped to 1,098,647 registered male veterans. This was close to fifty percent of the total college enrollment.

The returning servicemen brought with them a highly competitive spirit and turned out for intramural and intercollegiate competition in record-breaking numbers. Physical education and athletic facilities of prewar days were found to be inadequate at many schools. But those institutions which had housed military training units and were the recipients of expanded facilities were now able to offer broad and diverse programs. By 1946, all colleges in the Third District (the South) formerly having football teams were again competing. Swimming, soccer, and other sports also showed an increase in participation. College football and basketball were reaching new heights in excellence with the great number of athletes enrolled. Public interest in competitive athletics ballooned, and spectators turned out in unprecedented numbers. The Associated Press estimated that 11,981,728 attended football games in 1946.

Although most colleges and conferences soon returned to prewar rules of regulations, exceptions in the transfer rule and "freshman rule" were made to returning servicemen. But as the athletes returned from the service and "shopped around" for the best offer in college, the problems of recruiting and subsidizing, dormant during the war, began to rear their ugly heads. Aware of these developing problems, the NCAA held a conference in Chicago on July 22 and 23, 1946, "to determine whether it would be possible to formulate a national program to cure the malpractices in college athletics, particularly evident in the immediate postwar period. Recruiting and subsidizing subsidizing were of specific concern." A tentative set of "Principles Conduct of Intercollegiate Athletics" (the "Sanity Code") was drawn up and these were distributed to more than 400 colleges and universities to determine their acceptance. The principles were approved at the NCAA Convention in New York on January 8, 1947, and adopted as amendments to the Constitution at the 42nd Annual Convention the following year. On January 10, 1948, the "Sanity Code," as it was popularly known, went into effect.

At the end of its first year in effect, the Southern schools were generally in agreement with the "Sanity Code," and serious efforts were made to bring all institutions into complete compliance with it. However, at the NCAA meeting in New York in January of 1950, it was reported that seven institutions had been found to be in noncompliance with the Constitution of the Association: Virginia, Maryland, Virginia Tech, Virginia Military Institute, The Citadel, Villanova, and Boston College. The vote to terminate their membership in the Association failed, but the institutions were prohibited from participating in NCAA tournaments during 1950, until the charge of noncompliance was lifted.

President H. C. Byrd of the University of Maryland proposed that a resurvey of NCAA members be made to determine if the "Sanity Code" regulations were equitable to all members. This proposal,

28

known as the "Byrd Resolution," was adopted. The smaller colleges were, as a rule, in favor of retaining the "Sanity Code" as stated. The larger universities felt that the provisions of the code, for the most part, were impractical and they urged their amendment or repeal. The major areas of contention were that permissible aid to athletes, based on need, included only tuition and fees. It was felt that room and board should also be included. At many institutions it was not possible for an athlete to work (after his class hours, study time, practice period, and in the case of military institutions, his military duties) a sufficient number of hours to pay for his college expenses. This led to subterfuge and the creation of nonexistent jobs. Many also felt that the NCAA should not be a regulatory body, and that the enforcement of rules and regulations should be left up to the regional conferences and institutional integrity.

On January 12, 1951, proposals for amendments to Article III of the Constitution (the "Sanity Code") were brought before the NCAA Convention. The Association voted to drop the provision governing financial aid to athletes and to abolish the enforcement machinery. After almost universal agreement three years earlier that a set of principles for the conduct of intercollegiate athletics was necessary, the "Sanity Code" was now dead.

During this postwar period there were many newsworthy events and personalities that brought national attention to athletics in the South. In August of 1947, Dean N. W. Dougherty of the University of Tennessee, a past president of the Southern Conference and a longtime secretary of the Southeastern Conference became acting Commissioner of the Southeastern Conference because of the serious illness of Mike Conner. Dougherty served until February 21, 1948, at which time Bernie H. Moore, football and track coach at Louisiana State University was appointed Commissioner. Later that spring, Dr. W. D. Funkhouser, Dean of the University of Kentucky Graduate School, died. Dr. Funkhouser had served as secretary-treasurer of the Southern Conference from 1925 until 1931, and as secretary-treasurer of the Southeastern Conference from 1935 until his death. He worked tirelessly to maintain the records and history of the two conferences, and he had a marked effect on their sound growth and development.

North Carolina and Clemson were cited in 1948 as the outstanding football teams in the area. This was the first time any future Atlantic Coast Conference teams were mentioned in the NCAA district reports since Duke was cited for its outstanding team in 1941. Clemson beat Missouri 24–23 in the Gator Bowl to finish the season undefeated with an 11–0 record. North Carolina, with only a 7–7 tie with William and Mary to blemish a perfect record, lost a close game to Oklahoma 14–6 in the Sugar Bowl. The following year North Carolina went to the Cotton Bowl and bowed to Rice 27–13. This was the third bowl appearance in four years for North Carolina. Earlier, they had lost to Georgia 20–10 in the 1947 Sugar Bowl. This was known as the Charlie (Choo-Choo) Justice era at North Carolina, and the great halfback capped his star-studded career by being the overwhelming choice for Most Valuable Player in the College All-Star game in Chicago in 1950. Against the Philadelphia Eagles, Justice carried the ball nine times for 133 yards, caught five passes, and scored a touch-down in the 17–7 victory.

In December 1949 the famous "Dixie Classic" was inaugurated. North Carolina State's basketball coach, Everett Case, was the father of this event, and it grew to be one of the outstanding holiday basket-ball tournaments in the country. It matched the "Big Four" schools of North Carolina against four of the nation's best teams each year. During its twelve years of existence no out-of-state team ever won the tournament, and North Carolina State alone won seven titles. Everett Case had brought big time basketball to the South, and in particular, to the future Atlantic Coast Conference. However, in 1961 the "Dixie Classic" was canceled by the college administrators because they were concerned that the highly publicized basketball tournament would attract the undesirable elements of gamblers and "fixers" who were plaguing college basketball at that time.

At the annual meeting of the Southern Conference on December 8, 1950, in Charlotte, North Carolina, Wallace Wade was elected the first Commissioner. Wade's appointment took effect January 1, 1951, and the Commissioner's Office was opened in Durham, North Carolina. Wade was Athletic Director at Duke University at the time, and had brought nationwide fame to Duke as its football coach from 1931 through 1950.

The basketball gambling and "fixing" scandals, and the West Point "cribbing" affair of 1950 and 1951, shocked the American public. It was disclosed that in the period between 1947 and 1950, 86 basketball games had been fixed in Madison Squre Garden and other arenas in 22 cities throughout the country. The investigation that followed resulted in the jailing of five players and 13 gamblers, while 13 other players got off with suspended sentences. In August 1951, 90 cadets were dismissed or forced to resign from the U.S. Military Academy at West Point for violations of the honor code in which "cribbing" (passing examination information) was the main offense. The Army football team was seriously effected.

This prompted the NCAA Council to issue to all its members on

September 11, 1951, twelve recommendations for the conduct of intercollegiate athletics. Among these, the NCAA urged that the number of games in each sport be limited, and that postseason games be reevaluated in the light of the pressures they were creating.

Dr. Gordon Gray, President of the University of North Carolina, called a meeting of the presidents of the Southern Conference institutions in Chapel Hill on September 28, 1951. This meeting was called "for the purpose of discussing ways and means of effecting improvement in the organization, management, and direction of intercollegiate athletics." At this meeting the presidents decided to "recommend" that the Conference adopt a rule to abolish bowl games, and the presidents expressed an intent to vote against giving permission for any school to participate in a bowl game on New Year's Day, 1952. At the Annual Meeting on December 14, the University of Maryland requested permission to participate in the Sugar Bowl on January 1. Although the Bylaws stated that postseason football games were not permitted without the consent of the Conference, Maryland had signed a contract with the Mid-Winter Sports Organization of New Orleans prior to the Conference meeting. Maryland had assumed that, as had occurred in the past, consent was only a formality, and that the recommendations of the Presidents' meeting were not binding or retroactive.

However when the motion was called, the Conference voted 14 to 3 to deny permission to Maryland. Furthermore, the Conference adopted, by a 12 to 5 vote, a resolution that any member institution participating in a postseason football game in 1952 or thereafter would be placed on probation for one year. Probation meant that said institution would not be able to vote as a Conference member, or participate in any football games with other members of the Conference. Maryland went to the Sugar Bowl anyway and beat Tennessee 28–13. Clemson also went to a bowl game, losing 14–0 to Miami of Florida in the Gator Bowl. The following football season, which turned out to be the last for both teams in the Southern Conference, Maryland and South Carolina were the only Conference games on Clemson's schedule, and both games were played and lost by Clemson. Maryland had no other Conference games.

By 1953 the public clamor against college athletics had begun to subside. The NCAA, the regional athletic conferences, and the colleges and universities made a concerted effort to correct the abuses of intercollegiate athletics. It was in this new period of stability and development that the Atlantic Coast Conference was born.

Part II

The Formation and Development of the ACC

7

Birth of a New Conference

On May 7, 1953, the presidents, faculty chairmen, and athletic directors of the Southern Conference gathered at the Sedgfield Inn in Greensboro, North Carolina for their annual spring meeting. The major items of business were the question of freshmen participation, and participation in bowl games.

Because of the Korean War, the rule against freshmen participating on varsity teams had been waived in 1951 and 1952. Effective September 1, 1953, the waiver would be lifted and freshmen again would be ineligible. Virginia Tech proposed that "a freshman shall not be allowed to compete on any intercollegiate athletic team during his freshman year." President Walter S. Newman, of Virginia Tech, explained that this proposal was a means of de-emphasis, and took into consideration the economic problems of fielding so many teams, and the interference with a student's academic work.

Maryland sought to have the ban on postseason bowl games lifted, and to amend the Bylaws so "a team of a member institution may compete in those extra events that meet the requirements of and are approved by the National Collegiate Athletic Association." Maryland and Clemson had been suspended for the 1952 football season after appearing in bowl games that January against the rules of the Southern Conference.

There was also some speculation in the newspaper that the Conference might split up if agreement could not be reached on the major items of business. Appearing in the *Durham Morning Herald* that day was a column by Ken Alyta in which he said, "The old talk of breaking up the sprawling conference into a sure compact group again is heard, but with no place on the agenda, it will be reduced to unofficial hotel lobby or smoke-filled room status."

Hugo Germino, writing in *The Durham Sun*, commented, "If the bowl question is not settled amicably, there is talk that the old suggestion of splitting up the ungainly Conference will come up again . . . However, since Conference realignment has no place on this weekend's agenda, nothing can be done officially at this meeting." Another article in *The Durham Sun* that day centered its attention on the meeting of the presidents, and the pressure on them to rescind the Conference ban on football bowl games. It went on to say that,

"Should the Maryland move fail, there might be action on a much talked-about but never officially considered plan to split the conference."

At the presidents' meeting Thursday afternoon, May 7 (which preceded the Conference meeting on Friday), the question of freshman participation and postseason bowls did come up, without any settlement, but there was no mention of breaking up the 17-member Southern Conference. Moreover, only six presidents, those from Davidson, Duke, North Carolina, Wake Forest, Virginia Tech, and Richmond, were present.

However later that evening, at 9:30 P.M., the following representatives met at a special session to put into effect the desire to separate from the Southern Conference and form a new organization. They were:

Clemson College
Lee W. Milford, Faculty Chairman
Frank Howard, Athletic Director

Duke University
Charles E. Jordan, Faculty Chairman
Edmund M. Cameron, Athletic Director

North Carolina State College
H. A. Fisher, Faculty Chairman
Roy B. Clogston, Athletic Director

University of North Carolina
Robert B. House, Chancellor
Allan W. Hobbs, Faculty Chairman
Charles P. Erickson, Athletic Director
Oliver K. Cornwell, Chairman, Physical Education and Athletics

University of South Carolina
James T. Penney, Faculty Chairman
Rex Enright, Athletic Director

Wake Forest College
Harold W. Tribble, President
Forrest W. Clonts, Faculty Chairman
James H. Weaver, Athletic Director

University of Maryland
Geary E. Eppley, Faculty Chairman
James M. Tatum, Athletic Director

James T. Penney of South Carolina was asked to serve as temporary chairman, and Oliver K. Cornwell of North Carolina was asked to serve as temporary secretary. The following motion, made by H. A. Fisher of North Carolina State, and seconded by Lee Milford of Clemson, was passed unanimously, and the Atlantic Coast Conference, as yet unnamed, was born.

In view of the increasing problems in intercollegiate athletics it is the opinion of the group present that the formation of a smaller conference is desirable.

We, therefore, propose to recommend that a new conference be formed consisting of the seven colleges and universities present.

That the colleges and universities present clear through proper channels the approval of this action.

That a meeting of the seven schools be called as soon as possible after proper clearance is obtained.

Left to right, 1st row: Gus Tebell, Virginia, Athletic Director; Oliver K. Cornwell, North Carolina, Secretary-Treasurer of the ACC; Rex Enright, South Carolina, Athletic Director. 2nd row: Charles P. (Chuck) Erickson, North Carolina, Athletic Director; Frank Howard, Clemson, Athletic Director and Head Football Coach; Wallace Wade, Duke, Athletic Director and Head Football Coach, and ACC Commissioner

Left to right, 1st row: H.C. (Curly) Byrd, Maryland, University President; Jim Tatum, Maryland, Athletic Director and Head Football Coach and Head Football Coach, North Carolina; Roy B. Clogston, North Carolina State, Athletic Director. 2nd row: James H. (Jim) Weaver, ACC Commissioner; Eddie Cameron, Duke, Athletic Director. 3rd row: Dr. James T. Penney, South Carolina, First Conference President

37

It was then decided that a committee of Clonts, Jordan, and Eppley would meet with Max Farrington, the President of the Southern Conference, before the Conference meeting scheduled for Friday morning, May 8th. They were to inform him of the action taken by the seven institutions, and to request that he order this Conference meeting immediately into executive session. Another committee of Penney, Fisher, and Cameron was appointed to meet with a committee of the Southern Conference to discuss the following problems: 1) commissioner's office; 2) booking office; 3) conference name; 4) conference assets and liabilities; and 5) attitude toward present commitments. Meanwhile, O.K. Cornwell was instructed to get clearance on the action taken from each of the institutions involved. A meeting of the representatives from each institution was scheduled for the weekend of June 12 in Raleigh.

The *Durham Morning Herald* printed a bulletin on the first page of their May 8 Sports Section.

In a telephone conversation with Sports Editor Jack Horner from Greensboro last night he reported that it looked like the split of the Southern Conference would come at Friday's opening session.

The presidents of the conference schools and their athletic directors met in a secret session which lasted until midnight at which final plans for the split were formulated.

At 10:00 A.M. on May 8, 1953, President Farrington called the meeting of the Southern Conference to order. After the roll was checked, Farrington requested those not officially representing a conference institution to leave, and he then ordered the Conference into executive session. Dr. Penney of South Carolina was recognized by the chair, and he presented the following resolution.

Mr. President, as most of you well know, for some time there has been under consideration a possibility of forming a new and smaller playing Conference. These ideas were crystallized at a meeting last night, in which Clemson College, Duke University, the University of North Carolina, the University of South Carolina, Wake Forest College, North Carolina State College, and the University of Maryland, decided that they should notify the Southern Conference that they propose to organize a new intercollegiate athletic conference.

This action was taken with mixed feelings, as all of us have formed many personal and institutional friendships through the years. It is our belief that this action will be the best for all concerned. We realize that there are certain obligations and commitments which we in no way wish to abrogate.

Where any large group separates, there are many administrative details to be considered, and for this reason, our institutions have appointed a Committee, consisting of Dr. H. A. Fisher of North Carolina State College, Mr. Eddie Cameron of Duke University, and J.T. Penney of the University of South Carolina. It is hoped that the remaining institutions in the Conference will appoint a similar committee to meet with ours as soon as possible.

President Farrington asked the representatives of the seven institutions to recess at this time in order that the ten remaining members might confer. They were: The Citadel, Davidson, Furman, Richmond, George Washington, Virginia Military Institute, Virginia Tech, William and Mary, Washington and Lee, and West Virginia. They appointed a committee headed by President Farrington to meet with the committee of the seceding group. The two committees met with Commissioner Wallace Wade at a two-hour luncheon session, and then each reported back to its own group.

Dr. Penney asked representatives of the seven institutions, "Would it be possible for the seventeen institutions making up the Southern Conference to use the same policies, same facilities, but build schedules among the seven institutions as they saw fit and remain in the same conference?" It was moved by Hobbs and seconded by Clonts that the proposal be rejected, and the motion was passed. This would have amounted to a conference within a conference but allowed all 17 schools to share tournament and bowl games profits.

President Farrington reconvened the Southern Conference meeting at 6:10 P.M. that night. This would be the final meeting of all 17 institutions together. Farrington reported on the three propositions proposed to the Southern Conference committee as possible solutions to the problems of Conference division, and stated that Proposition I had been accepted. It stated: "That the Southern Conference keep all assets and assume all liabilities, but that the new Conference will have the services of the Commissioner's Office and the Booking Office until January 1, 1955." Wallace Wade agreed to be Commissioner of both Conferences, but expressed doubt whether this was advisable in view of the many problems that would probably arise.

The feeling of understanding and good will that pervaded throughout the meetings was expressed by George Modlin of Richmond and R.B. House of North Carolina. President Modlin stated that though he did not know the consensus of opinion of all 10-member institutions, he felt that he was speaking in behalf of his other colleagues, by saying that they appreciated the fine spirit in which the separation of the Conference was taking place. Chancellor House stated that he responded 100 percent to Dr. Modlin's statement and expressed the feeling that they (the 7-member institutions) as the initiating group had less legal right to the generosity with which they had been treated. He expressed the feeling that as the 17 representative institutions adjourned, they did so in a spiritual unity, recognizing certain problems in each distinct Conference.

At 8:30 that night, the seven institutions met again to discuss certain details pertinent to the formation of a new conference. The meeting was chaired by Dr. Penney; and Clonts, Eppley, and Jordan were appointed as a temporary executive committee. It was agreed that the rules and regulations of the Southern Conference (with possible amendments) would be adopted for the first year, 1953–1954. Erickson, Tatum, and Cameron were requested to arrange a meeting of the athletic directors prior to the June meeting in Raleigh, and Roy Clogston was asked to make the arrangements for the Raleigh meeting. All institutions were requested to obtain and file a clearance with regard to their withdrawal from the Southern Conference and the formation of the new conference.

Although the newspapers had speculated about a possible "split" in the Southern Conference, no one really suspected it would materialize at this meeting in Greensboro. When the "split" was announced, the reaction of most people was one of surprise. M. P. (Footsie) Knight, Supervisor of Officials for the Southern Conference at the time, stated that it came as quite a surprise to him.

Prior to the meeting at Sedgfield, I had heard nothing about any division at all. We went up to the meeting there and all of a sudden somebody got up and made the provision that these seven were going to drop out and form a new conference. Well, to me it was just like dropping a thunderbolt. I had heard it discussed from time to time, but nobody ever had any idea that there would be any substance to it.

When asked if the members in the Southern Conference were surprised at the announcement of the "split," Wallace Wade, Conference Commissioner at that time, replied:

Yes. I think most of the people left in it were surprised. It was a complete surprise to me, and I thought I knew Duke about as well as anybody. I knew there was interest in it and I knew they were talking about it, but I had no idea that they had developed a program to the extent that they had when they sprang it in Greensboro that day. I believe that was true with most of the people.

Hugo Germino, Sports Editor of *The Durham Sun*, commented:

We had heard rumors several months before the meeting, but then all of a sudden it came out like a thunderbolt and a whole gang of sportswriters gathered to see what was going to happen. I thought it was pretty much a well-kept secret until they met up there, although there had been some comments about there being too many teams in the Conference.

The reaction in the press was almost unanimous that the break up of the Southern Conference would be in the best interest of all.

Jack Horner wrote in the *Durham Morning Herald*:

This corner is delighted to see the seven more athletic minded members of the Southern Conference pull out and form a new conference of their own. It's a forward step no less. The sports-loving public should welcome the move . . . Most everyone was caught by surprise at the sudden turn of events, but I believe they are glad to see it come about.

Hugo Germino wrote in *The Durham Sun*:

Happy days! At long last a division has been made in the unwieldy 17-member Southern Conference.

The seven top schools in the Conference have pulled out to form their own, more compact loop.

It's the finest move possible for all concerned—even for the 10 schools left behind, the so-called "weaker" sisters of the Conference. Now they can compete among themselves on more equal terms.

Wilton Garrison wrote in *The Charlotte Observer*:

The splitting of the Southern Conference, although not unexpected, came suddenly. Two years ago at the Richmond meeting, when Clemson and Maryland were suspended for accepting bowl bids, the breakup was inevitable. The football "career" schools wanted one thing and some of the others wanted something else.

The new group has the good wishes and blessing of the old. Several of the new members said they would not join unless they had the approval of their good friends, which they got.

Both the new and old conferences have fine opportunities ahead of them. There are many problems to settle, especially in scheduling, but it is an opportunity to have two strong leagues (according to their own strength) due to better matching and more equality. N.C. State must improve in football in the new conference but that is evidently planned. Here's wishing good luck to both and with capable leadership, both should succeed.

Dick Herbert wrote in the Raleigh *News and Observer*:

For years there has been agitation for a division of the unwieldy Southern Conference. Today it became an acutality, startling some with its suddenness, yet being achieved with a minimum of acrimony. The inevitable brought some disappointment, some uncertainty, many questions, but no real hard feelings.

Successful operation of the new conference should not be difficult. Each of the seven members has extensive athletic programs. Their physical plants are adequate.

The new conference should be able to create more interest nationally than the old one, for it will be much easier to keep up with seven or eight schools than with 17. There won't be many weak links placing a burden on the strong.

Because of the difficulty in keeping up with the Southern Conference and making its prestige great nationally sports writers for years have been advocating a division which would place the large schools with strong athletic programs in the same league.

Parting was sad, but almost everyone agreed, "It was inevitable." They were happy it happened without much bitterness.

The feeling of understanding and good will expressed earlier by Dr. Modlin and Chancellor House had truly permeated the two groups involved in the division of the Southern Conference, but it was inevitable there would be some disappointment. The much respected Dr. C. P. (Sally) Miles, Faculty Chairman from Virginia

Tech, was quoted, "It's the saddest day of my life. We hate to lose Duke, North Carolina and the other schools, but maybe we can get along." As "Footsie" Knight recalled, "There were no hard feelings that I could detect anywhere. I mean it just worked right on out."

This sudden announcement of the division of the Southern Conference immediately raised the questions: what brought about the split, and how did the withdrawal of seven members come about? Talk of splitting the Conference had appeared from time to time through the years but without any substance. Dr. Hollis Edens of Duke had commented in Greensboro, "I've been hearing talk of a new conference from time to time ever since coming to Duke (1949). This isn't anything new. Maybe it's the first time anyone has decided to do anything about it."

According to Duke Athletic Director Eddie Cameron, the groundwork for the new conference was actually laid in January 1952 at the NCAA Convention in Cincinnati. There at the Netherland Plaza Hotel, Rex Enright, (South Carolina), Jim Tatum, (Maryland), Chuck Erickson, (North Carolina), and Cameron agreed that something ought to be done about the scheduling problems in the Conference. They decided to go back and talk with their faculty chairmen and presidents about these problems and the possibility of forming a new conference. Duke and North Carolina were the key schools involved in forming a new conference. If they agreed to join, then it was felt that North Carolina State, Wake Forest, and Clemson would follow their lead. With Maryland and South Carolina already agreed, the conference would then be formed. President Gordon Gray of the University of North Carolina stated that if they formed a new conference, it ought to be a "playing conference," one in which everyone plays everyone else. Duke was somewhat reluctant, however, to commit itself to playing every Conference school every year in football. Duke and North Carolina had no problem in scheduling football games with the big schools in other conferences— the Southeastern, Southwest, Big Ten, etc. In fact, both schools felt it was necessary financially in order to carry out their large athletic programs to continue scheduling schools like Georgia Tech, Tennessee, Army, Navy, Notre Dame, Michigan, and Ohio State. It was only after certain guidelines were established and Duke was assured of some flexibility that it agreed to join. The importance of flexibility in scheduling was emphasized by Eddie Cameron's remarks:

If it hadn't worked out, we would have gone independent. I mean it was either the Conference or independent because we weren't about to saddle ourselves with a local schedule. The whole principle of Duke's operation from the adminstrative level has been to make it a national institution, and we wanted the right to schedule teams from California, or New Orleans, or Ohio, or Michigan. Yes, we would have gone independent. We would not have stayed with the old Southern Conference.

President Gray had been given approval by The University Trustees Executive Committee to determine whether North Carolina and North Carolina State should enter the new Conference. Entrance was based upon the following conditions:

1. That as early as practical each member of the conference regularly schedule football games with each other conference member each year.
2. That the conference not permit freshman participation in varsity sports.
3. That the conference set up adequate standards for admission of students and scholarship requirements looking toward degrees.
4. That so far as possible the conference encourage participation by all members in all sports so as not to limit competition to the major sports of football, basketball and baseball.
5. If a majority of the members wish to permit postseason contests, to permit such participation under a conference rule which would prohibit institutions from profiting. The conference in its organizational meeting would determine the disposition of receipts from such contests after the expenses of participating teams had been met.

Although other factors were important, scheduling in the unwieldy 17-member Southern Conference was the key factor that brought about the "split." The larger institutions (with 40,000 seat stadiums) felt it was impractical to schedule games with the smaller schools (with 10,000 seat stadiums). There was also the problem of determining a Conference champion when it was impossible for all the teams to play each other. In 1950, Washington and Lee had the best record in the Southern Conference, 6 and 0, and 8 and 2 overall. They went to the Gator Bowl and lost to Wyoming 20–7. However they did not play Clemson, which was 9-0-1 overall, but only 3 and 0 in the Conference. Nor did they play any other member of the seceding seven. Scheduling problems were not limited to football. In basketball it was necessary to play 12 conference games in order to qualify for the eight-team tournament. There was a scramble by some schools each year to schedule the weakest teams in the Conference to ensure a winning record and a place in the tournament.

There was some talk the suspension of Maryland and Clemson by the Southern Conference, and the ban against postseason bowl games had caused the "split." However neither Eddie Cameron nor Wallace Wade seemed to think the bowl ban had been an important factor in organizing the new conference. President Edens of Duke had stressed this fact at time of the "split," pointing out that it was Duke and North Carolina who were instrumental in passing the bowl ban and getting Clemson and Maryland suspended. Now they were all in the same conference. Representatives from Miami, including the general manager of the Orange Bowl, were present at the meetings in Greensboro, however.

The big question left unanswered when the announcement of the "split" was made was what school, if any, would become the eighth member of the new conference. The three schools most often mentioned were West Virginia, Virginia Tech, and Virginia. West Virginia, a newcomer (1950) to the Southern Conference, was disappointed when the larger schools withdrew and was very interested in joining them. Their athletic director, Roy M. (Legs) Hawley, was well liked and West Virginia had a strong athletic program, but Morgantown was a hard place to travel to. It was felt that West Virginia was severely hindered by its geographical location, particularly in scheduling "minor sports." Virginia Tech was not considered very likely because it did not field strong football teams. The situation with Virginia was a mystery. Some representatives opposed Virginia because they had pulled out of the Southern Conference in 1936 and remained an independent. Others felt quite favorable toward Virginia, believing it would be a natural geographically and would balance the Conference numerically. Athletic Director Gus Tebell said, "Virginia would consider seriously joining the new Conference but the ultimate decision would have to be made by President Colgate Darden, and the Board of Visitors." Tebell hastened to add that Virginia had had absolutely no part in breaking up the Southern Conference, although he had heard reports in might be done.

Some even wondered why North Carolina State was invited by the football powers in the new conference. State was in the process, however, of developing plans to move up in football and had formed a committee to talk with coaches Jim Tatum, Bobby Dodd, Wallace Wade and Bob Neyland about this. Plans were made to enlarge the football stadium and to become a power in the Conference by 1955. It is interesting to note that two years from this target date (1957), North Carolina State won the Atlantic Coast Conference football championship.

The weekend following the "split," the Southern Conference wound up their last championships as a 17-member conference. In spring sports North Carolina copped golf and tennis, Duke won the baseball, and Maryland took the track title. According to Wilton Garrison, "the only championship left is lacrosse and we suggest a round-robin between Carolina, Duke and Maryland in Kenan Stadium at Chapel Hill—right behind the new hospital where all the players would probably wind up."

44

8

The Development of the ACC

The athletic directors of the seven seceding institutions met in Durham on May 25, and in Chapel Hill on May 26 to work out schedules for all sports. Commissioner Wade, "Footsie" Knight of the Booking Office, and temporary Secretary O.K. Cornwell were also present. Sports committees were set up and plans were made to make it a "playing conference" in a wide variety of sports. It was agreed that the Basketball Tournament would be held at the North Carolina State Coliseum, and that Eddie Cameron, as Chairman of the Basketball Committee, would contact the NCAA about participation in the National Tournament.

On Sunday, June 14, 1953, representatives from the seven seceding institutions of the new conference met at the Sir Walter Hotel in Raleigh, along with Commissioner Wade, "Footsie" Knight, and William Friday of the Consolidated University of North Carolina. Secretary Cornwell reported that all the schools had filed letters of authorization to withdraw from the Southern Conference except Duke. Dr. Jordan stated that Duke was not free to file a letter of authorization until a policy concerning football scheduling was definitely established. After some discussion, the following policy was passed, and Jordan stated that the authorization statement from Duke University would be filed immediately.

It is resolved that in line with our basic principles of making this a playing conference, all teams shall play each other team in football as soon as practicable.

Pending the successful attainment of this goal, the following requirements are agreed upon. Should the conference remain in a seven (7) member conference, each school shall play at least five (5) other schools in the conference beginning no later than 1956. Should the conference become an eight (8) member conference, each school shall play at least six (6) other schools in the conference beginning no later than 1957. Each school must play all other members at least once in three years.

Many suggestions for a name for the new conference had appeared in the North Carolina newspapers prior to this meeting in Raleigh. Some of them were: Dixie, Mid-South, Mid-Atlantic, East Coast, Seaboard, Colonial, Confederate, Tobacco, Cotton, Blue-Gray, Piedmont, Rebel, Big 8, Southern Seven, Shoreline, and Atlantic Coast. Eddie Cameron recommended that the name of the new conference be the Atlantic Coast Conference and the motion passed unanimously. Cameron, claiming no credit for the originality of the name, said it seemed logical since there was a Pacific Coast Conference at that time, and all seven institutions in the new conference were in states bordering on the Atlantic Coast.

The first officers elected in the Atlantic Coast Conference (ACC) were: James T. Penney of South Carolina, President; Forrest W. Clonts of Wake Forest, Vice-President; and Oliver K. Cornwell of North Carolina, Secretary-Treasurer. A committee on Constitution and Bylaws, with Cornwell as chairman, was appointed to report back at the next meeting of the Conference on August 7, in Greensboro, North Carolina, and each member institution was assessed $200 to pay the Conference expenses. This was necessary because all assets of the Southern Conference (approximately $150,000) were left with the remaining ten members. In Cameron's words, the new Conference started "cold," without any money. This was one of the reasons that the Basketball Tournament at the end of the season was continued. The Conference needed the revenue from the tournament in order to pay the Commissioner, develop tournaments in other sports, and meet the general operating expenses.

It was then moved by Dr. Hobbs that the University of Virginia be invited to become a member of the Conference. Dr. Jordan seconded the motion and it was passed. The procedure for extending the invitation was delegated to Penney and Cameron. The question of Virginia Tech and West Virginia was then brought up. Dr. Hobbs again moved that an invitation to membership be extended to both institutions, but the motion failed for lack of a second. There were no representatives from any of these three schools present at the meeting.

In other business at the first official ACC meeting, the proposal to ban freshmen from all intercollegiate competition was rejected. The ACC kept the same rules as the Southern Conference that freshmen were not eligible for varsity competition but could participate on freshman teams. Most of the recommendations concerning schedules in the various sports, which were made at the athletic directors' meeting in May, were adopted. This, and the referral to the Constitution Committee of new amendments allowed the meeting to run smoothly and effectively. The Secretary was requested to file an application for Conference membership in the NCAA, and a week later the request was granted. The question of a post-season bowl tie-up was never raised at this meeting.

On August 7 the ACC met again at the Sedgfield Inn in Greensboro and adopted a Constitution and Bylaws. The major item of business was the report by Commissioner Wade on the alleged violations of North Carolina State of the rules and regulations of the NCAA and

Top: Sedgefield Country Club
and Inn, Birthplace of the
ACC, May 7, 1953

Left: King Cotton Hotel,
Greensboro, N.C., Confer-
ence Office, 1954-1966

the ACC. Wade presented the material sent to him by Walter Byers, Executive Secretary of the NCAA, pertinent to charges against State:

1. Holding tryouts for basketball players.
2. Using Athletic Association funds to pay transportation expenses for prospective athletes visiting North Carolina State's campus.
3. Grants-in-aid or scholarships to athletes that exceeded the amount allowed under NCAA and the Atlantic Coast Conference rules and regulations.

It was alleged that fourteen athletes were brought to Raleigh in the Spring of 1953 for basketball tryouts, and their expenses were paid. It was rumored at the time that future All-American "Hot Rod" Hundley was one of the athletes involved. This was later denied, but Hundley did enroll at West Virginia instead. The other reports involved payments of $75 a month and other benefits to basketball star Ronnie Shavlik. After much discussion concerning the charges, it was agreed by the ACC and the officials at State that there was sufficient evidence to prove charges one and two, but not enough evidence to prove charge three. President Penney then made the following motion which was passed by the Conference:

That North Carolina State College be placed on probation in the Atlantic Coast Conference for one year and that the boys concerned in the violation of the NCAA and the Atlantic Coast Conference rules and regulations be ineligible for intercollegiate athletics at N.C. State College.

According to Wallace Wade, this resolution was the key to the future success of the ACC. A problem of this magnitude could have wrecked the Conference before it had had an opportunity to develop. The NCAA and others were watching how this new conference would react to this situation. Some figured it would be easier to turn their backs and overlook violations by a friend or neighboring institution when an admonition might upset future financial arrangements. However, the founders of the Atlantic Coast Conference were so intent on developing the ACC as a leading athletic conference that they were able to put the welfare of the Conference ahead of their own institutional advantage. The ACC hoped to demonstrate to the NCAA that they were capable of handling their own problems, and they proved this capability by placing North Carolina State on probation. The NCAA later announced that it was removing the 1954 Eastern Regional Basketball Tournament from Reynolds Coliseum in Raleigh because of the recruiting violations.

It was also recommended at the August meeting that the Conference approve restricted competition beyond the regular schedule. A general discussion of bowl games followed, centering around three factors: 1) an institution should not be compelled to participate in a bowl; 2) an institution should not profit by participating in a bowl; and 3) players should receive no payment for participating in a bowl game. The Conference then passed a motion by Eppley to approve participation in bowl games according to the rules and regulations set forth by the NCAA and the ACC. Furthermore, the bowl receipts would be divided as follows: The participating team would be allowed to keep one-half of its share of the gate receipts; of the remaining half, the Conference would receive 25 percent and the other 75 percent would be divided equally among the other members of the Conference. Now it remained to be seen if the ACC would tie-up with a major bowl.

The Orange Bowl had shown an interest in the ACC right from the start. Orange Bowl representatives were present at the Southern Conference meeting in May when the "split" occurred. Competition was keen each year among the Bowls to secure the best football teams, particularly among the "Big 4" Bowls. The Rose Bowl had a tie-up with the Pacific Coast and Big Ten Conference, the Cotton Bowl was tied-up with the Southwest Conference, and the Sugar Bowl usually had the champion from the Southeastern Conference. This put the pressure on the Orange Bowl to secure top flight teams, and they were anxious to insure this with a "major conference contract."

The Bowl Committee of the Conference explored the possibilities of a tie-up with all the major bowls. They met with representatives of the Sugar Bowl, the Cotton Bowl, and the Big Seven Conference in Chicago on August 14. Four days later they met with representatives from the Orange Bowl in Durham. On October 2, Dr. H.C. (Curly) Byrd, President of the University of Maryland and a prime mover in the "split," expressed his opinion that the ACC would sign an agreement with the Orange Bowl to meet a representative from the Big Seven Conference soon. On October 11, six Orange Bowl representatives from Miami, three representatives from the Big Seven Conference, and the ACC Bowl Committee along with Wallace Wade met in the Washington Duke Hotel in Durham. The meetings were held in secret until Commissioner Wade released the following statement:

Representatives of the Atlantic Coast Conference, the Big Seven Conference and the Orange Bowl met here today and they are exploring the possibilities of a permanent tie up for an annual Orange Bowl game between representatives of the two conferences. No decision has been made and none will be made today.

It was later discovered that the contract had not been signed at this time because the representatives from the Big Seven did not have full authorization to act, and they needed additional information regarding the terms of the contract. One of the problems was the fact that the Big Seven did not want the same team to appear twice in succession (like the Big Ten rule at that time for the Rose Bowl). The ACC would not agree to this. Faculty representatives of the Big Seven Conference met in Kansas City on October 18, and approved a two-year contract. The announcement was made by Orange Bowl President W. Bruce Mac Intosh, who said, "I'm just as happy as I can be with our agreement with these great conferences. The initial agreement is for two years, but we hope and I believe it will become a permanent fixture."

The Big Seven Conference was composed of Kansas, Kansas State, Nebraska, Missouri, Iowa State, Oklahoma, and Colorado. The Missouri Valley Intercollegiate Athletic Association, as it was officially named at that time, added Oklahoma State as its eighth member in 1957, and became known officially in 1964 as the Big Eight Conference.

Morris McLemore of the *Miami Daily News* had this comment about the new agreement:

Nobody around here claims the Big Seven or the Atlantic Coast, as a conference, will produce the number of powerful teams found year after year in the SEC. . . But the Big Seven and the Atlantic Coast are willing to guarantee their best teams in each case. This assures the Orange Bowl a fair match of real consequence and with honor, not with a hat-in-hand, please gimmie-a-break attitude that has been necessary when approaching some of the SEC wheels up yonder in the bush.

In Washington, D.C. on November 15, the ACC and the Big Seven Conference officially signed a contract to appear in the 1954 and 1955 Orange Bowl. Each team was guaranteed a minimum of $110,000. Only a two-year contract was signed at this time because the ACC wanted to study the results before adopting a permanent policy. The radio and television contracts with the Orange Bowl also expired in two years and, according to "Chuck" Erickson who was Chairman of the Bowl Committee and had played a major part in working out the contract details with television, a new contract would then have to be negotiated.

President Penney announced on November 24 that the Conference had unanimously selected Maryland to represent the ACC in the Orange Bowl on New Year's Day. Maryland, undefeated with a 10 and 0 record and the nation's No. 1 team, was paired against fourth-ranked Oklahoma, loser only to Notre Dame. Duke actually had a 4-0 Conference record (7-2-1 overall) compared to Maryland's 3-0 record, but the Conference had agreed to select, "the most representative team" as there was no official Conference champion.

An editorial in the New Orleans *Times-Picayune* discussed the upcoming bowl games and had this to say:

One circumstance. . . the tying up of five conference champions by three other 'bowls'. . .is changing the whole face of post-season football as it used to be. Luck certainly attended the first casting of this die by the Orange Bowl, for it has the game of the year in Maryland vs Oklahoma.

In a hard fought defensive struggle, Oklahoma upset Maryland 7–0. Oklahoma was coached by Bud Wilkinson, who had been an assistant to Jim Tatum before Tatum left Oklahoma for Maryland. The attendance under perfect skies was 68,718.

Meanwhile the question of who would be the eighth member in the Conference was still unanswered after the August meeting in Greensboro in spite of the previously accepted motion to invite Virginia. Dr. Colgate Darden, President of the University of Virginia, had said back in May, "We have had close and happy relations with several members of the new conference and we hope to continue these relations." However, Darden declined to say if Virginia was interested in joining the new conference. The student newspaper at Virginia, *The Cavalier Daily*, suggested that Virginia join the Southern Conference where all its state rivals (Virginia Tech, Virginia Military Institute, William and Mary, Washington and Lee, and Richmond) were and forget about the new conference. President Darden admitted that there was strong sentiment by many alumni and supporters for Virginia to join the Southern Conference. The possibility was also raised that the Southern Conference might extend an invitation to Virginia before the ACC did.

On June 12 the Board of Visitors at Virginia had met to discuss the policies of the athletic program and the advisibility of joining the new conference. At the conclusion of the meeting, the Board did not announce a stand on the question of membership in the new conference. However, they did remove one of the obstacles to admission in the new conference by revising their athletic grant-in-aid program. The Board authorized "institutional control of grants-in-aid to student athletes in compliance with the regulations of the Sanity Code of the NCAA." Previously all scholarships and funds were controlled by alumni groups. Ever since Virginia withdrew from the Southern Conference in 1936 in apparent disagreement with the "Graham Plan," they had operated independently with their own eligibility and recruiting policies. Virginia was concerned with the strict transfer rule that the ACC had adopted. The rule prohibited an athlete from competing in the same sport after transferring from one member institution to another member institution. Virginia had also gone on record as opposing postseason football games.

Meanwhile, Virginia Tech, in an apparent move toward acceptance by the ACC, announced that it had signed Athletic Director and

51

Football Coach Frank Mosely to a new eight-year contract, and had decided on a big time athletic policy. There was also speculation that Virginia's reluctance to join hinged on the acceptance of Virginia Tech. It was assumed that Virginia wanted a "package deal" whereby both schools would be accepted together. It appeared that it might be a political problem with the state legislature and the appropriations to the two state schools. The ACC was not interested in increasing the membership to nine at this time however.

On October 8, ACC President Penney, in a telephone conversation with President Darden, extended an invitation to Virginia to join the Atlantic Coast Conference. Darden accepted the invitation. The acceptance was made possible by an earlier announcement from Rector Barron F. Black that the Virginia Board of Visitors agreed to join the ACC if an invitation was issued. President Penney stated that the invitation had been agreed on previously by the other conference members, but he could not say whether the Conference would be limited to eight schools. At the first annual winter meeting of the Conference on December 4, 1953, the University of Virginia was officially admitted to the ACC.

In other business, Eddie Cameron reported on the Basketball Tournament, and recommended that it be held at North Carolina State beginning the first Thursday in March. The winner of the Tournament was to be the ACC representative in the NCAA Tournament. Virginia was made eligible for the Tournament but would be seeded eighth regardless of their won and lost record. The first ACC Tournament was typical of those that would follow, as Wake Forest and South Carolina went into overtime in the first game of the Tournament before the Deacons won 58–57. State rallied in the second half to edge North Carolina 52–51 in the first round while Maryland beat Clemson 75–59 and Duke beat Virginia 96–68. In the second round State beat Duke 79–75, and Wake Forest went into overtime again to beat Maryland 64–56. Then in the finals a third overtime game was played as North Carolina State beat Wake Forest 82–80. There were a number of outstanding players in that first tournament including ACC Player of the Year, Dickie Hemric of Wake Forest, Gene Shue of Maryland, Ron Shavlik of State, and "Buzz" Wilkinson of Virginia. The Wolfpack went on to place third in the Eastern Regionals, beating George Washington 75–73, losing to La Salle 88–81, and beating Cornell 65–54.

A Planning Committee was appointed to project the future of the Conference beyond January 1, 1955, the time the contract with Commissioner Wade expired. Although planning to retire, Wallace Wade had agreed to stay on as Commissioner of the Southern

Conference until January 1, 1956. Wade felt that his loyalty lay with his friends in the Southern Conference, those who had employed him originally. There was a feeling by some that Wade had never been given enough authority by the Southern Conference. Wade acknowledged that he had not been given as much authority as some commissioners in other conferences. He reasoned that it was the old philosophy of "States Rights" that permeated the Southern institutions which made them not want to surrender too much authority and control over their institutions to a commissioner. Wade stayed on as Commissioner of the Southern Conference however until 1960.

At their spring meeting, the ACC met again at the Sedgfield Inn in Greensboro on May 6 and 7, 1954. In doing so, they returned to the site of their "split" from the Southern Conference exactly one year before. The Planning Committee made their report, and they recommended the hiring of a new Commissioner at the expiration of Wade's contract. Many people from outside the Conference were considered for the post, but it was felt that first consideration should be given to a men associated with athletics in the ACC. This person would be familiar with the Conference, its members, and the direction it was trying to move. Speculation on those in the Conference centered around three men: Jim Weaver, Athletic Director at Wake Forest; Gus Tebell, Athletic Director at Virginia; and Conference Secretary O.K. Cornwell, Chairman of the Department of Physical Education and Athletics at North Carolina.

"Ollie" Cornwell, who withdrew from the Planning Committee when his name was mentioned as a candidate, had a lot of support in the Conference. Cornwell was highly respected, had been instrumental in writing the Constitution and Bylaws, and was active as Secretary-Treasurer of the Conference. However, Cornwell later withdrew his name from consideration because he was close to retirement from the University of North Carolina and had accummulated many retirement benefits in his 19 years of service.

The election of a Commissioner was postponed until May 28 when a special meeting of the ACC was held at the Sir Walter Hotel in Raleigh. It was recommended that the Office of the Commissioner be located in Greensboro, and the term of the contract be for five years commencing July 1, 1954. The starting salary would be $12,500, with increases up to $15,000 over the period of the contract. These recommendations were approved, and two men were placed in nomination: Jim Weaver and Gus Tebell. James H. (Jim) Weaver was elected on the first ballot by a 6 to 2 vote (which was later made unanimous) as the first Commissioner of the Atlantic Coast Conference. Weaver had come to Wake Forest in 1933 as Head Football Coach, and in 1937 he became Athletic Director.

This ended the first year of operation for a new athletic conference, the ACC. It had been a busy and noteworthy year, and in the eyes of most, a very successful one. In this short period of time the Atlantic Coast Conference had become one of the major intercollegiate athletic conferences in the United States.

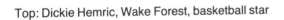

Top: Dickie Hemric, Wake Forest, basketball star

Center: Buzz Wilkinson, Virginia, basketball star

Bottom: Grady Wallace, South Carolina, basketball star

Top: Reynolds Coliseum, Raleigh N.C., Site of ACC Basketball Championships 1954-1966

Left to right, bottom: Ronnie Shavlik, North Carolina State, basketball star; Everett Case, North Carolina State, Head Basketball Coach

9

The Formative Fifties

As the Atlantic Coast Conference entered its second year of operation, it lost an individual who had played a significant role in the development of the Conference. At the same time it gained a new coach who would build a powerhouse on the football field. H.C. (Curly) Byrd resigned as President of the University of Maryland, effective January 2, 1954, to seek the Democratic nomination for Governor of the State. In 1912 Byrd started a reign of 23 years as Head Football Coach, the longest in the school's history. Byrd relinquished his coaching duties in 1934, and two years later he became President of the University. In his 18 years as President, Byrd was determined that Maryland would become a football power. This goal was achieved in 1953 when Maryland was acclaimed the "Number One" team in the nation. Byrd delayed his resignation as President until after Maryland had appeared in the Orange Bowl on New Year's Day, 1954. Byrd had been one of the leading instigators for the formation of a new athletic conference.

At the end of that same month, North Carolina State ended months of speculation by naming Earle Edwards as Head Football Coach. Much of the speculation had centered around the possibility of luring Jim Tatum away from Maryland as Head Coach to revive the football fortunes at State. Tatum had met with State officials earlier to discuss the development of their football program, and his name was linked as the successor to Horace Henrickson. However Earle Edwards, an end coach at Michigan State for six years, was signed to a three-year contract. At that time Michigan State completely reshuffled their personnel. "Biggie" Munn resigned as Head Coach to become Athletic Director; "Duffy" Daugherty moved up from line coach to replace Munn; Steve Sebo, the backfield coach, went to Pennsylvania as Head Coach; and Edwards came to North Carolina State. Sebo was later to become Athletic Director at Virginia.

On December 31, 1954, the ACC signed a new three-year contract with the Orange Bowl and the Big Seven. The terms of the contract called for each conference, starting in 1956, to receive about $203,000, as compared to the approximate $131,000 each conference would receive from the 1955 game. The Columbia Broadcasting System paid $825,000 for the radio and television rights to the three games in

1956, 1957, and 1958. The following day, Duke capped an outstanding year in which they had lost only to Army and Navy, by beating Nebraska 34–7 before a record Orange Bowl crowd of 68,750. Duke's tough defense limited Nebraska to only six first downs and 106 yards rushing. Captain Jerry Barger threw two touchdown passes and Bob Pascal rushed for 91 yeards in nine attempts. Vice-President Richard Nixon, a Duke alumnus, witnessed the game. The Miami newspapers were upset with the lopsided score and the selection of Nebraska since Oklahoma, the Big Seven champion, was not allowed to return two years in a row.

North Carolina State won the 1955 ACC Basketball Tournament in March by beating Duke 87–77. However, since State was ineligible to participate in the NCAA Tournament because of their one-year probation, runner-up Duke was selected. Duke lost a heartbreaker by one point 74–73 to Villanova in the first round. Meanwhile, State accepted an invitation to play in the AAU Championships and advanced to the quarterfinals before losing to the Olympic Club of San Francisco 70–60.

Upon the recommendation of the Conference basketball coaches, and approval by the Conference, the Basketball Committee informed the NCAA that they would not compete in the National Tournament the following year unless the ACC champion automatically qualified. The past two years the ACC had had to participate in a play-off game immediately after the Conference Tournament.

That spring Maryland won the first of its two back-to-back National Lacrosse Championships, and in July the ACC held a banquet in honor of Wake Forest for winning the NCAA Baseball Championship. In the fall, the Service Bureau inaugurated "Operation Football ACC," a flying tour of the member institutions in the Conference for the press, radio, and television. It provided a compact review of the coming football season, and has proven through the years to be an outstanding promotional event for the Conference.

The NCAA changed the National Basketball Tournament for 1956 to a later date in March, and as a result, the Conference in their December meeting voted to send the ACC champion, even though their request for automatic qualification was not granted. A move by the basketball coaches to allow participation in the National Invitation Tournament was not recommended and a clause was inserted into the Bylaws that prohibited participation in the AAU Tournament. Many felt that it had been embarrassing for the Conference champion to have participated in the AAU Tournament while the second place team had participated in the NCAA Tournament.

Although Duke and Maryland had both tied with 4–0 Conference football records, Maryland was undefeated overall and ranked third in both the AP and UPI polls for the 1955 season. Maryland represented the ACC in the Orange Bowl on January 2 and lost to top-ranked Oklahoma 20–6. Maryland had led 6–0 at halftime, but Oklahoma came roaring back to score 14 points in the third quarter and six in the final quarter to win their 30th consecutive game under Bud Wilkinson. Maryland's 15-game winning streak was halted. The Orange Bowl again had selected the two best teams, both of whom were undefeated, and the recored setting crowd of 75,561 was not disappointed.

On January 8, 1956, it was officially announced that Jim Tatum had accepted the position of Head Football Coach at the University of North Carolina, replacing George Barclay. In his nine years as Head Coach at Maryland, Tatum had three regular season undefeated teams (1951, 1953, 1955) and a record of 73 wins and only 15 losses. As a result of his outstanding record, his name was linked with every major coaching vacancy that occurred. Tatum was a North Carolina graduate, had coached there in 1942, and many felt he had turned down other coaching positions for the chance to return to Chapel Hill. Tar Heel supporters believed that Tatum would be the answer to six consecutive losing seasons, and six consecutive losses to arch-rival Duke. New football coaches were also named at four other Conference schools: Tommy Mont replaced Tatum at Maryland, Warren Giese replaced Rex Enright at South Carolina, Ben Martin replaced Ned McDonald at Virginia, and Paul Amen replaced Tom Rogers at Wake Forest.

One of the Conference highlights occurred that spring in the person of Dave Sime, a 19-year-old Duke sophomore. On May 5, Sime set a new world's record in the 220 yard low hurdles with a time of :22.2, breaking the old record of :22.3 set by Harrison Dillard in 1947. Sime also won the 100, the 220, placed second in the long jump, and was third in the discus to lead his team to victory over North Carolina. The following weekend in the ACC Meet, Sime set a new world's record in the 220 yard dash with a time of :20.1, breaking the old record of :20.2 set by Mel Patton in 1947. Sime also won the 100 and the 220 low hurdles before one of the largest crowds (over 6,000) ever to witness a track meet in the Conference. On June 3, in an AAU meet in Stockton, California, Sime tied the world's record for the 100 yard dash with a time of 9.3 seconds, and a week later at another AAU meet in Sanger, California, Sime bettered his record in the 220 with a time of :20.0. He also ran another 9.3 100 yard dash in that meet. At this point, Sime was being acclaimed as the "fastest human," and considered to be a sure medal winner that fall in the 1956 Olympic Games in Melbourne, Australia.

Above: Dave Sime, Duke, track star; left to right, bottom: Dick Christy, North Carolina State, football star; Bob Pellegrini, Maryland, football star

At the NCAA Meet in Berkeley on June 16, Sime qualified for the Olympic Trials by winning his heat of the 100 meters, but strained a groin muscle in finishing second in his heat of the 200 meters. The seriousness of the injury caused Sime to miss the National AAU Meet in Bakersfield, California the next weekend. The Olympic Trials were held in Los Angeles on June 29, and Sime reinjured his groin muscle in the 100 meter trials forcing him to drop out. Sime had received a special invitation from the Olympic Committee to compete in the 200 meter trials the next day, but he was physically unable to do it. Sime's injury prevented him from qualifying for the Olympic Games four months away. In November in Melbourne, Joel Shankle, a former teammate of Sime's, won the bronze medal in the 110 meter high hurdles, as Lee Calhoun of North Carolina Central University won the gold medal.

That fall a group of North Carolina Jaycees formed the Mid-South Athletic Club with the prime purpose of enlarging the ACC. They felt that by adding West Virginia, Pittsburgh, Penn State, and Navy to the Conference, the prestige and national reputation of the ACC would be enhanced. Their plan included two six-team divisions, with the teams playing their division opponents first, and then based on the record, their counterpart in the other division in the season finale. The proposed alignment, which failed for lack of popular support, would have been: *Southern Division*—Clemson, Duke, North Carolina, North Carolina State, South Carolina, Wake Forest; *Northern Division*—Maryland, Navy, Penn State, Pittsburgh, Virginia, West Virginia.

Clemson won its first ACC football title in 1956 with a 4–0–1 record, including a 6–6 tie with Maryland, and was selected to represent the ACC in the Orange Bowl. On New Year's Day, 1957, Colorado beat Clemson 27–21 in one of the most exciting Orange Bowl games yet played. Colorado dominated the first half and held a 20–0 lead at halftime. Clemson came roaring back to take a 21–20 lead at the beginning of the fourth quarter, but Colorado scored again when an onside kick by Clemson backfired, and won the game. Criticism over the selections had been heard again since undefeated Oklahoma was ineligible to return, and Clemson had been beaten during the regular season by the University of Miami (Florida), 21–0. For the first time in ten years, ads for tickets had been placed in the newspapers, but at game time, the crowd of 75,552 was the second largest in history. Still the rumors persisted that the Orange Bowl pact would not be renewed after January 1, 1958.

The Conference met for their annual winter meeting in Greensboro on December 6, 1956, faced with an unprecedented amount of recruiting troubles. The problems began when the Executive Committee declared Don Coker, a former Reidsville, North Carolina high school halfback, ineligible for athletics at the University of North Carolina. Coker had been given a country club membership by a friend and alumnus of North Carolina, and Commissioner Weaver had ruled that this was aid beyond what was permitted by the Conference regulations. The following spring, after further investigation, Coker was allowed two years of eligibility.

Prior to the last game of the year with Duke, the University of North Carolina suspended football player Vince "Olen" when it was learned that he had falsified his application and eligibility papers by using an assumed name. "Olen" had played at Temple for two years, entered the Army, and then enrolled at North Carolina as a freshman. In December, Commissioner Weaver ruled that:

In accordance with the Atlantic Coast Conference Bylaws (Rule 15 Section B) The University of North Carolina football games of the 1956 season in which Vince Olenik participated shall be forfeited.

This office did not make an investigation but called the matter to the attention of the officials of the University of North Carolina. They acted promptly. The office received the full cooperation of their administrative officials. No one feels that any person at the University of North Carolina had any knowledge of the facts in the matter.

This office is hereby notifying the conference Service Bureau that in future records the 1956 season football games of the University of North Carolina in which Olenik participated shall be listed as forfeits.

Olenik had participated in nine games, and the forfeits changed the season record from 2–7–1 to 0 and 10.

Then it was announced that the NCAA Policy Council meeting in Detroit had placed North Carolina State on probation for a period of four years, effective immediately. During this period State was prohibited from participating in any NCAA championships and post-season events. Also, State was not allowed to participate in any NCAA televised event, be on any NCAA committee, nor allowed to vote on any questions before the Association. This was the stiffest penalty ever imposed by the NCAA at that time. Auburn and UCLA had previously received three-year suspensions. The NCAA had taken into account the fact that State had been on a one-year probation in 1954. The NCAA had found State guilty of violating the rules in recruiting the much sought after Jackie Moreland, a 6′ 8″ basketball star from Minden, Louisiana. The violations were:
1. Promising Moreland $200 a year for clothing during his college career.
2. Promising him an annual gift of $1000.

3. Promising Moreland's girlfriend an expense paid trip to Raleigh to meet Moreland at Thanksgiving time.
4. Promising his girlfriend a seven-year college medical education.
5. Giving Moreland $80 for transportation to enroll at State.
6. Promising Moreland a five-year scholarship at State.

Commissioner Weaver had ruled Jackie Moreland ineligible to play at North Carolina State in accordance with the findings of the NCAA. As a result, Dr. Carey H. Bostian, N.C. State Chancellor, requested that the ACC investigate the case. Dr. Bostian was invited to appear before the Faculty Chairmen of Athletics of the Conference, and after meeting with Dr. Bostian and members of the State Athletic staff, the faculty representatives "concluded that excessive financial aid was given to Moreland in violation of ACC regulations . . ."

A meeting of the State Athletic Council resulted in a vote of confidence for the athletic staff, and Bostian stated in a telegram to Weaver, "reaffirming again our belief, based on all the evidence known to us at this time, that State College is not guilty of the violations as charged in your telegram—we request the administrative officials of State College be permitted to appear before the faculty chairmen to answer the charges." Commissioner Weaver, in his telegram to Dr. Bostian, stated:

It is the decision of this office (1) that Jackie Moreland be declared ineligible for athletics at North Carolina State College; (2) that all basketball staff members be denied the privilege of contact with a prospective athlete for a period of one year; (3) that North Carolina State College be assessed a fine in the amount of $5,000, said fine to be cancelled should Jackie Moreland remain a student at North Carolina State College without athletic eligibility and under his present scholarship arrangement.

At the hearing of N.C. State officials, the Faculty Chairmen agreed to make a complete investigation into the Moreland case, and final action in the appeal by State would not be taken until this further investigation was completed. North Carolina State then asked for an open public hearing on the case with NCAA representatives invited to attend. The ACC rejected this request, however, and at the end of the fall semester, Moreland withdrew from State and enrolled at Louisiana Tech. He later played professional basketball with the Detroit Pistons and the New Orleans Buccaneers of the old ABA. He died suddenly in 1971 of cancer at the age of 33.

On February 13, 1957, the ACC reaffirmed it findings of illegal recruiting by North Carolina State. The ACC found State guilty of giving Moreland $80 for transportation to enroll at State and promising him a five-year scholarship. The Conference upheld the previously announced penalties which made Moreland ineligible, and banned recruiting for one year. However the Conference did reduce the fine from $5,000 to $2,500. In conclusion, the Conference ruled that the case was closed. Disappointed with the ACC findings, Dr. Bostian asked all the principal witnesses to appear at a hearing in Louisiana at the end of the month. State later dropped its efforts to hold a hearing because of its inability to get witnesses to appear.

Due to at least three conflicting versions by Moreland of the part State officials played, Bostian did not consider him a creditable witness. Before enrolling at State, Moreland had signed a letter of intent with Texas A & M, a grant-in-aid with Kentucky, and made plans to enroll at Centenary College. In his report to President Friday, Bostian stated that since it had not been established that any member of the athletic staff willfully violated any Conference regulations, he recommended that no action be taken against any members of the staff, and the case be closed. Those in question were Assistant Athletic Director Willis Casey, Assistant Basketball Coach Vic Bubas, and Harry Stewart. This report was accepted and approved by President Friday. In a letter sent by the mother, Mrs. J. B. Moreland, to Chancellor Bostian concerning the case, she concluded with these remarks:

It was no purpose to blame any one person or group of persons for this thing that has happened. Modern high pressure athletics has brought this about and until this has changed there will always be a "Jackie Moreland" or a "State College" for the goat.

The gloom over the Conference during the dark winter months of controversy eventually led to events that saw the ACC and one of its member institutions regain nationwide prestige and glory. On March 1, 1957, North Carolina beat Duke 86–72 in Durham to finish their regular basketball season undefeated in 24 games. At the ACC Tournament in Reynolds Coliseum the Tar Heels beat Clemson 81–61 in the opening round behind Lennie Rosenbluth's 45 points, a Tournament scoring record that still stands. In the semifinals, the Tar Heels trailed Wake Forest 59–58 with 55 seconds to play when Rosenbluth connected on a three-point-play to pull out a 61–59 victory. In the finals against South Carolina, Rosenbluth scored 38 points and Pete Brennan 22 points to lead the Tar Heels to a 95–75 victory. North Carolina had won the ACC Championship to remain undefeated. Lennie Rosenbluth, the ACC Player of the Year, had scored an incredible 106 points in the three games for a Tournament record. Grady Wallace, the nation's No. 1 scorer had scored an even 100 points for South Carolina.

In the NCAA Eastern Regionals in Philadelphia, North Carolina beat Yale 90–74, Canisius 87–75, and Syracuse 67–58 to advance to the NCAA finals in Kansas City as the only undefeated team in the tournament. In the semifinals, Kansas beat San Francisco 80–56; and in three overtimes, the Tar Heels beat Michigan State 74–70 behind

Top: University of North Carolina NCAA Basketball Champions 1957

Right: Lennie Rosenbluth, North Carolina, basketball star

Rosenbluth's two steals for layups and Tommy Kearns' two free throws in the closing minutes. In the championship game, the underdog Tar Heels played deliberately and shot 65 percent in the first half. However in the second half they got into foul trouble and eventually lost their All-American Lennie Rosenbluth with 1:45 left in the regulation game. The game then went into three overtimes and Kansas was leading 53–52 with six seconds to go in the third overtime when Joe Quigg of North Carolina was fouled. Quigg sank both free throws and then knocked away a pass to Chamberlain to preserve the upset, 54–53. The Tar Heels had won 32 consecutive games without a loss to win the National Championship. Rosenbluth had scored 20 points before fouling out, and All-American Wilt Chamberlain led Kansas with 23 points. Rosenbluth won the Helms Award as Player of the Year, and Frank McGuire was selected as the National Coach of the Year, to go along with his award as ACC Coach of the Year.

In July, Orange Bowl Committee President Joe Adams announced that, by a unanimous vote of the 41 members present, the contract with the Atlantic Coast Conference would not be renewed after January 1, 1958. The Orange Bowl agreed to invite a representative from the Big Eight Conference (formerly Big Seven) in 1959, 1960, and 1961. The Big Eight, in turn, waived its rule that the same team could not appear two years in a row. President Adams stated:

We are very happy about this. The policy of continuing with the Big Eight and selecting the other team from the wide open field was recommended by both the Columbia Broadcasting System and the National Broadcasting Company.

The Orange Bowl people were upset over the fact that the Big Eight had not sent the Conference champion every year, particularly when it had been Oklahoma, which had been undefeated and nationally ranked. They also were not satisfied with the ACC, which had a record of only 10 wins and 4 ties in 34 games against nonconference opponents in 1956. The primary reasons for severing the pact with the ACC, however, appeared to be the pressure on the Orange Bowl Committee to make it possible for the University of Miami or the University of Florida to appear in the Bowl, and the desire to have Oklahoma as often as they were nationally ranked.

Officials in the ACC did not seem to be surprised at the announcement, as the break in the agreement had been rumored for some time. Many felt the financial loss in not having a bowl contract would be offset by the opportunity to send more than one team to a bowl game—an option that had been prohibited in the Orange Bowl agreement. This feeling was expressed by Rex Enright, Athletic Director at South Carolina:

Naturally we hate to lose the Orange Bowl contract. It paid us about $250,000 a year. But we might have more than one team going to future bowls. Too there's nothing to keep us from being invited to the Orange Bowl if we have a good enough team to merit a bid.

Duke, with a 5–1–1 Conference record and a 6–2–2 overall record, was selected as the ACC representative that fall for the Orange Bowl. North Carolina State won their first Conference championship with a 5–0–1 record and a 7–1–2 overall record, but was ineligible to participate because of the NCAA probation for its basketball infractions. On New Year's Day, 1958, Oklahoma beat Duke 48–21 by scoring 27 points in the final period. This 24th annual Orange Bowl game played before 76,518 spectators, was the final game in the Orange Bowl contract for the ACC. In the five games with the Big Eight Conference representative, Duke's victory over Nebraska in 1955 was the only ACC win. Clemson had beaten Miami 15–14 in 1951 before the ACC was formed. To date, no ACC team has appeared in the Orange Bowl since the end of the pact in 1958.

At the Conference meeting in December, approval was given to the appointment of M. P. (Footsie) Knight as Supervisor of Basketball Officials. Knight's duties of training and assigning basketball officials were similar to those designated to H.C. (Joby) Hawn in football the year before. After three years of deliberation, the Conference finally approved a letter-of-intent agreement which stated:

When a prospective student has fulfilled the Conference entrance requirements and has been tentatively admitted to a member institution; and when he has submitted an application for financial aid signed by himself and his parents or guardian; and when the above has been certified by the said member institutions to the Commissioner of the Conference on or after July 1st, his decision shall be accepted as final by other member institutions. However, if said prospective student in good faith, requests that he be released from this decision, he shall be eligible to participate at another member institution upon approval of the Commissioner.

A new section was also added to the Bylaws under Conference competition as follows: "Beginning with the 1961 football season, each member institution shall play a minimum of six other members and in 1962, shall play a minimum of seven and from that date thereafter." According to Bill Cobey, Athletic Director at Maryland, the adoption of a round robin football schedule by 1962 "would make the ACC 'a playing conference,' and that's why I thought the conference was formed."

Maryland surprised everybody in March by winning the Basketball Tournament after finishing fourth in the regular season standings. Led by Nick Davis and Charles McNeil, the Terrapins beat North Carolina in the finals 86–74. Coach "Bud" Millikan had guided

Top: Bud Millikan, Maryland, Head Basketball Coach and Gene Shue, Maryland basketball star

Right: William W. (Bill) Cobey, Maryland, Athletic Director

Maryland to its only ACC Championship to date. Maryland went on to finish third in the Eastern Regionals, beating Boston College 86–63, losing to Temple 71–67, and beating Manhatten 59–55.

Clemson won its second ACC football title in 1958, losing only to archrival South Carolina 26–7 in the Conference, and to Georgia Tech 13–0 outside the Conference. They were invited to the Sugar Bowl to face the number one ranked team in the country, undefeated Louisiana State. In a hard fought struggle, Clemson (a 16 point underdog) lost when late in the third quarter, in punt formation, a bad pass from center was recovered by LSU on the Clemson 12 yard line. LSU went in to score and won 7–0 before 82,000 spectators in the Silver Anniversary game New Year's Day, 1959.

North Carolina State and North Carolina ended the regular basketball season tied for first place, and both teams met in the final game of the Tournament. There was some concern when North Carolina coach Frank McGuire pulled his starters during the game, saying he wanted to rest them for the regionals. Since State was on probation, they could not participate in the NCAA Tournament. The Wolfpack won 80–56, and North Carolina went on to lose to Navy 76–63 in the opening round of the Eastern Regionals.

The Atlantic Coast Conference and the entire sports world were stunned at the announcement of Jim Tatum's death on July 23,1959. Tatum, 46 years old, had been hospitalized in Chapel Hill with a highly contagious virus that quickly reached the critical stage. The sudden death of the nationally famous football coach came as a shock to everyone. Tatum had come to North Carolina as Head Coach in 1956 to rebuild the football program of the Tar Heels. He had beaten Duke in 1957 (21–13) for the first North Carolina victory in that traditional series in eight years. The 1959 season was supposed to be the best yet in his rebuilding program. Under Jim Hickey, one of Tatum's assistants, North Carolina, still stunned by Tatum's sudden death, played erratic football until the last two games of the year. Then North Carolina beat Virginia 41–0, and before 33,000 spectators and a national television audience on Thanksgiving Day, the Tar Heels handed Duke their worst football defeat in history, 50–0. Quarterback Jack Cummings directed a near perfect game as Carolina scored the first three times they had the ball. When senior fullback Don Klochak returned the second half kickoff 93 yards for a touchdown, the outcome was never in doubt. The Tar Heel defense held Duke to only 59 yards rushing. In Coach Jim Hickey's words, "I think the boys won it for Coach Tatum…I don't think there's any doubt that the memory of him had a lot to do with this ball game."

Clemson repeated as ACC football champion that fall, losing only to Maryland 28–25 in the Conference, and for the second year in a row to Georgia Tech 16–6. They were invited to the inaugural Bluebonnet Bowl in Houston, Texas on December 19, which was their second bowl appearance in the same year. There they upset Texas Christian, ranked 7th by the Associated Press and the tri-champion of the Southwest Conference, 23–7 before 55,000 spectators. Clemson overcame a 7–3 deficit by exploding for three touchdowns within seven minutes in the fourth quarter. Clemson's second string quarterback, Lowndes Shingler, who played sparingly until late in the game, led the comeback and was voted the Most Valuable Back. The ACC had ended the first seven years of its existence on a high note, and as it prepared to enter the "Sixties," there was great optimism for the future.

Top: Maryland 1953 football champions
Bottom: University of North Carolina NCAA basketball champions 1957

10

The Action Packed Sixties

As the Atlantic Coast Conference began the decade of the "Sixties," a new face appeared on the horizon who was to make his presence felt for the next ten years. Duke had hired Vic Bubas away from North Carolina State in May of 1959 to head up its basketball program. While at State, Bubas was Everett Case's chief assistant for eight years and did a major share of the scouting and recruiting. In his first year at the helm Bubas took his fourth place team to the ACC championship by upsetting regular season co-champions North Carolina 71–69 and Wake Forest 63–59 in the Tournament. After beating Princeton 84–60 and St. Joseph's 58–60, the Blue Devils lost to N.Y.U. 74–59 to finish second in the Eastern Regionals.

In April, the ACC was saddened by the second death in less than a year of a prominent figure in the development of the Conference when Rex Enright died at the age of 59 in Columbia, South Carolina. Enright had come to the University of South Carolina in 1938 as Athletic Director and Head Football Coach. In 1955 he stopped coaching to devote all his time to directing the athletic program. Enright had been as assistant coach at North Carolina (1928–1931) when Jim Tatum played there. Rex Enright's contribution to the Conference was noted in a Resolution adopted at the spring meeting.

Those of us who were associated with him know of his unfailing courtesy, his deep sense of personal integrity, and his constant interest in athletics and the Atlantic Coast Conference. He was one of the organizers of the Atlantic Coast Conference, rendered valuable service on its various committees and had a lot to do with its development into one of the outstanding athletic conferences in the country. His fellow coaches, athletic directors and faculty chairmen knew his worth as a coach and administrator and respected him and his teams, but it was from his personal actions in bringing harmony and achievement out of chaos and failure in attempts to establish a new conference that caused him to be truly loved by the men in his own profession.

At their meeting on May 6, the ACC moved to strengthen the academic requirements for football and basketball players when they made it necessary for them to achieve a score of 750 or better on the verbal and math sections of the College Entrance Examination Board Scholastic Aptitude Test (SAT) in order to be eligible for a scholarship or grant-in-aid. Dr. M. M. Caplin, Faculty Chairman from Virginia, stated that this action was a significant step forward, and would place the ACC among the athletic conference leaders in the nation.

At the 1960 Olympic games in Rome in September, Dave Sime was nosed out by Armin Hary of Germany in a photo finish in the 100 meter dash. It took 15 minutes for the judges to decide that Hary won the gold medal and Sime the silver medal. Both athletes were given the same time of 10.2 seconds, tying the Olympic record. Sime had passed up an opportunity to play professional baseball to compete in the Olympic games, an opportunity that was denied him by an injury when he was at his peak four years earlier. Jim Beatty, the great distance runner from North Carolina, competed in the 5,000 meter race but did not place.

The Conference unanimously approved a new five-year contract for Commissioner Weaver at their December meeting. The Conference also changed the division of bowl game receipts so that the participating institutions received a larger share. This action was precipitated by the bowl policy that allowed members to accept invitations to bowls that were not as lucrative financially as the "Big Four" bowls.

On January 2, 1961, 10th-ranked Duke played 7th-ranked Arkansas before 74,000 spectators in the Silver Anniversary game of the Cotton Bowl. Duke quarterback Don Altman threw a nine-yard pass to All-American end "Tee" Moorman for the tying touchdown with 2:45 left in the game. Captain Art Browning kicked the extra point to give Duke a come-from-behind 7–6 victory. Duke had now played in all four major bowls, the only ACC team ever to do so.

In his Third District report to the NCAA in January, 1961, Dr. Cornwell expressed concern over certain problems in intercollegiate athletics.

Those that seem to require immediate attention relate to entrance requirements, eligibility requirements, letters-of-intent, limiting grants-in-aid both as to number and to college and university costs, and outside participation during the college year. There seems to be general feeling that these problems are the most pressing and deserve NCAA attention.

Dr. Cornwell's concern was well founded, as the events in the next few months shook the Conference, and the Consolidated Unversity of North Carolina in particular. It began in December when Billy Galantai, a freshman basketball player at North Carolina, was declared ineligible for intercollegiate athletics in the ACC for a year. Galantai's suspension resulted from a violation for knowingly making false statements regarding his eligibility.

Then in January the NCAA announced that the University of North Carolina was placed on probation for one year. The penalty, applicable to the basketball team only, prohibited them from competing in the NCAA Basketball Tournament. The probation was a result of excessive entertainment expenses in recruiting basketball players, providing lodging and entertainment for the parents of players during the "Dixie Classic" Tournament, and ineffective and inadquate accounting procedures. It was reported that North Carolina had been under investigation since 1957, the year of their National Championship, but their cooperation in the investigation had prevented their other athletic teams from being penalized as was the case with North Carolina State. State had just been taken off their four-year probation in November.

Chancellor William B. Aycock said that the school's basketball program was being penalized by the NCAA "for errors in judgement rather than for a deliberate violation of rules." Aycock further stated: We have cooperated fully with the NCAA throughout the long and extensive investigation into our basketball recruiting practices. The University of North Carolina will take every precaution to insure that its future activities adhere strictly to the rules and regulations of the NCAA."

Two weeks late North Carolina officials asked permission to withdraw from the ACC Basketball Tournament, "in the interest of fair play to the other teams in this conference." The Conference granted permission but stated that withdrawal was not mandatory. North Carolina was trying to avoid a situation where an ineligible team might win the Conference Tournament. This situation had occurred twice before in the Conference. In 1955, Duke went to the NCAA Tournament because North Carolina State, the Conference champion, was ineligible; and again in 1959 when State, the Conference champion, was again ineligible, North Carolina went to the NCAA Tournament. After meeting with Conference officials, Chancellor Aycock announced that the University of North Carolina would reimburse the ACC for any expenses incurred in investigating the recruiting violations. Aycock added North Carolina "has been informed that no further action is contemplated by the Atlantic Coast Conference in regard to this matter."

On February 4, 1961 Duke beat North Carolina in a basketball game in Durham 81–77. During the last nine seconds of the game a fight broke out between the two teams. As a result, Commissioner Weaver suspended the three main principals in the fight—Art Heyman of Duke, and Larry Brown and Don Walsh of North Carolina —from participating in Conference games for the remainder of the regular season. Heyman, however, was allowed to participate in the ACC Tournament at the end of the season. Wake Forest, runner-up to North Carolina in the regular season standings, was seeded first in the seven-team Tournament and given a bye in the first round. Wake Forest then beat Maryland 98–76 and Duke 96–81 behind Len Chappell and Billy Packer to win the Tournament. In the NCAA Eastern Regionals, the Deacons beat St. John's 92–74, St. Bonaventure 78–73, and lost to St. Joseph's 96–86 to finish second.

On March 21, Chancellor Aycock announced that two representatives from the District Attorney's office in New York had visited North Carolina's campus. They were seeking information with regard to the nationwide basketball investigation which had just hit the front pages. It was reported that the latest scandal might be bigger than the one in 1951 in which it was disclosed that 86 games had been "fixed" in Madison Square Garden and other arenas in 22 cities during the period between 1947 and 1950.

In April, New York City District Attorney Frank Hogan who was conducting the investigation, announced that Aaron Wagman, a convicted football "fixer" from New York, was indicted on 37 counts of corruption and one charge of conspiracy by the New York County Grand Jury. One of the players mentioned in the indictment was Lou Brown, a senior at the University of North Carolina. Brown was used as a contact man by Wagman, but his efforts to bribe any players at North Carolina were unsuccessful. Brown had been dropped from the North Carolina basketball team at the close of the 1959–1960 season, but had returned to the squad when Larry Brown and Don Walsh were suspended for fighting in the Duke game.

All-American basketball star Doug Moe was given an indefinite suspension by Chancellor Aycock in May for "misstatement and concealment of fact" in the basketball scandal. Moe had failed to report the attempts by Brown to involve him in "point shaving," or the $75 he received from Wagman as a "softening up." Moe was not named as a co-conspirator with Wagman in any of the counts of indictment, but he failed to report his contacts to the North Carolina authorities until eight months after the bribe attempt. Meanwhile Brown had withdrawn from the University in March while the investigations were still going on.

On May 13, warrants were issued by the State Bureau of Investigation against three basketball players at North Carolina State. Captain Stan Niewierowski and Anton Muchlbaur of Brooklyn and Terry Litchfield of Louisville were charged with accepting money to influence the results of various basketball games during the 1960–61 season. Niewierowski and Muchlbaur, who had reportedly received $1,250 each, had left school; and Litchfield, who had reportedly received $1,000, was immediately dismissed. Head Coach Everett Case, who had made it a practice to bring in an SBI representative to talk to his basketball squad every year since the 1951 scandals, had initiated the investigation when State did not play well in early season games against Georgia Tech and North Carolina. It was later learned that Don Gallagher, who had been voted the 1960 Alumni Trophy as the Outstanding Senior Athlete, had also been bribed. However, the State players were not prosecuted when the Grand Jury did not indict them in September because of their confessions and cooperation with the investigators.

Two days later Governor Terry Sanford indicated his concerns about "big-time athletics" to the Trustees of the Consolidated University of North Carolina. President Friday then met with Chancellor Caldwell and Chancellor Aycock in a series of meetings to discuss appropriate action that would reduce the pressures that led to these problems. This "de-emphasis" was announced by President William C. Friday of the Consolidated University after the annual commencement meeting of the trustees a week later. The sports public was shocked to hear that the annual "Dixie Classic" was cancelled. This three-day Christmas holiday tournament held in Reynolds Coliseum since 1949 had grown to be one of the most popular basketball tournaments in the country. Over 70,000 spectators had attended the tournament in 1960, which pitted the "Big Four" colleges of North Carolina against four outstanding teams from across the nation. Contracts for the 1961 Classic with Colgate, Tulane, Illinois, and Stanford now had to be cancelled. This ended the 12-year tournament, conceived by Everett Case, in which no outside team had ever won the championship. North Carolina State had won seven championships; North Carolina, three; Duke, one; and Wake Forest, one.

President Friday reported that consideration had been given to the suggestion of discontinuing intercollegiate basketball competition, but that it had been decided instead "to eliminate or correct conditions that have discredited the sport." Friday went on to say that although there were no direct links between the "Dixie Classic" and the bribing scandals, tournaments of this type "exemplify the exploitation for public entertainment or for budgetary or commercial purpose of a sports program which properly exists as an adjunct to collegiate education." Additional changes in athletic policies for the two schools were also announced. They were as follows:

1. Limit basketball schedules to 14 ACC games and two intersectional games, plus the ACC and NCAA Tournaments.

2. Outlaw organized summer basketball competition with the loss of eligibility for violators.

3. Limit the number of basketball scholarships to two and football to twelve that could be awarded to athletes outside the geographical area of the ACC.

In June, New York City District Attorney Frank Hogan announced that former North Carolina basketball player Ray Stanley had failed to report an offer of $1,000 to shave points. Later that month North Carolina State placed basketball player Ken Rohloff on disciplinary probation for failing to report what he knew about "game-fixing" incidents. By this time the public concern over the basketball scandals had grown to such a degree that state legislatures were being asked to do something about stopping or controlling it. In North Carolina, the General Assembly voted to give Governor Sanford and the Council of State the power to allocate up to $50,000 for investigations and prosecutions in the bribing scandals.

On August 3, Frank McGuire resigned as Head Basketball Coach at North Carolina to accept a position as Vice-President and Head Coach of the Philadelphia Warriors in the National Basketball Association. Dean Smith, chief assistant to McGuire for the previous three years, was named as the new Head Coach. In nine years under McGuire, North Carolina had won 164 games and lost 58, climaxed by the National Championship in 1957.

In December, the William D. Carmichael, Jr. family offered the Atlantic Coast Conference a trophy in honor of the late Billy Carmichael that would be emblematic of overall sports excellence. Carmichael, a former vice-president and finance officer of the Consolidated University had died on January 27, 1961. He was captain of the 1920 North Carolina basketball team and a member of the 1922 Southern Conference championship team. Carmichael was widely known as a friend to sports, and as Jack Horner said: "The late W. D. (Big Billy) Carmichael, Jr., enjoyed and promoted all athletics—not just his first love of basketball—and he stood up and fought for sportsmanship character-building and the importance of being a good loser as well as a good winner."

The award was planned to honor the Conference institution that achieved the best overall record in all the Conference sports. Participation as well as excellence was emphasized, as each Conference sport would be weighed equally. Points would be awarded in each sport depending on the order of finish, with eight being awarded the 1st place team on down to one point to the 8th-place team. At the end of the academic year a rotating trophy and a permanent plaque would be awarded to the Conference institution that accumulated the highest number of points. Since the Conference adopted the award in 1961, the Carmichael Cup has been dominated by the University of Maryland which has won it a total of 10 times. The University of North Caroina is the only other school in the Conference that has won the award—a total of seven times.

In addition to adopting the Carmichael Cup, the Conference paid tribute at their winter meeting to another outstanding sports figure at North Carolina. The resolution, adopted by a rising vote of thanks for his long and meritorious devotion to college athletics, was stated as follows:

Dr. Oliver Cornwell, one of the founders of the Atlantic Coast Conference and one of its officers since its origin, is retiring as Faculty Chairman of Athletics from the University of North Carolina. The Atlantic Coast Conference wishes to express its appreciation for his diligent service and activity in its behalf. It is therefore, hereby resolved that he be named Representative Emeritus with all the rights and privileges pertaining thereto.

In 1962, Wake Forest won their second consecutive ACC Basketball Championship by beating Clemson 77-66 in the final game of the Tournament. The Deacons were again led by All-American and ACC Athlete of the Year Len Chappell, and All-Tournament Billy Packer. They beat Yale 92–82 in overtime, St. Joseph's 96–85 in overtime, and Villanova 79–69 to capture the Eastern Regionals. In the NCAA Championships Wake Forest lost to Ohio State 84–64 before beating UCLA 82–80 for third place under Coach "Bones" McKinney.

Duke won its third Conference football title in a row that fall with the first undefeated (6–0) record ever recorded. Overall Duke was 8–2, losing only to top ranked Southern California 14–7, and Georgia Tech 20–9; but no ACC school was invited to a bowl.

At the NCAA Convention in 1963 it was reported that many of the larger institutions in the Third District were in favor of adopting a national or interconference letter-of-intent. It was felt that this action would eliminate many of the problems associated with recruiting. By April 1, six major conferences: the Southeastern, Southwest, Big Ten, Big Eight, Missouri Valley, and ACC had agreed along with four independents: West Virginia, Pittsburgh, Penn State, and Syracuse to a voluntary program of an interconference letter-of-intent agreement.

Duke finished the 1963 regular basketball season with a 14–0 record, for the first clean sweep since North Carolina did it in 1957. In the Tournament, the Blue Devils beat Wake Forest 68–57 in the finals behind Player of the Year Art Heyman and All-Conference Jeff Mullins. Duke beat NYU 81–76 and St. Joseph's 73–59 to win the Eastern Regionals. In the NCAA Championships they lost to Loyola (Illinois) 94–75 before beating Oregon State 85–63 for third place. Their overall record was an outstanding 27–3.

In College Park, Maryland, on the eve of the 10th anniversary of the ACC, President Penney remarked that each of the seven charter members had invested $200 to form the Conference in 1953. Now, ten years later, Penney estimated that each member had received about $100,000. (According to the Bylaws, any surplus that exceeds twice the annual Conference budget shall be equally distributed among all the members.) He also commented on the cooperation and achievment of the Conference.

We are a closely knit group, and while we may disagree now and then, we respect each other. The National Collegiate Athletic Association has adopted many of our ideas.

For instance, we were the first conference to adopt scholastic achievement as a requirement for financial grants-in-aid to athletes.

In his Commissioner's Report for 1962–1963, Weaver had stated that of the 300 athletes on football grants-in-aid in the Conference, only 42 scored below 800 on the College Board Exams and the average score for the 300 athletes was 945. A proposal by Virginia to raise the cutoff score on the College Board Exams from 750 to 800 failed, however.

The United States and the entire world were shocked on Friday, November 22, 1963, when President John F. Kenndy was assassinated in Dallas. The saddened sports world reacted in different ways upon learning of the death of the President who took such a fervent interest in youth, fitness, and sports. The administrators at Duke and North Carolina postponed their football game scheduled for November 23 until November 30. Then, since classes ended on Wednesday the 27th for vacation, the students' request to change the football game to Thursday, November 28, was honored. Before a sell-out crowd of 47,500 in Duke Stadium on Thanksgiving Day, North Carolina won 16–14 on a field goal by sophomore Max Chapman in the last 33 seconds of the game. This victory gave North Carolina an 8 and 2 record, their best since 1948, and earned them a bid to the Gator Bowl in Jacksonville, Florida. Before a capacity crowd of 50,018 fans, under 70 degree temperatures, the Tar Heels crushed the Air Force Academy 35–0 to win their first bowl game. North Carolina opened up a 20–0 half-time lead, and behind the running of Ken Willard and the play calling of quarterback "Junior" Edge, cruised to victory. The Gator Bowl had grown in size and prestige since the inaugural game on January 1, 1946, when Wake Forest beat South Carolina 26–14 before only 10,000 spectators.

A week earlier, North Carolina State, co-champions of the ACC with North Carolina, lost to Mississippi State 16–12 in the Liberty Bowl in Philadelphia. Mississippi State, the favorite, built up a 16 point lead and held on to win the game. State quarterback Jim Rosse was named the Outstanding Back in the game. A sparse crowd of only 8,309 fans, including Governor Terry Sanford, turned out to witness this game played in freezing 22 degree weather with high winds. The Liberty Bowl, plagued by poor weather and poor attendance since its inception in 1959, later moved from Philadelphia to Atlantic City and then to Memphis, Tennessee.

At the NCAA Convention in January 1964, conditional certification was given by the Extra Events Committee for a Tobacco Bowl football game in the Raleigh-Durham area. An organization of 15 sportsmen, headed by the executive vice-president William P. Johnston of Raleigh, sponsored the proposal. Final NCAA approval depended on the organization's ability to raise $100,000 in ticket sales 30 days before the game which was scheduled for December 19, 1964. This requirement was not met, and as a result the bowl game was never played.

In March, Duke beat Wake Forest 80–59 behind Jeff Mullins' 24 points to win their second consecutive ACC Basketball Tournament. The Blue Devils beat Villanova 87–73 with Mullins getting a career high of 43 points and Connecticut 101–54 to win the Eastern Regionals. They advanced to the NCAA Championships and beat Michigan 91–80 before losing in the finals to undefeated UCLA 98–83. In finishing second, Vic Bubas had led the Blue Devils to another outstanding year (26–5). That same month, Frank McGuire returned to the ACC as Head Basketball Coach and Associate Athletic Director at the University of South Carolina.

At the Conference meeting in May the ACC approved an 800 score on the College Board Exams as a requirement for athletic grants-in-aid. The Conference also adopted a memorial resolution in honor of Dr. Penney who had passed away in March.

Dr. James T. Penney was Faculty Chairman of Athletics at the University of South Carolina for over a quarter of a century. He was active in the formation of the Atlantic Coast Conference and served as its first President. A powerful force toward progress in the Conference, he served with distinction on many committees. Dr. Penney was a rare combination of a distinguished scholar and a man of action. His unselfish service in the cause of intercollegiate athletics was instrumental in strengthening these programs in his University and in the Atlantic Coast Conference.

In the latter part of May, President William Friday announced that North Carolina State and North Carolina were given permission to set up a two-day, four-team Christmas Basketball Tournament. The other restrictions concerning the number of basketball games and the number of scholarships outside the Conference area that were imposed in 1961 when the "Dixie Classic" was cancelled were also lifted.

Everett Case planned to retire as Head Basketball Coach at North Carolina State after the 1964–65 season. It would be his 19th season

Clockwise from left: Duke Basketball Head Coach Vic Bubas and Duke stars Jeff Mullins, Art Heyman, and Bob Verga

81

at the helm of the Wolfpack, and he was optimistic that his last year would be a good one. State beat Furman 73–60 in its opener, and then travelled to Wake Forest where they lost a hard-fought struggle 86–80. Unfortunately, the excitement was too much, and Case, a 64-year-old bachelor who had been in poor health in recent years, resigned after the game. In his words:

> I tried to finish out my 19 years of active coaching at State, but after two games of the season, I found it impossible to do so due to poor health . . . The emotion and tension was just too much . . . I felt terrible after our win over Furman . . . But I felt I would give it one more try . . . The game with Wake Forest at Winston-Salem did it.

In his 19 years at State, Case had only three losing seasons, and his record was an outstanding 379 wins against only 134 losses. Case came to North Carolina State in 1946, and in the next 10 years (1947–1956) the Wolfpack won 15 of the 17 Southern Conference, Atlantic Coast Conference, and "Dixie Classic" tournaments it entered. Case had brought big time basketball to the South, the Atlantic Coast Conference, and the state of North Carolina. Press Maravich, Case's assistant coach, took over the reins and guided the Wolfpack to the ACC Championship in 1965 by upsetting regular season champion Duke 91–85 in the finals behind the hot shooting of Larry Worsley who scored 30 points. State placed third in the Eastern Regionals after they lost to Princeton 66–48, and beat St. Joseph's 103–81 behind Larry Lakin's 33 points.

The Conference at their Winter meeting in 1964 voted to establish an Everett N. Case Award in his honor for the Most Valuable Player in the ACC Basketball Tournament. It was a fitting tribute to Case that the first recipient of the award was one of his players, Larry Worsley, and the ACC Coach of the Year was one of his assistants, Press Maravich.

The following spring the Conference adopted a new policy in selecting the site for the Basketball Tournament. It was decided to rotate the site of the Tournament for three years among Raleigh, Greensboro, and Charlotte. Representatives from these cities had appeared before the Basketball Committee to present their cases and the Conference basketball coaches had voted 7 to 1 (North Carolina State opposed) to move to a neutral court. Eddie Cameron, Chairman of the Basketball Committee, said: "We can pretty well count on the tournament being rotated in future years. The No. 1 reason for the decision to move the tournament from Raleigh was the continual request that we play on a neutral court. That is the main and best reason."

In the fall of 1965 the ACC lost two of its most successful head coaches by retirement. Horace "Bones" McKinney, the colorful Head

Basketball Coach at Wake Forest, resigned in September because of poor health. In eight seasons under McKinney, an ordained Baptist minister, Wake Forest had won 122 games and lost 94 games. The Deacons won the Atlantic Coast Conference Championship in 1961 and 1962, and finished third in the NCAA Tournament in 1962.

Immediately after Duke beat North Carolina 34–7 in the last football game of the season, Bill Murray announced his resignation to accept the position of Executive Secretary of the American Football Coaches Association. Murray, a graduate of Duke, class of '32, returned to his *alma mater* in 1951 to succeed Wallace Wade. In 15 years at Duke, Murray's teams had a 93–51–9 record, including a Conference record of 54-15-2. The Blue Devils went to two Orange Bowls and one Cotton Bowl, and won seven Conference championships under Murray, a member of the National Football Foundation's Hall of Fame.

On December 3, Commissioner Weaver announced that Clemson University had been fined $2,500 by the Conference for violating the Conference rule limiting the total football and basketball grants-in-aid to 140 in any one year. It was also ruled that 18 members of the freshman football squad who were currently receiving aid must be withheld from competition during the 1966–67 season. Furthermore, if any of those 18 later competed, they would count toward the 35 incoming prospects allowed each year to receive aid. Professor R. R. Ritchie, Faculty Chairman at Clemson, had reported the violation to the Conference office, and when asked why Clemson had 18 more students on scholarship than allowed, he replied, "We usually lose 15 to 20 a year from the freshman and varsity squads for academic and other reasons, but this fall they all showed up." Clemson President Robert C. Edwards notified the Conference that "Clemson University accepts without question your evaluation of our violation of Rule 14 and your decisions as to penalties which are to be imposed due to that violation. We have neither the desire nor the intent to appeal."

Less than a week later, the University of South Carolina was also fined $2,500 by the Conference for having more than 140 athletes on football and basketball grants-in-aid, and their athletic department was reprimanded by Weaver. In addition, South Carolina was penalized five scholarships for the 1966–67 season. Marvin Bass, Athletic Director at South Carolina, said the violation was inadvertent and added:

> We were under the impression that several injured boys who had been permanently ruled out of further competition by doctors did not have to be counted toward the grant-in-aid limit.

The Athletic Department of the University of South Carolina regrets any inconvenience it may have caused Commissioner Weaver and other members of the Atlantic Coast Conference and we will certainly abide by Commissioner Weaver's ruling.

The Duke basketball team beat defending National Champion UCLA twice (82–66 and 94–75), Michigan, and Notre Dame in the month of December to launch their drive to the ACC Championship. In the March Tournament in Raleigh, Duke blasted Wake Forest 103–73 in a fast paced opening game, only to run up against a North Carolina "stall" in the second game. The score at half-time was an incredible 7–5, Duke's favor. The Blue Devils hung on for a 21–20 victory, and then edged past State 71–66 in the finals. In the Eastern Regionals, also held in Reynolds Coliseum, the Blue Devils beat St. Joseph's 76–74 and Syracuse 91–81 to advance to the 1966 NCAA Championships at College Park, Maryland. Duke lost to Kentucky in the opening game 83–79, as an ailing Bob Verga, who had been the Most Valuable Player in the Regionals, saw only limited action and scored four points. The next night Duke squeaked by Utah 79–77 for third place. This was Vic Bubas's third trip to the "Final Four" in four years.

Two famous athletic figures in the South died that spring within three days of each other. The first to succumb was Everett Case, the "Old Gray Fox" as he was affectionately known, on April 30 in Rex Hospital in Raleigh. A native of Anderson, Indiana, Case's record in 48 years of coaching in high school, the military, and collegiate ranks was an unbelievable 1161 games won and only 213 lost. Vic Bubas, a former player and coach for Case, said this upon his death:

The world has lost a great man and a great basketball coach . . . From his life I was fortunate to learn what made him and his teams great. It was discipline, desire, sacrifice, organization, and loyalty. His influence is felt today by every coach, player, fan, official and basketball administrator in the state of North Carolina.

At their spring meeting, the Conference paid tribute to Everett Case in the following resolution:

An illustrious era in North Carolina State athletics came to a close when Everett Case retired in his 19th season as Basketball Coach of the Wolfpack. Now, we record with sorrow his death, April 30, 1966, and the end of a career which continued beyond retirement, with a keen and profound interest in the activities, not only of his institution, but the Conference which he served with honor and distinction.

BE IT RESOLVED THAT the Atlantic Coast Conference expresses its everlasting recognition of the contributions Coach Case made in the formation years of the Atlantic Coast Conference and his contributions in bringing it recognition as one of the nation's outstanding centers of intercollegiate athletics.

Two days after Case's death, Dean C. P. (Sally) Miles, Faculty

Chairman of Athletics at Virginia Tech, died at the age of 86 in Blacksburg, Virginia. Miles came to Virginia Tech as a student in 1897 and stayed on after graduation, serving as Athletic Director from 1920 to 1935 and Dean of the College from 1943 to 1951. He was one of the founders of the original Southern Conference in 1921, was President of the Southern Conference in 1932 when the Southeastern Conference was formed, and Faculty Chairman at Virginia Tech in 1953 when the ACC was formed. Colonel D. S. McAlister, Faculty Chairman at The Citadel, paid tribute to Miles in this way: "He was one of the unfortunately vanishing Americans who really were pioneers in the development of the idea of regional athletic conferences."

During the summer, Commissioner Weaver ruled that South Carolina would have to forfeit all Conference football games in 1965 in which two ineligible players had participated. The players in question had received financial assistance without attaining a minimum score of 800 on the College Board Exams. This was a violation of the Conference rules. One freshman player had also received illegal aid. Weaver further ruled that: the athletes who received illegal aid were ineligible for further participation in the ACC; any athlete at South Carolina whose eligibility was questioned must be withheld from participation until his status had been settled; and South Carolina had to reimburse the Conference for the cost of the investigation. South Carolina President, Thomas F. Jones, said:

We are greatly disturbed at the irregularities which have come to light.

Paul Dietzel, director of athletics, and Dr. James A. Morris, faculty chairman, are making every effort to find out how such irregularities could have occurred and will take every reasonable step to assure that there can be no question of the propriety of actions of our athletic department in the future.

South Carolina, which had tied Duke for the Conference championship, fell to last place in the standings. Clemson and North Carolina State, as a result of their forfeit victories over South Carolina, were declared co-champions, and Duke finished second.

On October 28, the Executive Committee of the Conference met in a motel at the Raleigh-Durham airport. The purpose of the meeting was to discuss the recruitment and admission of Mike Grosso to the University of South Carolina. Back in December of 1965, Commissioner Weaver had ruled that Grosso, a 6'8" basketball sensation from Raritan, New Jersey, was eligible to play freshman basketball. Although Grosso's 789 College Board scored did not meet the 800 requirement for a grant-in-aid, he had met the entrance requirements at South Carolina, and his family reportedly was paying his tuition.

However, at the Conference meeting in the spring of 1966, a move to tighten the athletic eligibility rules was approved. An amendment to the Bylaws was added which stated that an athlete, regardless of financial assistance, was required to meet the 800 College Board score in order to be eligible to participate. No mention was made of this ruling having retroactive application, but there was still some question about the recruiting policy concerning Grosso.

After deliberating nearly four hours at the closed meeting, President Fadum announced that the Executive Committee had ruled Mike Grosso ineligible. Dr. Fadum later stated:

> The University of South Carolina requested an opportunity to review the Michael Grosso case with the executive committee of the conference. After full deliberation of the facts before it, the executive committee concluded that the evidence presented to it was in its judgment not sufficient to satisfy the conference that eligibility requirements were met.
>
> In particular there still remains a question of substance concerning his eligibility as related to the admissions procedures that were followed in this area.

When news of the Conference's ruling was made public, a petition began to circulate in South Carolina urging the University to withdraw from the ACC. This prompted South Carolina President Thomas Jones to issue the following statement:

> In our present situation, I have to say that it does not seem right or proper for USC to take any action toward withdrawing from the ACC, which it helped to form and in which it participates actively.
>
> The right and proper thing is to work out any and all problems within the conference, vigorously protecting the interests of the University of South Carolina in the process.

A request by South Carolina to meet with the Appeals Committee before the regular Conference meeting in December was not successful because of the shortage of time and other conflicts. As a result, South Carolina decided to take the case before the NCAA Committee on Infractions. This committee reports its findings to the NCAA Council which in turn takes whatever action it deems appropriate. At the Conference meeting on Hilton Head Island, South Carolina President Jones apologized to the Conference for certain statements made by Coach Frank McGuire in the aftermath of the Grosso controversy. Jones' apology on behalf of the trustees and administration of the University of South Carolina was made to the faculty chairmen, athletic directors, and to the presidents of the member institutions who were present at a Conference meeting for the first time.

In an unprecedented move, the Conference, "because of the climate created by events of the past several months and conscious of the fact that basketball games can create an explosive situation," made an exception to Article III, Section 1 of the Bylaws. Instead of requiring every team to meet every other team twice in the season, the Conference allowed any school that considered it inadvisable to bring its basketball team to South Carolina to reschedule the game on a neutral court. South Carolina was given the same option. If it was not feasible to hold the contest on a neutral court, the game could be cancelled by mutual consent.

The following week Duke and South Carolina announced that they were cancelling their games for the 1966–67 season. Much controversy had arisen over whether Duke was to blame for Grosso's ineligibility, and the climate was not conducive to holding a hotly contested basketball game between the two schools. Eddie Cameron, Athletic Director at Duke, issued the following statement.

Due to the unfortunate series of events connected with the determination of the eligibility of a South Carolina basketball player this year, it is the feeling of the athletic officials at Duke that the regular season games between USC and Duke should not be held this season.

In no way should this be construed as a break in athletic relations between the two universities, since we have future scheduled meetings in other major sports. Rather this is merely the cancellation of two basketball games. This does not preclude the possibility that our teams may meeting during the ACC. Tournament next March.

It is our hope that this action will provide sufficient time for the clarification of unanswered questions concerning the eligibility of the player and at the same time prevent any confrontation which might jeopardize the good relations between our universities.

In his statement, South Carolina Athletic Director Paul Dietzel said:

When I questioned the commissioner of the Atlantic Coast Conference, Jim Weaver, this morning, he told me that it was the intent of the Atlantic Coast Conference that any member institution had the prerogative that Duke has exercised. Therefore the officials of Duke University are within the rights granted them by the Atlantic Coast Conference at the December 7 meeting held at Hilton Head Island, S.C.

We have enjoyed a long and pleasant rivalry in all sports with Duke University, and the University of South Carolina plans that this will continue.

At the NCAA Convention in Houston in January 1967, the NCAA Council found South Carolina had violated the principles governing sound academic standards, financial aid, and recruiting. The violations were as follows:

1. An athlete was admitted contrary to the regular published entrance requirements.

2. Three athletes, ineligible to receive institutional financial assistance, were given assistance from a personal fund.

3. Financial assistance to athletes was not administered through the regular institutional channels.

4. A secret fund was created to entertain high school coaches.

5. A basketball tryout game was arranged at a summer camp in New Jersey.

6. The educational expenses of an athlete were paid by a corporation upon which the individual "was neither naturally nor legally dependent."

The corporation referred to was Grosso's Bar and Grill in New Jersey, which was operated by an uncle and was said to have been the source of Grosso's financial assistance. As a result of these violations, South Carolina was placed on probation for two years, and they were not allowed to participate in any postseason football or basketball games, nor allowed to participate in any NCAA-approved television programs during this period. In taking this action, the NCAA Council supported the findings and action of the ACC, its Executive Committee, and its Commissioner, "recognizing that their efforts give meaning to the cooperative principle and philosophy of the NCAA enforcement program . . ."

President Jones, in hearing the verdict, stated: "We accept the action of the NCAA and pledge our full cooperation in upholding the principles of that organization. We will continue our efforts in the development of a constructive athletic program at the University."

Since the ACC Basketball Tournament was not considered postseason play, South Carolina announced they would participate in it. However, if they won the Tournament, they would be ineligible to compete in the NCAA playoffs. At the end of the semester Mike Grosso held a news conference in New Jersey and announced that he was transferring to the University of Louisville.

In January, Commissioner Weaver directed the Conference basketball officials to strictly enforce the rules requiring basketball coaches to remain on the bench. The coaches were informed of this directive, and the athletic directors were reminded of their responsibilities in the conduct of basketball games at their facilities. Recent disturbances in Conference games brought about this action. Most notable was the North Carolina State-Maryland game at College Park in which the referees stopped the game with 1:15 remaining and declared Maryland the winner, the score being 60–55, Maryland's favor, at the time. This occurred after a double technical had been called against the North Carolina State coach.

In March 1967, the Conference Basketball Tournament was held in the Greensboro Coliseum. It was the first time in the history of the ACC that the Tournament had not been held in Reynolds Coliseum at North Carolina State. In fact, Raleigh had been the site of the

Southern Conference Tournament from the time that 13 of the 23 members had withdrawn in the winter of 1932 to form the Southeastern Conference. Clemson and Virginia Tech, because of their season records, did not participate in that first tournament in Raleigh in 1933 that saw South Carolina defeat Duke 33–21 for the championship.

The tournament originated in 1921 when Al Doonan of the Atlanta Athletic Club invited 15 teams to Atlanta to play off for the Basketball Championship of the South. Kentucky won that first championship 20–19 over Georgia. It was during this tournament in February that 14 colleges withdrew from the SIAA and organized the Southern Conference. According to "Sally" Miles, "There was a great need for a working collegiate conference, the basketball tournament just came along."

The tournament was moved from Raleigh's 3,500 seat Memorial Auditorium in 1947, because of the heavy demand for tickets, to the 8,800 seat Duke Indoor Stadium. When Reynolds Coliseum, with 12,400 seats, was completed in 1951, the tournament moved back to Raleigh. Reynolds remained the site of the Southern Conference Tournament until 1953, and then continued as the site of the ACC Tournament until it was moved to Greesboro in 1967.

That March, Dean Smith won his first of three straight regular season and three straight Tournament basketball championships for North Carolina. In the final Tournament game Larry Miller hit an incredible 13 of 14 shots from the floor, scored 32 points, and took 11 rebounds to lead the Tar Heels over Duke 82–73. In the Eastern Regionals North Carolina beat Princeton 78–70 and Boston College 96–80 and advanced to the NCAA Championships. There they finished fourth, losing to Dayton 76–62 and Houston 84–62. The ACC had approved the acceptance of an invitation to the National Invitation Tournament (NIT) at Madison Square Garden at their December meeting, and Duke received the first Conference bid. The Blue Devils lost to Southern Illinois in their first game 72–63.

The most significant legislation passed by the Conference at its meeting in May was the change in the Bylaws which allowed freshmen to compete on varsity teams in all sports except football and basketball. The limitations on the number of scholarships were changed again to read, "the total number of grants-in-aid shall not exceed 120 in football and 20 in basketball, effective July 1, 1968."

A complete review of the activities of the Service Bureau was given in a report by Smith Barrier, the Director, who tendered his resignation effective June 1. His associate, Irwin Smallwood, who had been in charge of the weekly statistics, had resigned in August 1966. Both men had received promotions and additional responsibilities with their employer, the *Greesboro Daily News*. Barrier had been Director of the Service Bureau since it was established in 1954. During this period the activities and responsibilities had increased greatly to include every aspect of promotions and publications connected with the ACC. Smith Barrier was commended by the Conference for his outstanding service, and in light of the magnitude of this job, the Conference decided to employ a full-time staff member to handle public relations functions and other duties assigned by the Commissioner. In June, Commissioner Weaver announced that Eugene F. (Gene) Corrigan was appointed as Assistant to the Commissioner, and Director of the Service Bureau. Corrigan, a 1952 graduate of Duke University, had been on the staff at Virginia for nine years, and was serving as Sports Information Director and Head Lacrosse Coach at the time of his appointment.

Dr. Ralph Fadum, Conference President and Faculty Chairman of Athletics at North Carolina State, in commenting on the harmonious spring meeting, said:

> We have come a long way since Hilton Head (the winter meeting involving the Grosso case). We cannot foresee any major problems in the immediate future and I feel we have recaptured a bit of the spirit of the conference. We have travelled some rough roads during the past year.

On Saturday, September 16, 1967, the first football double-header in the 79-year history of football in North Carolina was held. In Raleigh in the new Carter Stadium (only one year old), North Carolina met North Carolina State at 2:00 P.M. in the 57th game of a rivalry dating back to 1894. North Carolina led in the series with a 39-11-6 record. At 7:30 P.M. Duke and Wake Forest clashed in a series that started back in 1889. Duke led in the series with a 35-11-1 record. In this "Big Four" doubleheader, State edged North Carolina 13-7 behind Jim Donnan's 55 yard touchdown pass to Harry Hartell and Gerald Warren's two field goals. As exuberant crowd of 42,300 spectators watched this game, and 22,452 more fans turned out for the nightcap to see Duke beat Wake Forest 31-13, as Jay Calabrese scored two touchdowns.

Attendance at home games during the 1967 football season passed the one million mark for the first time in the history of the ACC, with an actual total of 1,044,228 spectators for the 35 home games. Clemson won the Conference championship with a 6-0 record, and North Carolina State, with an overall record of 8-2, was invited to the Liberty Bowl. State had appeared in the 1963 Liberty Bowl, the fifth and last one to be held in Philadelphia. In 1964 the Liberty Bowl was held indoors in Convention Hall in Atlantic City, and then in 1965 it

Above: Greensboro Coliseum, Site of ACC
Championships; below: Charlotte Coliseum, Site of
ACC Championships

moved to the new Memorial Stadium in Memphis. On Saturday, December 16, under sunny skies, 35,045 spectators watched North Carolina State upset Georgia 14-7 for their first bowl victory. Georgia scored first before State came back to tie it up and then go ahead early in the fourth quarter. The Wolfpack staged two goal line stands in the closing minutes to preserve the victory. State quarterback Jim Donnan was voted the Most Valuable Player in the game. This was the first victory by an ACC football team over a Southeastern Conference opponent in 24 games. Coach Earle Edwards had his best team ever, and only a 13-8 loss at Penn State and a 14-6 loss at Clemson kept them from a shot at the national championship.

At the NCAA Convention in January 1968, an amendment to allow freshmen to participate in all varsity sports except football and basketball was adopted. The amendment which passed by the narrowest of margins, 163 to 160, was effective for the 1967–68 school year. It permitted freshmen to compete for four years and in all postseason events. Previously, freshmen could not participate in NCAA championships, and athletes were limited to three years of varsity competition unless their institution had an undergraduate male enrollment of less than 1,250 students. The ACC had approved freshman participation six months earlier, and the Southeastern Conference and Western Athletic Conference were already allowing freshmen to participate.

In March, the Basketball Tournament was played in the Charlotte Coliseum for the first time. North Carolina won its second consecutive Conference championship by beating North Carolina State 87–50. Duke had lost in the semifinals to State by the score of 12 to 10 (4 to 2 at half-time) as the Wolfpack held the ball in the greatest slow down in ACC history. North Carolina beat undefeated St. Bonaventure 91–72 and Davidson 70–66 to win the Eastern Regionals. In the first round of the NCAA Championships, the Tar Heels beat Ohio State 80–66 before bowing to the Lew Alcindor-led UCLA Bruins in the finals 78–55. The second place Tar Heels were led throughout the season by ACC Athlete of the Year Larry Miller, and super sophomore Charlie Scott. Meanwhile Duke went to the NIT for the second time, beating Oklahoma City 91–81 before losing to St. Peter's 100–71.

At the spring meeting the Conference approved the recommendation by the Basketball Committee to return to Charlotte in 1969 for the Tournament. The Charlotte Coliseum, seating 11,666 spectators, was the "largest available neutral facility in the Conference area," and the 1968 Tournament had returned $145,680 to the Conference.

The University of Maryland soccer team finished the 1968 campaign undefeated with a 14–0 record under Coach Doyle Royal. In the title game for the national championship, Maryland and Michigan State played to a 2–2 tie and both teams were declared NCAA Co-champions. The attendance at 1968 ACC football games surpassed the 1967 record with 1,101,767 spectators for 38 home games. South Carolina had the highest average with a mark of 41,804 fans, and the Clemson-South Carolina game in Clemson's Memorial Stadium drew 53,247 spectators. This was the largest crowd to see a Conference game in the 16 years of ACC competition.

At its winter meeting the Conference adopted the recommendation of the Booking Office Committee to hire a Supervisor of Officials to work full time out of the Conference Office. His primary responsibility would be the recruitment and supervision of football and basketball officials. The present Supervisors, "Joby" Hawn in football and "Footsie" Knight in basketball, were both employed in other businesses outside of their Conference responsibilities. Gene Corrigan was given this responsibility as Supervisor of Officials.

The Basketball Tournament returned to the Charlotte Coliseum in 1969 for the second straight year, and North Carolina won the championship for the third year in a row. In the title game, after falling behind 43-34 at half-time, the Tar Heels rallied to beat Duke 85-74. Charlie Scott hit 12 of 13 shots from the floor in the second half to finish with a total of 40 points in a dazzling one-man performance. North Carolina again won the Eastern Regionals by beating Duquesne 79–78 and Davidson 87–85 as Scott hit an 18 foot jump shot with two seconds to go. In the NCAA Championships the Tar Heels finished fourth, losing to Purdue 92–65 and Drake 104–84. This was the seventh time in the past eight years that the ACC representative had reached the "Final Four" of the National Tournament—a record unsurpassed by any other conference. South Carolina received a bid to play in the NIT and beat Southern Illinois 82–63 before losing to Army 59–45. At the NCAA Convention in January, the probation imposed in 1967 against South Carolina had been lifted.

The 1969 Basketball Tournament held a special significance for the Conference in that it was the final tournament for five men who had played important roles in the development of the Atlantic Coast Conference. A week earlier Vic Bubas had seen his Duke Blue Devils upset second-ranked North Carolina 87–81 behind Steve Vandenberg's 33 points. This was Bubas' 100th and last game as Head Basketball Coach in the Duke Indoor Stadium where his teams had won 87 home games and lost only 13. Now the Conference Tournament was his last appearance before becoming Director of Public Relations at Duke University. His ten year record at Duke showed 213 victories, 67 losses, four ACC Championships, and three NCAA

Above: Billy Cunningham, North Carolina, basketball star

Left: Charlie Scott, North Carolina, basketball star

94

Regional titles.

Three athletic directors who had made important contributions in the formation and growth of the Conference were also participating in their final tournament. Charles P. (Chuck) Erickson had actually announced his resignation from the University of North Carolina the previous May. Erickson, a 1930 graduate of North Carolina, had returned to his *alma mater* in 1933, and had been active in the athletic department ever since. In June 1952, Erickson was named to succeed the late "Coach Bob" Fetzer as Athletic Director. (Fetzer had served as the first athletic director since 1923.) Many of the present athletic facilities, including the second deck on Kenan Stadium and Carmichael Auditorium were the result of his 16 years of planning and direction. Erickson was one of the leaders in the formation of the ACC, and he played an important role as Chairman of the Bowl Committee and as a member of the Basketball Committee.

Roy B.Clogston had been Director of Athletics at North Carolina State since August of 1948. Clogston, a 1928 graduate of Springfield College, had been Athletic Director at St. Lawrence University prior to assuming those duties at North Carolina State. During his 21 years of leadership, Reynolds Coliseum and Carter Stadium were built, making the Wolfpack athletic facilities some of the finest in the Conference. Clogston served the Conference from the beginning as Chairman of the Public Relations Committee and a member of the Basketball Committee. He was also the first Chairman of the ACC Athletic Directors group. Clogston's retirement was effective July 1, 1969.

Another athletic director whose retirement was effective on July 1 was William W. Cobey of the University of Maryland. Cobey began his career at Maryland in 1931, one year after his graduation. He first served as the University's Cashier and then became Graduate Manager of Athletics in 1948. When Jim Tatum left Maryland in 1956, Cobey became the Director of Athletics. Cobey served on many Conference committees, including Television, Public Relations, Booking Office, and Basketball. During his 13 years of leadership, Maryland won the coveted Carmichael Cup six out of the eight years of its existence.

The newest member of the Conference family and the Tournament Manager was also participating in his last ACC Basketball Tournament. Gene Corrigan had announced his resignation in late January to become Athletic Director at Washington and Lee University at the conclusion of the Tournament. Corrigan had been appointed Director of the Service Bureau in July, 1967, and in the short period that followed, had made a significant contribution to the effectiveness of

95

the Conference and its relationship with the press and the public.

Later in the spring, another athletic director who had played a prominent role in the Conference, passed away. Gus K. Tebell, Athletic Director at the University of Virginia, died on May 28, 1969. Tebell received the Big Ten Scholar-Athlete Award when he graduated from Wisconsin in 1923, and was Head Football Coach at North Carolina State from 1925 to 1930. He joined the athletic staff at Virginia in 1930, and from 1934 to 1936 he had the unique distinction of being Head Coach of football, basketball, and baseball at the same time. In 1951 he became Director of Athletics and served in this capacity until his retirement in 1962. Tebell was a nominee for the position of Commissioner of the ACC, and held many important committee positions in the Conference.

The NCAA Council reprimanded and censured the University of North Carolina that spring for recruiting and football practice violations. The violations involved the off-campus entertainment of a prospective basketball player during his visit to the University, and the practice of the center snap in offseason football physical conditioning sessions. The censure did not involve any penalities. The Council commended North Carolina for its diligence in correcting the situation, and Athletic Director Homer Rice said, ". . . the athletic department of the university will strive as it always has to comply with all the NCAA, Atlantic Coast Conference, and institutional policies."

Two new assistants to the Commissioner joined the Conference during the summer of 1969. Marvin A. (Skeeter) Francis was named Director of the Service Bureau. Francis had been Sports Information Director at Wake Forest since 1955, and had been Assistant Sports Editor of the *Durham Morning Herald* prior to that. He was a past president of the College Sports Information Directors of America, and a member of the Helms Hall of Fame for Sports Information Directors.

Norvall Neve was named as Supervisor of Officials, after serving as Commissioner of the Missouri Valley Conference for 12 years. Earlier he had been a football coach and served as Athletic Director at Wichita for five years. He had had 24 years of officiating experience in basketball and football, and served as Secretary-Treasurer of the Collegiate Commissioners Association.

That fall South Carolina won its first outright ACC Football Championship by winning all six of its Conference games. Coach Paul Dietzel's team became only the third team in Conference history to post a 6-0 record. South Carolina represented the ACC in the second annual Peach Bowl in Atlanta, Georgia, on December 30.

There, before 48,542 fans who sat through a driving rain, the Gamecocks lost to West Virginia 14-3. Billy Du Pre's 37 yard field goal in the second period was the only score for South Carolina.

Just before the winter meetings in December, Frank Howard announced his resignation as Head Football Coach at Clemson. Howard had joined the staff in 1931 as an assistant coach to Jess Neely, and took over as Head Coach in 1940. In 30 seasons the 60-year-old Howard won 165 games, lost 118, and tied 12. Under the colorful Howard, the Tigers won four of the seven bowls they appeared in, won five ACC titles, and tied for another. Howard would remain as Athletic Director however.

When the Conference met, much concern was expressed over the poor football record against non-conference teams (7-23). Proposals were submitted that would make the Conference more competitive in recruiting. However the plan to reduce the ACC academic entrance requirements to that of the NCAA was given to a committee to study and report on at the spring meeting in May. The NCAA used a 1.6 grade point projection for prospective athletes, but the ACC was requiring an 800 minimum college board score in addition. In other action, fencing was added to the list of sports in which a championship meet would be held.

As the ACC entered the decade of the "Seventies," other new faces joined the Conference who would have an impact on its future. Notable among these were three new atheletic directors: Homer Rice at North Carolina, Willis Casey at North Carolina State, and Jim Kehoe at Maryland. There were also five new head coaches: Charles (Lefty) Drisell, basketball coach at Maryland; Raymond (Bucky) Waters, basketball coach at Duke; Calvin Stoll, football coach at Wake Forest; Roy Lester, football coach at Maryland, and Cecil (Hootie) Ingram, football coach at Clemson.

Left: Roman Gabriel, North Carolina State, football star

Below: Brian Piccolo, Wake Forest, football star

Right: Len Chappell, Wake Forest, basketball star and Horace (Bones) McKinney, Wake Forest, Head Basketball Coach

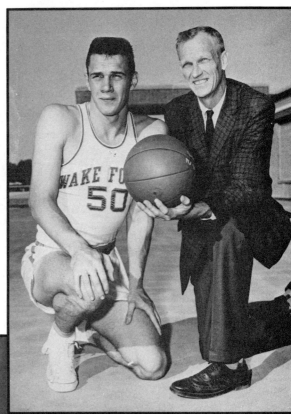

Left to right, below: Randy Mahaffey, Clemson, basketball star; Rusty Adkins, Clemson, baseball star

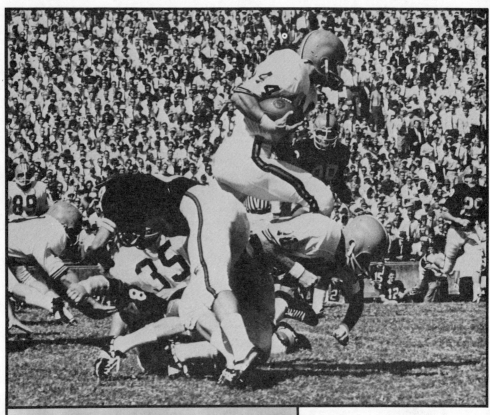

Above: Buddy Gore, Clemson, football star

Left: Frank Quayle, Virginia, football star

11

The Glory of The Seventies

As the decade of the "Seventies" began, officials and fans throughout the Conference were relieved to hear that the Academic Council at Duke University had reversed the recommendations of its *ad hoc* committee on athletics. Back in November the sports public was surprised to read that this committee had recommended that Duke withdraw from the ACC and, in an effort to curb athletic expenses, all athletic grants-in-aid should be awarded on a basis of financial need only. In its report the faculty committee cited differences in academic standards, programs, and aims as the chief reasons why Duke should leave the ACC. The other recommendations in the report pertinent to nonrevenue sports, intramurals, and physical education went by almost unnoticed. Meeting in February, for the fourth time, the Academic Council instead adopted amendments that called for Duke to review its conference membership, and to take the initiative in establishing a national policy of athletic scholarships based on need. Athletic Director Eddie Cameron called the reversal "a vote of confidence for our athletic program."

South Carolina swept through the 1970 regular season basketball campaign undefeated (14–0) in Conference games, behind ACC Player of the Year John Roche. This was only the third time in 17 years a team had not lost a Conference game. In the Tournament, South Carolina edged Clemson 34–33 in a very deliberate ball game, and then beat Wake Forest 79–63. In the finals against North Carolina State, the regulation game was tied 35–35 as Roche's shot missed at the buzzer. In the first overtime Roche again missed the last shot and the score remained tied 37–37. North Carolina State finally pulled ahead in the second overtime to win 42–39. Disappointed at the upset, the Gamecocks refused to come out of the dressing room to accept their consolation trophies, dampening an otherwise outstanding year in which they finished 25–3 overall. State went to the Eastern Regionals and finished third, losing to St. Bonaventure 80–68, and beating Niagara 108–88. Duke and North Carolina both went to the NIT, and both lost in the first round, the Tar Heels to Manhattan 95–90, and the Blue Devils to Utah 78–75. Since South Carolina was hosting the Eastern Regionals in Columbia, NCAA rules prevented the Gamecocks from going to the NIT.

At the Conference meeting in the Spring the question of entrance requirements for athletes was again brought up. Maryland proposed that the ACC drop the 800 minimum score required on the SAT exams, but action on this proposal was postponed until the Winter meeting in December. Dr. Jack Sawyer, ACC President, told a news conference that this was done in order to give the presidents of the Conference schools "time to make a study of the academic regulations as applied to athletes."

South Carolina's proposal that the regular season Conference winner automatically qualify for the NCAA Tournament, while the winner of the ACC Tournament (excluding the Conference champion) be the NIT representative, failed for lack of a second. South Carolina's proposal to increase the number of grants in football (from 35 in one year to 80 in two years) and basketball (from a total of 20 to a total of 24) was postponed until December.

The following week the Board of Trustees of the University of South Carolina met to discuss whether or not it would withdraw from the ACC (because of the strict academic requirements) in order to pursue an independent program. After the Trustees had heard a report from the athletic committee, the following statement was read by President Jones:

. . . After prolonged and careful consideration of all aspects and possibilities, the board of trustees of the University of South Carolina has voted unanimously to take no action at this time to change or jeopardize the status of the University of South Carolina in the Atlantic Coast Conference.

In June, Commissioner Weaver announced that four athletes who planned to attend South Carolina would be allowed to retake their SAT exams. One of the athletes would be allowed to accept a scholarship as a hardship case even if he failed again to make the 800 minimum score required. This decision was reached by the Executive Committee of the ACC, and was considered by many as an effort to restore harmony within the Conference.

On Saturday, July 11, 1970, the Atlantic Coast Conference was shocked by the sudden death of Jim Weaver. Commissioner Weaver, who was attending the Collegiate Commissioners Association meeting in Colorado Springs, died of a heart attack at the age of 67. Weaver, a native of North Carolina, graduated from Centenary College, and later returned to North Carolina to coach at Oak Ridge Institute. In 1933 he became Head Football Coach at Wake Forest, and in 1937 he relinquished his coaching duties to become Athletic Director. In May of 1954, Jim Weaver was elected as the first Commissioner of the ACC. It was under his guidance and direction that the Conference developed into national prominence. At the time of his death he was serving his second term as Chairman of the Commissioners and he was a member of the NCAA Executive Committee. Dr. James R. Scales, President of Wake Forest said:

Mr. Weaver had a very special place in the hearts of Wake Foresters. He guided the institution's athletics on to high ground when he was director of athletics. Wake Forest was proud when he became the first commissioner of the ACC. He was a gentleman of compassion, good judgment and courage.

Tributes to Jim Weaver came from all the Conference members, and from colleges and conferences throughout the country. Willis Casey, Athletic Director at North Carolina State said:

He was a guiding force in the formation and development of the Atlantic Coast Conference and helped make it one of the nation's strongest conferences. His loss will be felt by all in intercollegiate athletics and not only in the ACC. He represented our conference well on national committees and with the NCAA. He was so familiar with the ACC family and soothed many of its potential problems with his patience and sound judgment.

Tom Hamilton, Commissioner of the Pacific 8 Conference and Vice-Chairman of the Commissioners said:

We have all suffered a deep personal loss and intercollegiate athletics will sorely miss one of its outstanding leaders. Jim Weaver's contributions to college sports have been outstanding and national in scope. His influence will continue to be a significant force in our university sports programs.

The Conference adopted the following resolution (at their Winter meeting) and sent copies to Mrs. Jim Weaver and Miss Florence Weaver:

WHEREAS, JAMES H. WEAVER became Commissioner of the Atlantic Coast Conference on July 1, 1954, and was its Commissioner until the time of his death on July 11, 1970; and

WHEREAS, JAMES H. WEAVER was an inspiration to all those privileged to know him; a man of unique and extensive abilities, possessed of a keen, perceptive mind, and unusual human spirit and an engaging sense of humor; Therefore,

BE IT RESOLVED that his colleagues of the Atlantic Coast Conference record their deepest affection and highest respect. None among us will forget the strength of his courage and wisdom, or the generosity with which he gave of himself to all. Each of us will be forever better for having shared some part of his life. What any such recital cannot convey, however, is the deepest sense of attachment to this man, which was felt by all who convened in the fellowship of this Conference.

Mrs. Weaver and her daughter initiated the Jim Weaver Memorial Graduate Scholarship to be awarded annually to an outstanding Conference athlete who distinguished himself by his academic record and leadership qualities. Their request that the Conference administer the fund was approved, and a donation of $4,000 ($500 in the name of each member) was made by the Conference. The Faculty

Chairmen appointed Norvall Neve (present Supervisor of Officials) to serve as acting Commissioner while a four-member committee headed by Dr. John Faber of Maryland made recommendations for fulfilling the Commissionership.

As fall classes resumed in September, North Carolina supporters were outraged to learn that Tom McMillen had changed his mind and had decided to enroll at Maryland. McMillen, a 6'11" basketball star from Mansfield, Pennsylvania, was one of the most sought after high school basketball players in the country. In July, he announced that he would attend North Carolina but changed his mind when school began. Norvall Neve ruled that McMillen, an outstanding student, would be eligible to play at Maryland since he had not signed an interconference letter-of-intent, but had only made an institutional agreement with North Carolina.

On September 30, President Shannon of the University of Virginia announced that Gene Corrigan would become Director of Athletics Programs, effective January 1. Corrigan was presently Director of Athletics at Washington and Lee, and had been Assistant to the Commissioner and Director of the Service Bureau of the ACC. Corrigan, in addition to overseeing the athletic program, would also be in charge of intramurals, recreation, facilities, service class physical education, and the women's intercollegiate program.

In October, the Trustees of the University of South Carolina authorized the athletic department to recruit prospective athletes under the NCAA entrance requirements only (1.6 grade prediction) and stated that these standards would be in effect in September 1971 regardless of what action the ACC took. Clemson, also unhappy with the added burden of the ACC's 800 SAT requirement, stated that they would also reconsider their position. Both schools felt that the ACC standard made it difficult for them to recruit against neighboring Southeastern Conference schools that did not have this requirement.

When asked to comment on the possible withdrawal of South Carolina and Clemson from the Conference, Duke Athletic Director Eddie Cameron philosophized to a group of reporters:

A group of people were sitting around a table just as we are today and wanted a conference closely knit geographically with high academic standards. All the schools talking about this new conference were schools with good reputations, and we feel the conference has progressed. It has a fine reputation and it is the only conference in the country with such high academic requirements for athletes.

Now we must decide if conditions have changed to the point where lowering of standards is advisable. It is time, I believe, for the conference to take a long, hard look at the matter. Until we do that, I don't think anyone can clearly predict what will happen.

104

Tom McMillen, Maryland, basketball star

When the Conference met in Greensboro for their Winter meeting in 1970, many observers felt that this might be the most crucial meeting in its 17-year history. There was the uncertainty over the status of South Carolina and Clemson, the indecision over the eligibility requirements, and the search for a new Commissioner. It was hoped that a Commissioner would have been named earlier in the fall, but now the selection would not be made until the Conference meeting. On Thursday, December 10, it was announced that Robert C. (Bob) James would be the new Commissioner of the Atlantic Coast Conference, effective March 1, 1971. James, 49, had been Commissioner of the Mid-American Conference for seven years, and before that had been civilian Athletic Director at the Air Force Academy for four years. James was a native of Harrisburg, Pennsylvania and attended the University of Maryland prior to World War II. After the War, James returned to Maryland where he graduated in 1947. After graduation he remained at Maryland, becoming Associate Dean for Student Life in 1958 before accepting the position at the Air Force Academy in 1960.

The Presidents of the member institutions, headed by Chancellor John Caldwell of North Carolina State, reported that by a 5–3 vote their group had approved a proposal that the Conference continue their present rule of requiring both an 800 SAT score and a 1.6 grade point prediction for athletic eligibility. However they added a provision that students who scored between 700 and 799 and projected a 1.75 score of a possible 4.0 would also be admissible. The change, as explained by Chancellor Caldwell, "gives more emphasis to class rank rather than college boards. It does not weaken academic standards; it strengthens some areas for athletic ability." It was hoped that this compromise would be acceptable to all members. This proposal was later adopted by the Faculty Chairmen by a 6–2 vote. However South Carolina and Clemson still did not think that the rules had been relaxed enough, and both schools announced that they would begin recruiting immediately under only the 1.6 NCAA rule. President Edwards of Clemson added that they hoped this matter would be resolved within the Conference framework because Clemson wanted to remain in the ACC. The Conference did approve an amended proposal by South Carolina which stated that the number of football grants-in-aid should not exceed 70 in a two-year period or 40 in a one year period. This is called the "banking concept."

Then to add to the troubled waters of the Conference, a free-for-all broke out in a basketball game in Columbia between South Carolina and Maryland the following week. The Gamecocks were leading 96–70 with almost five minutes remaining to play when the fight broke

106

out and the officials stopped the game. There was concern expressed over South Carolina's return visit to College Park, but Maryland Athletic Director Jim Kehoe assured South Carolina Coach Frank McGuire that all steps woud be taken to assure his team's safety. In January, before 14,312 fans, Maryland held the ball while South Carolina stayed in a zone and the half time score was an incredible 4–3, Maryland's favor. At the end of the regulation game the score was tied 23–23. Then in overtime, Jim O'Brien won it for Maryland with two seconds to go, 33–31. South Carolina had won 35 of 39 games before this defeat.

The first annual "Big Four" Basketball Tournament was held in Greensboro on December 18 and 19, 1970. It was the answer to the famous "Dixie Classic" which had thrilled basketball fans for 12 years before it was cancelled in 1961. The new format included only the "Big Four" schools of North Carolina, and would serve as a preview in the years to come of the ACC season. The idea had been proposed by Bob Kent, then manager of the Greensboro Coliseum, back in 1968 at the spring meeting of the ACC in Hot Springs, Virginia. The athletic directors of the four schools realized the income producing potential of the tournament, particularly since the seating capacity of the Coliseum was being enlarged from 9,000 to 15,000, and agreed to it. Although the games did not count in the ACC standings, they did not lack in intensity and thrills as evidenced by the first tournament. In the opening game, Wake Forest beat Duke 83–79; and in the second game, North Carolina State beat North Carolina 82–70. On the second night, North Carolina edged Duke 83–81; and in the championship game, North Carolina State beat Wake Forest 73–70.

While the future of the Conference was making all the news that fall, Wake Forest was winning its first football title by compiling a 5–1 Conference record, losing only to South Carolina 43–7 in the second game of the season. Overall, Wake Forest was 6–5 under Cal Stoll, who was to resign in January to become Head Coach at Minnesota. North Carolina, with a better overall record of 8–3, however, was selected for the Peach Bowl. All-American tailback Don McCauley of North Carolina set a national rushing record of 1,720 yards and shattered a total of 23 ACC and school records during the season. The Tar Heels faced eighth-ranked Arizona State (unde-feated with a 10–0 record) before a record crowd of 52,126 fans. North Carolina lost the services of quarterback Paul Miller with an injury in the second quarter and fell behind 21–7 before coming back to take a 26–21 lead. As snow was falling, Arizona State scored three times in the third quarter to regain the lead, and eventually went on to win this see-saw contest 48–26. Don McCauley rushed for 132 yards and scored three touchdowns.

The first month of 1971 brought further incidents of controversy, as it was reported that the ACC had placed a number of basketball players on probation for fighting during games. Although there was no specific confirmation of the report, since it is against league policy to release action of this nature in order to protect the players from fan abuse, the *Spartanburg* (S.C.) *Herald* said the players penalized were: John Roche and John Ribock of South Carolina, Randy Denton of Duke, Bill Gerry of Virginia, Bill Chamberlain of North Carolina, and Jay Flowers and Sparky Still of Maryland. A later report stated that it was not Randy Denton, but Rick Katherman from Duke who had been placed on probation for his ejection from a game during the Big Four Tournament. Norvall Neve, acting Commissioner, although not commenting specifically, expressed concern over the general increase in rowdiness by players and fans and urged that member institutions take a bigger role in controlling these situations.

At the NCAA meetings in Houston that month, North Carolina Central University presented a grievance that since star halfback Kenny Garrett of Wake Forest never was released from an athletic grant-in-aid that he had signed with NCCU, he should not be allowed to play for Wake Forest. Garrett, a native of Fayetteville, had enrolled at Northeast Oklahoma Junior College before transferring to Wake Forest. Wake Forest officials claimed that Garrett had the right to change his mind and they had discussed his signing with the Conference Commissioner and the Collegiate Commissioners Association. After hearing the grievance the Collegiate Commissioners Association ruled that the differences should be settled between the conference commissioners of the two schools involved. Since there was no violation of the interconference letter-of-intent, Garrett was allowed to continue playing for Wake Forest.

There were continued reports that South Carolina and Clemson would drop out of the ACC because of the controversy over eligibility requirements, and the *Atlanta Journal* reported on January 30 that a new conference of Southern schools was being considered. The proposed conference would be made up of the following schools in addition to South Carolina and Clemson: Florida State, Memphis State, Tulane, Southern Mississippi, Virginia Tech, and West Virginia.

In the meantime, Frank Howard had stepped aside as Athletic Director at Clemson to become an assistant to the Vice-President, and he was replaced by Bill McLellan, who had been Associate Athletic Director. McLellan was a Clemson graduate and had been a member of the athletic staff since 1958.

It was in this air of uncertainty that Robert C. James assumed his duties as Commissioner of the Atlantic Coast Conference on March 1. James succeeded the later Jim Weaver, and Norvall Neve who had been serving as acting Commissioner since Weaver's death in the summer of 1970. He took office just in time for the Basketball Tournament two weeks later in Greensboro. North Carolina won the regular season championship and reached the Tournament finals by beating Clemson and Virginia. South Carolina reached the finals for the second year in a row by beating Maryland and North Carolina State. On the first night, the Maryland players had swapped uniforms with each other so that the names on the jerseys did not match the player wearing them. However, the Gamecocks were not confused and went on to beat the Terrapins 71–63. In the finals, the Tar Heels had the game apparently won, 51–50, when Lee Dedmon blocked a shot by South Carolina's Kevin Joyce with four seconds remaining. A jump ball was called, however, between the 6'4" Joyce and the 6'10" Dedmon and the tap went to the Gamecocks' Tom Owens who was alone under the basket. Owens scored and South Carolina won the ACC Championship 52–51. Dedmon and John Roche of South Carolina shared the Everett Case MVP Award. In the Eastern Regionals, South Carolina placed fourth, losing to Pennsylvania 79–64 and Fordham 100–90. Meanwhile North Carolina and Duke were both invited to the NIT. Duke beat Dayton 68–60 and Tennessee 78–64 while North Carolina beat Massachusetts 90–49 and Providence 86–79. This set up a semifinal game between the Tar Heels and the Blue Devils, and North Carolina won 73–67. North Carolina went on to win the NIT Championship by beating Georgia Tech 84–66, and Duke finished fourth, losing the consolation game 92–88 in overtime to St. Bonaventure. The Tar Heels were led by Bill Chamberlain who won the Most Valuable Player Award.

Monday, March 29, 1971, the long speculated rumors were confirmed when the University of South Carolina announced it would resign from the Atlantic Coast Conference effective August 15. T. Eston Marchant, Chairman of the USC Board of Trustees made the following remarks:

We'd like to stay in the ACC, but that isn't possible right now . . . 'under the present circumstances and in the best interest of all concerned' the university would submit its resignation effective August 15 . . . Because USC has enjoyed and hopes to continue to enjoy its relationship with fellow conference members, we hope that this separation will be of a temporary nature and for a minimum amount of time . . . It is our intention of continuing the long existing relationships with our old and valued opponents which presently comprise the membership of the Atlantic Coast Conference.

There were mixed reactions around the league on South Carolina's withdrawal—some regret, but little surprise. Gene Corrigan, Virginia's Athletic Director said, "I am not surprised. I don't think anybody is. But I think it's a shame that they have taken this course of action." Willis Casey, Athletic Director at North Carolina State commented, "I am sorry they're withdrawing from the conference. I had no idea the statement was coming Monday. South Carolina preferred to do some things differently." Dr. Jack Sawyer, Faculty Chairman of Athletics at Wake Forest said, "I hate to see one of the original schools pull out of the conference. Scheduling is something that will have to be kicked around quite a bit." Athletic Director Homer Rice said, "In a way this comes as a shock, I didn't expect it to happen at this moment. Those of us at the University of North Carolina still had hoped that the problems would be resolved, but South Carolina has made the decision and I suppose that's final."

Commissioner Bob James called a special meeting of Faculty Chairmen and Athletic Directors the following Monday to discuss the scheduling problems, particularly in football and basketball, presented by South Carolina's withdrawal. The Conference had a rule which prevented its members from playing independent schools in the ACC territory unless they competed under the rules of eligibility of the Conference.

Clemson had also been recruiting under the NCAA rules of a projected 1.6 of a 4.0 grade average instead of the stiffer ACC requirement of 1.6 plus 800 on the College Board exams. However Clemson President Robert Edwards had announced two weeks earlier at the Tournament that "the institution is now a member of the Atlantic Coast Conference in good standing, and further, has no intention of withdrawing from the conference now, or at any foreseeable date."

At the special meeting held in Greensboro, ACC President Fadum read to the membership the letter of resignation addressed to Commissioner James and signed by William F. Patterson, Secretary of the USC Board of Trustees, dated March 31, 1971. The letter, which was "accepted with profound regret." said:

This letter is to formally advise you of the action taken by the Board of Trustees of the University of South Carolina on Monday, March 29, 1971, relative to its membership in the Atlantic Coast Conference. By motion duly made, seconded, and unanimously carried, the Board approved the resignation of the University of South Carolina as a member institution in the Atlantic Coast Conference effective August 15, 1971.

The Conference then voted unanimously to delete Article VI, Section 3 of the Bylaws which would have prohibited ACC members from competing with South Carolina. It was also agreed that the 1971 football contracts would be fulfilled, and South Carolina would not use any players ineligible by Conference academic standards. Scheduling for basketball and other sports would be left up to the institutions involved. South Carolina agreed to honor the ACC members' grants-in-aid commitments, and it was agreed that South Carolina would share in the normal distribution of Conference revenues for 1970–71.

ACC President Ralph Fadum stated that, "Deliberations and action taken were engaged in a spirit of good will. No action taken in any way should be interpreted to be punitive in nature."

At the annual Spring meeting in May, South Carolina changed their withdrawal date from August 15 to July 1 to coincide with the new operating year of the Conference. A recommendation by the Basketball Committee was approved that would give the regular season winner a bye in the first round of the seven-team basketball tournament. The No. 2 team would meet No. 7 at 1:00 P.M., No. 3 and No. 6 would play at 3:30 P.M., and No. 4 and No. 5 would play at 8:00 P.M. The schedule for the last two nights would remain the same.

The following resolutions honoring two of the leaders in the formation and development of the Conference were adopted.

1. Dr. Harry Clifton Byrd, President of the University of Mayland from 1935 to 1954, was truly an early pioneer in intercollegiate athletics. As a player, coach, faculty member and administrator he rendered valuable and outstanding service to the youth of our nation.

Dr. Byrd assisted in the organizing of the original Southern Conference in 1921, which was later to spawn the Southeastern Conference and the present Atlantic Coast Conference.

His dedicated interest in the welfare of intercollegiate athletics and the contributions they could render to colleges and universities played a prominent part in his life.

BE IT RESOLVED that the Atlantic Coast Conference express deep sorrow at the passing of Dr. Byrd and recognize his outstanding contributions to intercollegiate athletics.

2. WHEREAS, he is the last of the original Faculty Chairmen of the Atlantic Coast Conference to retire;

AND WHEREAS, he has served the Atlantic Coast Conference in numerous capacities, including being its president twice;

AND WHEREAS, he has been one of the leaders in moulding the Atlantic Coast Conference into one of the most respectable and competitive conferences in the nation;

NOW, BE IT THEREFORE RESOLVED, that the Atlantic Coast Conference go on record in offering its grateful thanks, with deep appreciation, to R. R. (Red) Ritchie of Clemson University for his untiring efforts in the formation, support and leadership within the ranks of the Atlantic Coast Conference during the past eighteen years, and that the member institutions wish him well in his retirement, not only for his long service to the Atlantic Coast Conference, but also for his influence in shaping the lives of thousands of young men during his forty-five year teaching tenure at Clemson.

On Friday, June 25, it was announced that the dean of the ACC football coaches, Earle Edwards, was resigning effective July 1. Edwards was in his 18th year as head mentor at North Carolina State. During that time the Wolfpack had won three ACC championships, tied for two others, finished second four times, and Edwards was ACC football coach of the year four times. At the time of his resignation Edwards was president of the American Football Coaches Association. Chancellor Caldwell announced that Edwards' new duties would be as Assistant Director of Foundations and Development, and that Al Michaels would be the interim head coach for the 1971 season. Michaels had come from Penn State in 1954, soon after Edwards was named as head coach, and was the defensive coordinator.

The Conference was saddened in September with the tragic death of Bill Arnold, a sophomore defensive guard at North Carolina who collapsed during a preseason Labor Day football practice. Arnold had been in the Intensive Care Unit for fifteen days before passing away. The cause of death was given as heat prostration complicated by liver and kidney failure.

In a move to curb the spiraling costs of intercollegiate athletics, the financial aid committee of the NCAA recommended that: athletic scholarships be awarded in cases of financial need only (excluding tuition and fees) and be for a period of one year only; a limit be placed on the number of grants awarded in football and basketball; a limit be placed on the size of the coaching staffs in these two sports (this was subsequently dropped); and a national letter-of-intent be adopted. At a special meeting of the Conference in October, Dr. Ralph Fadum, ACC President and Faculty Chairman at North Carolina State, asked that the ACC consider the four recommendations of the NCAA committee, and the Conference also changed the dates of the annual Winter meeting from December to February.

The month of November witnessed the departure of two of the most influential men in the formation and development of the Atlantic Coast Conference and in intercollegiate athletics in general. On November 17, Oliver Kelly Cornwell died at the age of 75 at North Carolina Memorial Hospital. He was a former Chairman of the Department of Physical Education at the University of North Carolina, and long time Secretary-Treasurer of the Atlantic Coast Conference. He served the University for 34 years, and was the mayor of Chapel Hill in the fifties. Dr. Cornwell was one of the most knowledgeable and respected men in physical education and athletics in the country. The Conference adopted the following resolution in memorium:

Dr. O. K. "Ollie" Cornwell was Faculty Chairman of Athletics at the University of North Carolina until May, 1962. He was one of the founders of the Atlantic Coast Conference and served as an officer from its inception until his retirement as its President in 1962.

He also contributed significantly to the National Collegiate Athletic Association by distinguished service on its Eligibility Committee, Executive Committee, as well as District Vice-President.

In appreciation of his diligent service and activity in its behalf, the Conference named "Ollie" Representative Emeritus in May, 1962 upon his retirement as Faculty Chairman.

"Ollie" Cornwell will be greatly missed by all who have been privileged to associate with him in intercollegiate athletics over the years. The Conference is immeasurably better for having the benefit of his wisdom, courage and perseverance in its formative years.

THEREFORE, BE IT RESOLVED THAT the Atlantic Coast Conference expresses its deepest sympathy to the family of Dr. O.K. Cornwell, and that a copy of this resolution be sent to his family.

That same week it was announced that Edmund McCullough Cameron would retire as Athletic Director at Duke University on August 31, 1972. Eddie Cameron, a graduate of Washington and Lee, joined the Duke staff in September 1926 as freshman football coach. In 1929 he was named Head Basketball Coach, and in 14 seasons his teams rolled up an oustanding 226–99 record, and won three Southern Conference championships. In 1942, Cameron was named acting Head Football Coach when Wallace Wade left for duty in the Army, and in four years his record was 25–11–1. He won three Southern Conference football championships and in 1945 he guided the Blue Devils to an exciting 29–26 win over Alabama in the Sugar Bowl. He is the only coach in Duke history never to lose to North Carolina in football. In 1951, Cameron succeeded Wade as Athletic Director, and two years later he was one of the leaders in the founding of the Atlantic Coast Conference. Cameron was chairman of the influential basketball committee of the Conference for many years and a member of the Helms Foundation Hall of Fame. In his 46 years of service to Duke, Cameron had a significant impact not only on athletics at his University but on intercollegiate athletics in the ACC and the NCAA. The Conference adopted the following resolution upon his retirement:

WHEREAS, EDMUND MCCULLOUGH CAMERON has been associated with the affairs of the Atlantic Coast Conference since its founding May 8, 1953, and with intercollegiate athletics for many years prior to that time, and

WHEREAS, Mr. Cameron has served in many capacities within the Atlantic Coast Conference, the most noteworthy being the Chairman of the Basketball Committee for nineteen years during which time he carried out his duties with distinction and devotion, and

WHEREAS, his wholesome influence on the regional and national athletic scenes has brought much distinction upon the Atlantic Coast Conference,

BE IT RESOLVED THEREFORE that the membership of the Atlantic Coast Conference congratulate Mr. Cameron upon his retirement and proclaim to him and for all to note the heartfelt gratitude for the quality of his devotion to the Conference and to the athletic causes which he has represented so extraordinarily well.

The second annual "Big Four" Tournament was held on December 17 and 18, 1971, in Greensboro. On the first night, North Carolina beat Wake Forest 99–76, and North Carolina State beat Duke 67–62. On the second night, North Carolina beat State for the championship 99–68, and Duke beat Wake Forest 70–58 for third place.

North Carolina won its first outright football championship that fall with a perfect 6–0 league mark. They had tied for the crown in 1963. Overall the Tar Heels were 9–2, losing only to Tulane 37–29 and Notre Dame 16–0. North Carolina was invited to the Gator Bowl to face fifth-ranked Georgia with a 10–1 record. The Bulldogs, a 12 point favorite, were coached by Vince Dooley, the brother of North Carolina Coach Bill Dooley. This was the first time two brothers had faced each other as head coaches in a bowl game. In a rugged defensive game before 71,208 fans, in 71 degree weather, the Georgia Bulldogs won 7–3. All the scoring took place in the third quarter as the Tar Heels scored first on a 35 yard field goal by Ken Craven, only to see Georgia come back and score a touchdown to win the game. Linebacker Jim Webster was voted the Most Outstanding Player for North Carolina.

The new year, 1972, started with an announcement by the NCAA that would have a lasting effect on intercollegiate athletics. In a surprise move at their annual convention in Hollywood, Florida, a proposal to allow freshmen to play football and basketball was approved over the objections of the major college football coaches. The vote for football was 94–67 in favor of freshmen participating, and the vote for basketball passed by a hand-raised majority. Technically, the new rule only meant that freshmen were eligible to participate in postseason and championship NCAA events. Regular season participation would still be up to individual schools and conferences. This proposal was made by the ACC and the Western Athletic Conference. Freshmen had been made eligible in other sports four years earlier.

The Conference had postponed their annual meeting from December to February in anticipation of the action taken by the NCAA. At their meeting in February, the Conference voted to make freshmen eligible for varsity football and basketball beginning in the 1972 season. They also voted to establish junior varsity programs in these sports. In other business, the Conference voted 4–3 to retain its 800 College Board test score requirement. A Virginia proposal to allow women to compete in fencing, golf, swimming, track, and tennis was withdrawn for lack of support by the other members.

The 1972 Basketball Tournament was the first seven-team tournament, and North Carolina received a first round bye as the regular season champion. In the finals, the Tar Heels beat Maryland 73–64 behind Dennis Wuycik's 24 points. North Carolina beat South Carolina 92–69 and Pennsylvania 73–59 to win the Eastern Regionals and advance to the "Final Four." There the long awaited showdown between No. 1 ranked UCLA with Bill Walton and No. 2 ranked North Carolina with Robert McAdoo failed to materialize as the Tar Heels were upset by Florida State 79–75 on the first night. North Carolina came back to beat Louisville 105–91 for third place, and ended the season with an outstanding 26–5 record.

Meanwhile Maryland, with a 23–5 record, went to the NIT and beat St. Joseph's 67–55, Syracuse 71–65, Jacksonville 91–77, and Niagara 100–69 to win the Championship. The Terps were led by All-American Tom McMillen who won the Most Valuable Player Award. Virginia, with a fine record of 20–7, was also invited to the NIT, but the Cavaliers were edged by Lafayette 72–71 in the first round.

At the Spring meeting in Virginia Beach, the Conference established a counseling service to aid basketball players in dealing with agents and professional basketball organizations. It was emphasized that the Conference would not negotiate financial arrangements with professional teams, but their service would be entirely educational in that it would explain "pro" contract offers in financial terms to the players. It would include legal advice on contractual matters, tax assistance, and investment counselling.

Virginia won the second annual NCAA Lacrosse Championship in June by beating Johns Hopkins 13–12 in a thriller at Maryland's Byrd Stadium. The Cavaliers had struggled through the regular season and had lost the ACC Championship to No. 1 ranked Maryland. But in the Tournament, Virginia swept by Army and Cortland State en route to the Championship, while Maryland was being upset by Johns Hopkins 9–6 after an opening round win against Rutgers. The Cavaliers were led by Pete Eldridge who won the Player of the Year Award.

Above, top left: Virginia vs. Maryland, lacrosse, 1975; bottom left: 1972 NCAA Lacrosse Champions, Virginia; right: Pete Eldridge, Virginia, lacrosse star. Below: 1973 NCAA Lacrosse Champions, Maryland

There was still a cloud hanging over the ACC as the school year drew to a close in 1972. This uncertainty was brought about by a suit filed back in December by two Clemson University students. The students, Joey Edward Beach and James Marion Vickery, had asked a federal court to enjoin an ACC academic requirement (of a score of 800 on the SAT) that barred them from participating in intercollegiate athletics at Clemson. Beach said he wanted to go out for football but was not eligible since he only had a 760 SAT score. Vickery, a diver who wanted to go out for the swimming team, reported his SAT score was 799. The students claimed that the ACC requirement violated the 14th Amendment and denied them equal protection of the law. They contended that as qualified students they had the right to participate in all of the University's activities including varsity athletics.

At a pretrial hearing on January 31, the date of March 13 was set as the opening day for the suit in federal court in Anderson, South Carolina. Judge Robert W. Hemphill who presided in the case then took depositions the following month from the two students; Robert Edwards, Clemson President; Ken Vickery (no relation), Dean of Admissions at Clemson; Bob James, ACC Commissioner; and Ralph Fadum, President of the ACC. President Edwards told the court that the previous year there had been 8,200 students at Clemson and 113 had scored below 800. Edwards went on to say that:

It is essential to our program that we continue to be members of the Atlantic Coast Conference. As long as we are members of the conference we must comply with the rules of the conference. We have lived by these rules and will continue to do so until they are changed.

Arguments pro and con were heard throughout the spring but no decision was reached until August 7 when Judge Hemphill signed an order enjoining the Atlantic Coast Conference and Clemson University from enforcing the "800 rule" for student athletes. In the order, Hemphill said,

The evidence . . . convinces this court that the requirement of 800 on the SAT test is not based on valid reasoning . . . They do not refer to this 800 score for entrance . . . Clemson cannot withhold grants-in-aid from students and the privilege of engaging in intercollegiate athletic activities on the same basis as those rights and privileges now accorded students who pass the score of 800 and above on scholastic aptitude tests.

The Faculty Athletic Chairmen of the Conference met immediately to discuss the implications of this momentous decision, and it was decided to delay any action until this decision could be discussed with the university presidents and attorneys. They were also concerned about the possible effects this decision might have on other policies at the member institutions. On August 10, in a conference telephone hook-up, the Faculty Chairmen decided to appeal Judge Hemphill's decision. They also decided to request that the order to eliminate the "800 rule" be delayed until the Appeals Court ruled. Then a week later, in a surprise announcement, the ACC said that its members had voted to rescind the "800 rule," and in the future they would only use the NCAA requirement of the 1.6 prediction, on a 4.0 scale, in order for students to take part in intercollegiate athletics. As a result, the Conference dropped its appeal, and the court dismissed the suit. The issue which had brought about South Carolina's withdrawal from the Conference a year earlier was now finally resolved. The ACC no longer had an academic eligibility requirement that was higher than any other conference in the nation. Ironically, the Conference had just completed a year in which an all-time high of 354 athletes had made the ACC Honor Roll by maintaining a "B" average (3.0 or better) for the academic year. Duke topped the list with 85 athletes, which was only five short of the individual school record set by Virginia in 1971.

On the same day that this issue was being finalized, August 18, the NCAA announced that Duke University was being reprimanded, censured, and placed on probation for one year because of illegal basketball recruiting violations. The violations involved entertaining and transporting a prospect, David Thompson of Shelby, North Carolina, who later enrolled at North Carolina State. The probation specified that Duke's basketball team could not go to a postseason tournament, NCAA or NIT, in 1973. The announcement came as a surprise to Duke officials since they did not believe any violations had been committed, and there had been no charges made after the Conference itself had investigated the matter. It was also considered to be a rather severe penalty in light of the fact that Duke had always had a clean slate with the NCAA prior to this time.

Chancellor John B. Blackburn issued the following statement on behalf of Duke University:

In the spring of 1971, a friend of the university, who, under the NCAA interpretation of its rules, was a representative of the university's interests, took a high school senior whom the university was attempting to recruit for its basketball program, and his high school coach to the ACC basketball tournament.

He also purchased a sport's coat and trousers for the young man, without the knowledge of anyone in the university. The NCAA has determined that these actions constitute a violation of its rules. The young man did not enroll at Duke.

As the NCAA has indicated, the university provided "excellent assistance and cooperation" in its investigation. The university has made, and will make every effort to abide by the rules of the NCAA and recognizes that in this case the rules were violated.

We regret the incident and have taken steps to insure that the mistake will not be repeated.

Then on October 25, the NCAA announced that it was placing North Carolina State University on probation because of basketball recruiting violations. The violations involved an assistant coach, Eddie Biedenbach, who participated in at least one informal basketball game with five prospective athletes; two prospects who were given financial aid to attend a summer school session; housing a prospect free in a dormitory which was utilized to house counselors in a summer basketball camp; and employing three prospects as counselors in the summer basketball camp operated by the head coach, Norman Sloan. As a result of these and other violations, the North Carolina State basketball team was prohibited from participating in any post-season tournaments for one year. State had previously been placed on probation by the NCAA for one year in 1954 and for four years in 1956 for recruiting violations.

David Thompson was again the man in the middle of the alleged recruiting violations, and the rumors of illegal offers became so prevalent that both the NCAA and Commissione James conducted independent investigations of the charges. The Commissioner concluded that his investigation did not substantiate the charges that North Carolina State or its representatives offered excessive financial aid. However the circumstances involving the transportation to campus, and the free housing and work outs in the gym, gave indication "that acts of negligence by members of the North Carolina State University Basketball Coaching Staff did indeed place the University in a precarious position . . . because sufficient precautions were not taken . . ." James then reprimanded the State basketball coaching staff and sent a copy of his report to Chancellor John Caldwell and the NCAA.

The NCAA Infractions Committee reviewed the Commissioner's report and decided to continue its investigation since the report dealt only with the Thompson case, and the NCAA had charges against State dating back to 1970. Athletic Director Willis Casey in his report to the Chancellor on September 27 stated:

"I do not find any evidence of willful or knowing violation of either ACC or NCAA rules. Nor do I find any reason to suspect our staff of improper motives, that is, a purpose to gain an advantage, for the allegations mostly relate to athletes who had already signed a letter-or-intent with North Carolina State.

What I do find are several evidences of carelessness or bad judgment on the part of the basketball staff. These deficiences of attention or judgment or both permitted situations to occur quite unnessarily out of which allegations arose.

Casey then instituted internal control procedures, applicable to all coaches, that would prevent a recurrence of similar type situations. Chancellor Caldwell, Willis Casey, and Faculty Chairman Ralph Fadum went to Kansas City on October 6 to present the case for North Carolina State. Two weeks later the NCAA placed State on probation. Chancellor Caldwell reprimanded Sloan and Biedenbach but reiterated that his action did not "concede justification to the penalty imposed by the NCAA," but added that State "accepted the penalty and will continue our diligence in attempting to conform with the policies and regulations of the NCAA."

Commissioner James offered the following opinion concerning the NCAA probation of Duke and North Carolina State:

Confusion is the one word I feel that describes why these violations crop up . . . The rules in many cases are not specific enough. They don't clearly spell out what they mean.

Violations do not take place because a coach wants to defy the governing body. Or that he feels he can get away with something. I am confident that there are so many rules that there is confusion in getting the proper interpretation. Each January at the NCAA convention new rules are voted in and amended. At that session there is the necessity for an interpretation period.

No conference in the nation has spent as much time and money in trying to cite rules from a preventive standpoint than has the Atlantic Coast. Many conferences copy us. The Atlantic Coast is the only conference to have published a book on recruiting rules in all sports. We have also compiled a letter and sent it to high school coaches.

. . . If the NCAA had not been thoroughly impressed with the sincere intentions of the two schools involved to try and do what is right, we would really have been penalized.

In November, the Wake Forest University faculty authorized the dean of the college to appoint an *ad hoc* committee to study the University's athletic program. An earlier move to have Wake Forest withdraw from the ACC and seek a less competitive conference had been voted down. There was some feeling that the enrollment at Wake Forest, the smallest in the Conference with less than 3,000 undergraduates, was a serious hinderance in competition against the much larger state universities. The faculty resolution followed the firing of Head Football Coach Tom Harper, who had won only one game so far that fall. Then after the firing was announced, the Deacons upset Duke 9–7 to win their second game. Athletic Director Gene Hooks, when asked to comment, stated that:

We have no intention of pulling out of the ACC . . . We are operating at the same level of scholarships, recruiting and virtually the same academics as the other ACC schools are. The trustees, administration, alumni and Deacon Club supporters are strongly in favor of a strong team on the ACC level.

In football that fall, North Carolina won its second straight championship with a 6–0 record and extended its winning streak to 15 in a row against Conference opponents. Overall the Tar Heels were 10–1, losing only to Ohio State 29–14. North Carolina State was runner-up in the Conference, losing to North Carolina by only one point in a 34–33 thriller that saw both teams score a touchdown in the final minute, and tying Maryland in the opening game 24–24. Both the Tar Heels and Wolfpack were invited to bowl games at the end of the season and both teams brought back victories, for one of the most memorable weekends for the ACC and the state of North Carolina.

The great weekend began on Friday night, December 29, 1972, in Atlanta, Georgia. There the Wolfpack, with a 7–3–1 record faced the Mountaineers from West Virginia with an 8–3 mark. A record crowd of 52,671 fans turned out in Atlanta Stadium to watch the Fifth Annual Peach Bowl. The first string quarterback for State, Bruce Shaw, broke his arm in drills after the team arrived in Atlanta and he was replaced by freshman Dave Buckey. At half-time the score was 14–13 in State's favor, but the Wolfpack completely dominated the second half to win a resounding victory 49–13. Buckey, who was named the Outstanding Offensive Player, threw for two touchdowns and ran for one as State rolled up 535 yards in total offense. Stan Fritts scored three touchdowns for the Wolfpack, and teammate George Bell won the Outstanding Defensive Player award. Lou Holtz, in his first season, had taken North Carolina State to a Bowl victory, and he was named ACC Coach of the Year.

The following day it was North Carolina's turn. The Tar Heels were the first team from the ACC ever invited to the Sun Bowl in El Paso, Texas and their opponents on Saturday were the Red Raiders from Texas Tech. Carolina, with a 10–1 record, was a slight favorite over Texas Tech, with an 8–3 record. The Tar Heels had been nick-named the "Cardiac Kids" for their ability to come from behind all season and squeak out victories in the closing minutes. This game would be no exception. North Carolina led at the half 9–7 but was behind 21–16 at the end of the third quarter. Early in the fourth quarter the Tar Heels went ahead 24–21 only to fall behind again 28–24. Then, before 31,312 fans on a windy day, North Carolina quarterback Nick Vidnovic threw a 12 yard touchdown pass to Ted Levering with one minute to play to put the Tar Heels up 30–28. The kick for the extra point failed but on the ensuing kick off the Tar Heels scored a safety for the final point margin, 32–28. Vidnovic led the victors by throwing for 215 yards and two touchdowns as the Tar Heels finished with an outstanding 11–1 season.

North Carolina State was also showing its strength in basketball as they captured the third annual "Big Four" Tournament on December 15 and 16. This was the first year that the tournament had been sold out and proved to be the big financial success that had been predicted (each school realizing about $60,000). In the opening game, State beat Wake Forest 88–83 while North Carolina defeated Duke 91–86. Then the next night, State beat North Carolina 68–61 for the championships, and Duke beat Wake Forest 80–67 for third place. The Wolfpack were paced by the much heralded sophomore David Thompson, and 7'4" Tommy Burleson, a junior from Newland, North Carolina. State's showing in Greensboro was an omen of things to come as the ACC entered 1973.

At the annual meeting in February, the Conference's major concern was how to select the ACC representative to the NCAA Basketball Tournament if North Carolina State and Duke, both of whom were on probation, met in the championship game. It was decided that a preliminary game between the two semifinalists would be held at 6:00 if this pairing occurred. If only Duke or North Carolina State were in the finals, their opponent would automatically become the ACC representative.

A second major item was the reorganizational plan of the NCAA to divide into two or three divisions according to school size and athletic strength. This proposal had been defeated at the NCAA convention in January, and now the major college conferences had called a special meeting in Chicago to discuss possible alternatives. The ACC, along with most of the major colleges, was firmly in favor of the divisional split and instructed Commissioner James to strongly support this action at the Chicago meeting, and also at the specially convened NCAA convention coming up in August. In other business, the Conference made women eligible for intercollegiate participation by deleting the sentence "athletic participation is limited to male student-athletes" from its Bylaws.

As the Basketball Tournament got underway in March, there was some rumblings of discontent over holding the Tournament in Greensboro every year. The out-of-state schools considered the site to be an advantage to North Carolina, Wake Forest, North Carolina State, and Duke since they played some regular season games there. This feeling was even more paramount now since the advent of the "Big Four" Tournament in the Greensboro Coliseum back in 1970. Commissioner James stated that the Conference was preparing a survey of other playing sites in the league area, and would contact the operators of arenas in Charlotte, Norfolk, Roanoke, Richmond, and the new arena being built in Landover, Maryland about their facilities.

North Carolina State swept through the regular season undefeated in all games, and entered the Tournament with a 12–0 league record. The Wolfpack, only the fourth team to ever go undefeated received a bye in the first round, and beat Virginia 63–51 in the semifinals. Meanwhile, Maryland had beaten Clemson and Wake Forest to reach the finals. Only one game remained for State to finish the season undefeated. At half-time the score was tied 32–32. Then David Thompson's two free throws in the final seconds gave State the victory over Maryland in a 76–74 thriller. The Wolfpack won their seventh ACC Championship, had an outstanding 27–0 record, and were ranked No. 2 in the country. But the long awaited showdown with No. 1 ranked UCLA would have to wait another year because of State's probation. Maryland went to the NCAA Regionals and finished second, beating Syracuse 91–75 and losing to Providence 103–89. North Carolina was invited to the NIT and finished third. The Tar Heels beat Oral Roberts 82–65, Massachusetts 73–63, lost to Notre Dame 78–71, and beat Alabama 88–69.

That spring, Maryland's lacrosse team, ranked No. 1 in the country, met Johns Hopkins, ranked No. 2, in the NCAA Championship at the University of Pennsylvania's Franklin Field. Both teams had lost only one game during the season. In an exciting game, Maryland won 10–9 in overtime on Frank Urso's third goal of the day. "Buddy" Beardmore was named Coach of the Year and Doug Schreiber the Player of the Year as the Terrapins captured the national title.

There was talk that fall that the legendary basketball coach from Kentucky, Adolph Rupp, would come out of retirement to lead the Duke Blue Devils. Head Coach "Bucky" Waters had resigned on September 11 to take an administrative position with the Duke Hospital, and the 72-year-old Rupp had been offered the position. Rupp had retired in 1970 with a career record of 879 wins and only 190 losses. The night before a scheduled press conference was to be held to make the announcement, Rupp's business partner died and Rupp declined the offer. Duke Assistant Coach Neil McGeahey was named shortly afterwards, ending five weeks of speculation and confusion.

North Carolina State finished the 1973 football season undefeated in league play with a 6–0 record. The Wolfpack were led by an outstanding trio of backs running out of the "veer" formation, Charlie Young, Stan Fritts, and Willie Burden. Burden won the ACC Player of the Year Award and was the first State player to rush for over 1000 yards in a season (1014 yards). North Carolina State, ranked 16th with an 8–3 record, received a Liberty Bowl bid and faced the University of Kansas with a 7–3–1 record. Stan Fritts ran for 83 yards on 18 carries and scored two touchdowns to lead the Wolfpack to a

31–18 victory before 50,011 fans. Fritts was named the Most Valuable Player, and Lou Holtz had guided the Wolfpack to their second consecutive bowl triumph.

Maryland finished second in the ACC, losing only to North Carolina State in a close game 24–22. The Terrapins finished with an 8–3 record, were ranked 18th, and were invited to the Peach Bowl to face Georgia with a 6–4–1 record. This was Maryland's first bowl appearance in 18 years. The Terrapins dominated the game statistically gaining 461 total yards to Georgia's 284 yards, but the Bulldogs relied on the big plays to win 17–16. The score was tied 10–10 at half-time, but Maryland was shut out in the second half except for two field goals in the fourth quarter by Steve Mike-Mayer, who also had kicked a field goal in the second quarter. Maryland tailback Louis Carter rushed for 126 yards on 29 carries and completed 2 of 3 passes for 83 yards to be named the Outstanding Offensive Player. Attendance was 38,107 fans.

The "Big Four" Basketball Tournament was moved to the first weekend in January in 1974. North Carolina State squeaked by North Carolina 78–77 in the opening game, and Wake Forest edged Duke 64–61 in the second game. The next night, North Carolina State beat Wake Forest 91–73 for the Championship, and North Carolina beat Duke 84–75 for third place. North Carolina State used this tournament to set their basketball machine in motion as Conference competition began. The Wolfpack swept through the regular season undefeated for the second year in a row and entered the ACC Tournament with only one loss. Back in December, in St. Louis, State had faced UCLA in a much ballyhooed showdown that pitted the No. 1 and No. 2 teams from the previous season against each other. Before a national television audience, the two teams battled back and forth for 30 minutes on an even plane, but in the last 10 minutes UCLA put it together for a decided victory 84–66.

Then in March, the Wolfpack beat Virginia 87–66 to advance to the finals of the ACC Tournament where they faced a red-hot Maryland who had blitzed Duke 85–66 and North Carolina 105–85 in the semifinals. In one of the most spectacular games ever played, Maryland shot 61 percent from the floor and scored 100 points only to lose 103–100 in overtime when Monte Towe hit two free throws with six seconds left. This was the sixth straight win by State over Maryland in the last two years. The Wolfpack were led by Tommy Burleson, who scored 38 points and snared 13 rebounds, and David Thompson with 29 points. The Eastern Regionals were played in Reynolds Coliseum and the Wolfpack enjoyed the friendly confines by beating Providence 92–78 and Pittsburgh 100–72. The victory over Pitt was marred by an

Above: North Carolina State, 1974
NCAA Basketball Champions

Right: David Thompson, North
Carolina State, basketball star

125

injury to David Thompson in the first half that stunned the packed house of 12,400 fans. In attempting to block a shot, Thompson flipped over a teammate and crashed to the floor hitting his head. Thompson was carried out of the gym on a stretcher and rushed to a hospital. The concern of the crowd turned away from the game as they waited for the verdict from the doctors. Shortly before the end of the game Thompson returned to they gym with his head bandaged, and he received an ear-shattering ovation. The long awaited rematch with UCLA was now at hand, but the condition of Thompson was still a question mark. Crowds ranging up to 10,000 watched the Wolfpack practice, wondering if Thompson was going to play. The Greensboro Coliseum was packed with 15,829 fans to witness the first round game that most people thought would decide the national championship. This time State was ranked No. 1 and UCLA No. 2. At half-time the score was tied 35–35. At the end of the regulation game the score was still tied 65–65. In the first overtime UCLA jumped out to a 7 point lead 74–67, but the Wolfpack fought back to win 80–77 in a tremendous game between two great teams. The final game against Marquette was almost anticlimactic as State won 76–64, clinching the National Championship. The Wolfpack, with a superb 30–1 record were led by Player of the Year David Thompson, ACC Tournament MVP Tommy Burleson, and the diminutive playmaker 5'7" Monte Towe. Coach of the Year Norm Sloan had fashioned an incredible two-year record of 57 wins against only one loss. Maryland, upset with their frustrating loss to State, turned down an NIT bid and ended their season with, in the eyes of many, the second best team in the country. North Carolina accepted an NIT bid and lost to Purdue 82–71 in the first round.

The NCAA still only selected one team from a conference to compete in the national tournament. However, in 1975 the tournament would expand from 25 teams to 32 teams and the ACC would push for a rule change to allow more than one team from the same conference to be selected.

At the Spring meeting in Myrtle Beach, S.C., the Conference heard proposals from representatives of the Charlotte Coliseum, the Richmond Coliseum, the Greensboro Coliseum, and Capital Centre regarding future Tournament sites. A decision was postponed until the following month however. Jim Kehoe, Athletic Director at Maryland, was a prime advocate for a move from North Carolina and was in favor of the new 18,000 seat Capital Centre in Landover, Maryland as the next site. The Conference Basketball Committee met in June and selected the Capital Centre as the site for the 1976 Tournament, with the 1977 and 1978 Tournaments returning to the

Greensboro Coliseum.

While the ACC Basketball Tournament was still the talk of the town, Tony Waldrop, North Carolina's premier miler, was running his seventh consecutive sub-four minute mile in Detroit at the NCAA Indoor Track Meet. Waldrop's winning time of 3:59.4 was off from his world mark of 3:55.0 that he had set earlier in the season. Waldrop extended his phenomenal streak to 9 straight sub-four minute miles before the year was over, and he was later selected as the ACC Athlete of the Year in 1974 for his outstanding track accomplishments.

The Conference had adopted the following resolution at their Winter meeting in honor of one of the original ACC Faculty Chairmen of Athletics, who had passed away earlier in the year:

Because Dr. Charles E. Jordan was one of the Founding Fathers of the Atlantic Coast Conference, diligently and effectively serving the Conference and his institution, Duke University, in a variety of major positions; and because Dr. Jordan, for many years, also rendered distinguished service to his community and this state in the field of public education, the Conference wishes to express its sorrow over the untimely passing of Dr. Jordan. We extend to his family and to Duke University our deep sympathy and concern.

In August, Moses Malone, the heavily recruited 6'11" high school basketball star from Petersburg, Virginia, announced that he was signing a contract with the Utah Stars of the American Basketball Association. Many colleges were upset with the idea that a high school player had been recruited and signed by a professional team. However Commissioner James said his signing, "does not eradicate responsibilities of any institution in the ACC or in the NCAA." The Conference was investigating illegal violations in the recruiting of Malone who had been heavily pursued by Clemson but had signed a grant-in-aid with Maryland. James also acknowledged that the ACC was checking on possible recruiting irregularities involving Phil Ford, the outstanding high school star from Rocky Mount, North Carolina, who signed a basketball grant with North Carolina. In October, it was announced that Tates Locke, Basketball coach at Clemson, had been disciplined for providing a private air trip to Clemson for Ford's father. Locke's recruiting work was restricted to the campus until August 1, 1975.

Commissioner James also ruled that freshman football player Elijah Marshall would be eligible to play for North Carolina State that fall. Marshall had originally signed an institutional agreement with Tennessee, but later changed his mind and signed an interconference letter-of-intent with North Carolina State. The Southeastern Conference, of which Tennessee is a member, has an agreement with the ACC to honor each other's signings. The ACC Executive Committee later reviewed the case and upheld the Commissioner's decision.

In football that fall, Maryland went undefeated in Conference competition with a 6–0 record and was 8–3 overall. Three Conference teams were invited to postseason bowl games, for the first time in history, as the ACC enjoyed its best mark ever against nonleague competition, 21 wins against 14 losses. Maryland, 13th-ranked, was invited to the Liberty Bowl to meet Tennessee with a 6–3–2 record. The Terrapins held a 3–0 lead at half-time on Mike-Mayer's 28 yard field goal, and their defense, led by All-American and Outland Trophy winner Randy White, held the Volunteers scoreless until the final quarter. Then Tennessee recovered a bad snap from center when Maryland was in punt formation, and took over on the Terrapin's seven yard line. With only 2:38 left in the game, Tennessee scored on an 11 yard touchdown pass to win the game 7–3 before 51,284 fans.

A week later North Carolina State, ninth-ranked with a 9–2 record, met Houston 8–3 in the Astro-Bluebonnet Bowl in Houston, Texas. State had set an ACC record of not losing to a non-Conference opponent, and both teams were averaging more than 400 yards total offense per game. The 35,122 fans were not disappointed in the offensive show. State scored first and led at the half 10–3. Both teams scored in the third quarter, but the Cougars came roaring out in the fourth quarter and jumped to a 31–17 lead. The Wolfpack roared back themselves in the final 3 minutes and 38 seconds by scoring two touchdowns and one 2 point conversion to tie the game 31–31. State quarterback Dave Buckey, who engineered the offense, completed 18 of 28 passes for 200 yards and one touchdown. North Carolina State ended the year ranked ninth in the UPI poll, the first time ever for State in the Top Ten, and the first time for an ACC team since 1960.

Then it was North Carolina's turn as they faced Mississippi State in the 40th Annual Sun Bowl in El Paso, Texas. Snow had to be cleared from the artificial surface before the game, as it had been raining and snowing steadily for two weeks. The Tar Heels entered the game with a 7–4 record and the Bulldogs were 8–3. Mississippi State took a 10–7 lead at half, fell behind 21–20 at the end of the third quarter, and then pulled out a 26–24 victory, as the Tar Heel's Mike Voight was stopped on a fourth and one on the 48 yard line with 1:18 left in the game. The Bulldogs rushed for 455 yards and came up with the big plays in stopping North Carolina before 30,151 fans.

The "Big Four" Tournament was held the first weekend in January 1975 again, and on opening night, Wake Forest beat North Carolina State 83–78 and Duke upset North Carolina 99–96. The following night State beat North Carolina 82–67, and in the Championship game, Wake Forest edged Duke 75–71.

At the NCAA Convention in Washington, D.C. in January, the "hardship rule" was amended that allowed a player another year of eligibility if he was hurt after playing in *one* game out of the first five. The new revision would allow a player to have appeared in *two* games and still have another year of eligibility. The decision whether to accept or reject this amendment was the major item of business as the Conference met for their annual Winter meeting in February 1975. The decision took on added importance since the status of North Carolina's All-Conference quarterback Chris Kupec, who set an NCAA record for passing accuracy in 1974, was in question. Kupec played briefly against Maryland (3 plays) and Missouri (8 plays) in his junior year, the second and third games of the 1973 season, before breaking his collarbone. North Carolina had requested that Kupec be declared a hardship case under the new NCAA rule. However the Faculty Athletic Chairmen voted not to accept the NCAA amendment, and therefore Kupec was denied another season of eligibility. The vote, which required a two-thirds majority or five out of seven votes, was not announced but Commissioner James said that, "the voting members sensed the new rule is far too loose to be accepted by our conference." Two Clemson players also missed getting another year of eligibility.

Later that month the *Washington Post* broke a story that two former Clemson basketball players had received free airline tickets for their personal use. It also said that the wide-ranging investigation by the NCAA included the soccer and football programs as well as the basketball program. Alleged violations involving the recruiting of Moses Malone were also being investigated, as were those involving freshman basketball star Skip Wise. Wise was later named to the All-ACC team but dropped out of school after his freshman year to sign a contract with the now defunct Baltimore Claws of the old American Basketball Association. The NCAA interviewed Clemson players, coaches, and officials, and Athletic Director Bill McLellan said, "the university and athletic staff cooperated fully with the investigation."

Maryland won its first regular season basketball championship with a fine 10–2 record and received a bye in the first round of the ACC Tournament. However in the semifinals the Terrapins were edged by their old nemesis North Carolina State 87–85 behind David Thompson's 30 points. In the other bracket North Carolina had gone into overtime twice to reach the finals. The Tar Heels nipped Wake Forest 101–100 and Clemson 76–71 behind Phil Ford. The freshman sensation from Rocky Mount then led the Tar Heels to a 70–66 triumph over North Carolina State to win the ACC Championship.

Maryland and North Carolina were both selected for the NCAA Tournament (the first year that two teams from the same conference had been selected). Maryland came in second in the Midwest Regionals, beating Creighton 83–97 and Notre Dame 83–71 before losing to Louisville 96–82. North Carolina finished third in the Eastern Regionals, beating New Mexico State 93–69, losing to Syracuse 78–76, and beating Boston College 110–90. The disappointed Wolfpack turned down an NIT bid and Clemson was invited. The Tigers lost to Providence in the opening round 91–86. Maryland, State, and North Carolina were all ranked in the top ten for the second consecutive year by the UPI.

Maryland won their second NCAA Lacrosse Championship in three years by beating Navy 20–13 in the finals at Johns Hopkins University. The Terrapins were led by their All-American Player of the Year Frank Urso who scored five goals and had one assist. For the second time the ACC winner did not win the NCAA crown. Virginia had beaten Maryland for the ACC Championship this year; while in 1972, when Virginia won the NCAA Championship, Maryland had been the ACC Champion.

Wake Forest won their second consecutive NCAA Golf Championship that spring at Columbus, Ohio and set a new NCAA record 33 stroke winning margin. The Deacons were paced by Jay Haas, a junior who won the Individual Championship and was Collegiate Player of the Year in 1975; and Curtis Strange, a senior who won the Individual Championship and was Collegiate Player of the Year in 1974. Jesse Haddock was selected as the National Collegiate Golf Coach of the Year in honor of these two national titles.

At the Spring meeting of the Conference in Myrtle Beach, the major items of business centered around money-saving proposals. The NCAA had called a special meeting on economy in Chicago for August 14 and 15. Contingent upon a national policy, the ACC agreed: to reduce their football and basketball coaching staffs, to limit the football travelling squad to 50, eliminate spring practice, and limit basketball scholarships to 15 overall and football scholarships to 25 a year and 90 overall. It was also agreed that, starting in 1977, football teams must play all six conference schools. The present rule required only five conference games.

President Faber reported that 505 student-athletes were named to the ACC Honor Roll for 1974–75. This was a new record, surpassing the previous high of 384. Eleven athletes were named for the fourth consecutive year and the first woman athlete in the history of the Honor Roll, Ellen Feldman, a swimmer at Virginia, was included.

There was talk that spring of possible expansion in the Conference.

First, it was speculated that South Carolina would like to get back in the ACC. These rumors were precipitated by the remarks made by Jim Carlen, the new Head Football Coach and Associate Athletic Director at South Carolina. Carlen had replaced Paul Dietzel back in December, and stated then that he thought a school was better off in a conference than as an independent. He later stated that, although he didn't necessarily mean the ACC, "geographically, there are only two feasible conferences—the ACC and the Southeastern. Of course from the standpoint of old rivalries—especially in football—we'd be better off in the ACC."

Then, in March, an article appeared in *The Atlanta Journal* discussing the pros and cons of Georgia Tech's membership in the ACC. Although Georgia Tech was considered to be football oriented and the ACC basketball oriented, it was felt that since Tech was already playing many of the Conference schools a union someday would be inevitable. Commissioner James was quoted as saying:

I think there would be interest on the part of our people . . . Georgia Tech's thinking is consistent with the aims and goals of our people. The question is whether it would be beneficial for the conference and the institutions. It's very difficult to make an assessment of that now.

However, Bobby Dodd, Tech's Athletic Director commented: "They've talked about this ever since we got out of the SEC . . . at the present time, I don't see any change (in Georgia Tech's position)."

Later, Commissioner James stated that the Athletic Directors of the Conference had discussed expansion and the possibility of South Carolina rejoining the Conference. He went on to say that league officials were "assessing South Carolina's interest in reaffiliation and other expansion possibilities and will be making responsible recommendations to their various institutions." South Carolina President William T. Patterson had requested that the possibility of readmission be discussed, but it was later announced that the University Board of Trustees had voted to withdraw its instructions to President Patterson concerning the feasibility of reentry. Carlen, who eventually became Athletic Director, later changed his mind as well and expressed a preference to remain an independent.

On July 8, in the U.S. Middle District Court in Winston-Salem, Judge Hiram Ward denied Chris Kupec's request for a preliminary injunction against the ACC. The University of North Carolina quarterback filed suit against the Conference on March 27, six weeks after the ACC voted against ratification of the new NCAA amendment to the "hardship rule." Kupec claimed his constitutional rights were violated because he wasn't present at the ACC meeting when the decision was made. He also claimed that antitrust laws were violated, and that denying him another season of eligibility would hurt him economically since the pros would have drafted him higher with another year's experience. Kupec was also seeking $200,000 punitive damages. Judge Ward, in his ruling said, "The Court fails to see irreparable damage to Mr. Kupec if the preliminary injuction is not granted but could perceive great injury to the defendant, the ACC." Kupec appealed the decision to the U.S. 4th Circuit Court of Appeals in Richmond, but Judge Braxton Craven upheld the lower court ruling. Kupec later signed with the Charlotte Hornets of the now defunct World Football League.

On October 7, the NCAA announced that Clemson had been placed on probation for a period of three years for violations in the conduct of its basketball program. The probation included sanctions which would prohibit the basketball team from participating in any postseason tournaments or NCAA television games in 1976, '77, and '78. The University was also limited to awarding only two basketball grants-in-aid for 1976–77 and three grants for 1977–78. Clemson was also reprimanded for a violation occurring in the conduct of its football program. The penalties imposed by the NCAA were for violations involving: financial aid and extra benefits to student-athletes, institutional control, ethical conduct, recruiting, tryouts, entertainment, precollege enrollment expenses, transportation, out-of-season basketball practice, and a questionable practice related to the university's certification of compliance with NCAA regulations.

The violations occurred between 1970 and 1974 while Tates Locke was Head Basketball Coach. Locke had left Clemson back in the spring while the investigations were going on. The Infractions Committee of the NCAA found Clemson guilty of 41 violations while Clemson admitted to only 21. Clemson President Robert Edwards decided not to appeal the penalties and stated that,

Clemson University accepts the sanctions imposed by the NCAA and will comply . . . Clemson respects the role and mission of the NCAA on the national level, and the Atlantic Coast Conference and its member institutions at the conference level.

Maryland won its second straight conference football championship that fall with a 5–0 mark, and extended its winning streak against league opponents to 15 in a row, tying a Conference record. The largest crowd ever to witness an ACC home game (58,973) attended the Maryland-Penn State game at College Park. The Terrapins, 8–2–1 overall, were invited to the Gator Bowl to face Florida, 9–2, and ranked 13th at the time. Before 64,012 fans, in a steady rain with temperatures in the low fifties, Maryland upset the Gators 13–0. The Terrapins scored in the first quarter on a 19 yard pass from Larry Dick to Kim Hoover. Mike Sochko added two field goals of 20 and 27

132

yards to complete the scoring. Steve Atkins rushed for 127 yards on 20 carries for the Terrapins and was selected as the Most Valuable Player. Maryland finished a fine season 9–2–1, and was ranked 11th by the UPI.

North Carolina State, with a 7–3–1 record, made its fourth bowl appearance in a row by accepting an invitation to the Peach Bowl. There the Wolfpack faced West Virginia, 8–3, on New Year's Eve, before 45,134 fans. This was the last game for Dave and Don Buckey, the Wolfpack twins who four years earlier had led State to a Peach Bowl victory over the same Mountaineers. However, this time West Virginia came out on top by a 13–10 score. The Wolfpack had jumped out to a 10–0 lead, but the Mountaineers scored on the last play of the first half to get back into the game, and then went on to win with a touchdown in the last period.

For the third consecutive year, the "Big Four" Tournament was held the first weekend in January, 1976. On opening night, Kenny Carr set a tournament record by scoring 45 points as he led North Carolina State to a 104–95 victory over Duke. In the second game, Wake Forest beat North Carolina 95–83. On the next night, Wake Forest won its second consecutive championship by beating North Carolina State 93–78. North Carolina edged Duke 77–74 for third place. Going into the tournament, the four teams had a combined won and lost record of 27–1. Wake Forest was 8–0, North Carolina State was 7–0, North Carolina 6–0, and Duke 6–1.

At the NCAA Convention in St. Louis in January, a proposal to put all scholarships on a "need basis" rather than the present practice of "full ride" grants was narrowly defeated by the major colleges 120 to 112. This surprisingly narrow margin reflected the active participation in NCAA affairs of college presidents who were concerned over the spiraling costs of intercollegiate athletics. The ACC voted 5–2 (Clemson and North Carolina against) in favor of the "need" proposal.

Later that month Homer Rice announced his resignation as Athletic Director at the University of North Carolina to accept the job as Head Football Coach at Rice University. He was later named Athletic Director as well. When Chuck Erickson resigned in 1968 to become a consultant until his retirement, Rice was named as his successor. In his seven years at the post, North Carolina won the Carmichael Cup three times, indicative of the overall strength of their athletic program. Bill Cobey, assistant athletic director at North Carolina, was named to replace Rice. Cobey, 36, had joined the University in 1968, and had been recommended by Rice to succeed him. Cobey's father, William W. Cobey, Sr. had been Athletic Director at Maryland in the late fifties and sixties.

North Carolina won the regular season basketball championship with a 11–1 record, and entered the ACC Tournament with a sparkling 24–2 record. For the first time in its 23 year history the Tournament was being held outside the state of North Carolina. The Capital Centre in Landover, Maryland had been selected as the site for the 1976 Tournament. The Centre had a seating capacity of 18,400 as compared to the Greensboro Coliseum with 15,500. The times of the opening games had been changed to 1:00, 3:00, and 5:00 P.M. rather than having a break between the second and third games as in the past. This was done to avoid the rush hour traffic around the Washington, D.C. area. The U.S. Navy and Marine bands provided half-time activities in honor of the nation's Bicentennial Celebration, and an award in honor of the late Virginia coach, Bill Gibson, was made by the ACC Basketball Coaches. Mrs. Gibson presented the award to the leading rebounder in the regular season Conference games, and Mitch Kupchak of North Carolina was the recipient.

The 1976 Tournament became the "Cinderella" tournament for the University of Virginia. The Cavaliers, mired in sixth place in the Conference, upset three nationally-ranked teams to win the ACC Championship. State (ranked 19th) was the first victim, falling 75–63 in the opening round. Then came Maryland (ranked 9th) by a score of 73–65. In the finals, before a record ACC Tournament crowd of 19,600, Coach Terry Holland's young team upset favored and fourth-ranked North Carolina 67–62. This was only the third time in ACC history (Maryland in 1958 and South Carolina in 1971) that a non-North Carolina team had won the Tournament. Wally Walker, who scored 25, 27, and 21 points respectively for the Cavaliers, won the Everett Case Award for his outstanding play. Virginia then lost in the first round of the Eastern Regionals to DePaul 69–60, and North Carolina lost in the first round of the Mideast Regionals to Alabama 79–64. North Carolina State and Maryland were invited to the NIT but the Terrapins declined. The Wolfpack finished third as they beat Holy Cross 78–68, lost to UNC-Charlotte 80–79, and beat Providence 74–69.

At their Spring meeting in Myrtle Beach, the Conference requested that the C.D. Chesley Company, producer of the ACC Basketball Television programs, provide for the telecasting of the Thursday Tournament games in 1977. This would be the first time that the opening games would be televised, and the announcement was received with great joy by ACC basketball fans. The Conference also agreed that an appropriate plaque should be presented to Castleman D. Chesley at the 1977 Tournament for his 20 years of service to the ACC. Later it was announced that Holly Farms of North Wilkesboro,

Top: Capital Centre, Landover, Maryland, Site of 1976 ACC Championship

Bottom: Greensboro Coliseum, N.C. State vs. Wake Forest, Big 4 Action

135

North Carolina would award, under a formula approved by the ACC, $1000 to the Athletic Scholarship Fund of the school of the outstanding player selected in each of the regular season televised games; and $5000 in the name of the outstanding player in the Tournament. The player would be selected by the announcers. Holly Farms later changed the $5000 award to the Player of the Year so as not to conflict with the Everett Case award for the Most Valuable Player in the Tournament.

Dean Smith was honored by being selected to be the U.S. Basketball Coach for the 1976 Olympic Games in Montreal in July. Tryouts were held in Raleigh and Chapel Hill in May and June and when the 12-man squad was announced there were seven players from the ACC, including four from the University of North Carolina. Those selected were: Tate Armstrong from Duke, Steve Sheppard from Maryland, Kenny Carr from North Carolina State, and Walter Davis, Phil Ford, Mitch Kupchak, and Tommy La Garde all from North Carolina. Smith was accused of loading the team with his players and ACC players, but the selections were based on those individuals who could adopt to the team concepts that had been so successful for Smith in the past. The skeptics were soon silenced as Dean Smith led the U.S. team into the finals undefeated. Then in the Championship game in the Montreal Forum, before 16,000 spectators, the U.S. beat Yugoslavia 95–74 to win the Gold Medal. Yugoslavia had beaten Russia 89–84 in the semifinals to prevent a rematch of the 1972 Championship game that Russia had won on a controversial decision in Munich.

That fall at a meeting of NCAA Division I schools in Chicago, the ACC adopted the NCAA "hardship rule" which the Conference had rejected 18 months earlier. The rule allowed a player an extra year of eligibility if he was injured and only played in *two* of the first five games of the year. The old rule limited a player to only *one* game. If this rule had been adopted back in May of 1975, Chris Kupec would have had another year of eligibility. Commissioner James said:

It was first considered last May when our athletic directors looked at it seriously. They decided at that meeting that they hadn't had proper time to consider it.

This particular time, before any emotions get involved in the situation, the conference felt it was the proper thing to do. We had received a request from a number of schools to reconsider our position, and it was put in front of the conference in this context.

The "Big Four" Tournament was moved to November for the first time and opened the 1976–77 season for all the teams. The NCAA had changed the starting date for basketball games from December 1

Above: 1976 USA Olympic Basketball Team

Below: Wake Forest, 1974 NCAA Championship team in golf

to the last Friday in November, and the "Big Four" teams used the new ruling to start the season off with a bang. On opening night, Wake Forest slipped by Duke 81–80, and North Carolina beat State 78–66. The next night, Duke edged State 84–82, and Wake Forest won their third consecutive championship by nipping North Carolina 97–96 in overtime. The Athletic Directors of the Big Four schools instituted a Most Valuable Player award in honor of Eddie Cameron, past Athletic Director at Duke. The recipient of the first award was Jerry Schellenberg of Wake Forest. The Thanksgiving holiday crowd in Greensboro was treated to typical ACC excitement as three of the four games were decided by two points or less.

Maryland won its third consecutive ACC football Championship that fall, and extended its Conference win streak to a record 20 games. The Terrapins were only the second team in league history to win three championships in a row. Duke was the first in 1960, 1961, and 1962. Maryland blitzed through the season undefeated with an outstanding 11–0 record and were ranked fourth in the country. They were invited to the Cotton Bowl to face sixth-ranked Houston, co-champion of the Southwest Conference. The attendance on New Year's Day, 1977, was the smallest in 30 years, as only 58,500 fans turned out in 29 degree weather in Dallas. The Cougars scored three first period touchdowns in less than six minutes and opened up a 27–7 half-time lead. The Terrapins pulled up to a 27–21 deficit before the Cougars kicked a last period field goal to win 30–21. Maryland, second ranked in total defense, gave up 428 yards to Houston. This was Maryland's fourth straight bowl appearance.

North Carolina was runner-up in the Conference with a 4–1 record, and 9–2 overall. Their year was highlighted by a come from behind victory over arch-rival Duke in their season-ending game. In one of the finest college games ever played, the Tar Heels, behind 38–31 with 2 1/2 minutes to play, scored a touchdown and won 39–38 on a two point conversion play by Mike Voight. Voight ran for 261 yards on 47 carries and scored four touchdowns. Quarterback Mike Dunn ran and passed for 239 yards and scored four touchdowns for Duke, in one of the greatest two-man displays ever witnessed. The Tar Heels were invited to the Peach Bowl and lost to Kenctucky 21–0. All-American Mike Voight, who rushed to 3971 yards in his four years at North Carolina and was the fifth leading rusher in NCAA history, sprained his ankle in practice and didn't play. In windy, frigid, 30 degree weather, a record crowd of 54,172 turned out at Atlanta Stadium and saw Kentucky's defense limit the Tar Heels to only five first downs and 108 yards total offense.

On January 15th, the 1957 North Carolina basketball team was

138

invited back to Chapel Hill to celebrate the 20th Anniversary of their National Championship. Frank McGuire, the coach of the '57 Tar Heels, was on hand for the festivities, and offered these comments regarding South Carolina and the ACC to the sports editor of the *Durham Morning Herald:*

The message I've been trying to get across all these years is that South Carolina got out of the ACC (in 1971) because of football, not basketball . . . We don't have the interest like the ACC anymore . . . If we were still playing North Carolina, Wake Forest, or Duke, we would have all sellouts. National teams are nice, but there's nothing like a good rivalry.

Dietzel wanted to lower the academic standards, and he argued with Maryland and some other schools over this player named Freddie Solomon (who eventually went to Tampa). The next year he talked the school into dropping out. I wanted to continue playing ACC teams, but all of them dropped us except Clemson. We dropped them for a cooling-off period. We play Clemson home-and-home starting next year.

. . . After we're all gone, South Carolina should be in the ACC. From the standpoint of geography, interest, everything, there's only one league.

. . . They've taken the sting out of the tourney. If you have a good year and lose in the tournament, you can still go somewhere. They're taking two for the NCAA tournament and one or two to the NIT. When I was here, it was the NCAA or nothing. Those are the things I fought . . .

The colorful Irishman, although taking the Gamecocks into six postseason tournaments in the last nine years, never liked the ACC Tournament and frequently referred to it as "Russian Roulette."

The 1977 Tournament returned to Greensboro, and North Carolina, the league champion with a 9–3 record, drew a bye in the first round. On opening day, Virginia edged Wake Forest 59–57, Clemson beat Duke 82–74, and N.C. State beat Maryland 82–72. On Friday, North Carolina beat State 70–56 behind Walter Davis' 22 points. Davis, however, broke his right index finger during the game and played only eight minutes the next night. Meanwhile Virginia beat Clemson 72–60 to set up a renewal of the 1976 finals. This time, the Tar Heels behind Phil Ford's 26 points (before he fouled out with 5:45 to go) and John Kuester in the "four corners" held off the Cavaliers 75–69 to win the Championship. In a first round game in Raleigh, North Carolina beat Purdue 69–66 without Davis. In the Eastern Regionals at College Park, the Tar Heels beat Notre Dame 79–77 behind Ford's 29 points. Ford injured his elbow during this game and saw only limited action in the 79–72 victory over Kentucky. John Kuester directed the team and repeated the MVP award that he won in the ACC Tournament by winning the MVP award in the Regionals. This was the sixth time that North Carolina won the Eastern Regionals and the fifth time for Coach Dean Smith. No other ACC school has won more than three.

In the "Final Four" of the NCAA Tournament held at the Omni in Atlanta, North Carolina edged Nevada-Las Vegas 84–83, as Mike O'Koren scored 31 points. In the other first round game, Marquette beat UNC-Charlotte 51–49. This set up a classic championship between two of the winningest coaches in America, Dean Smith and Al McGuire. McGuire had already announced his retirement with this final game. The Warriors prevailed in a game which was closer than the 67–59 score indicated. Phil Ford, hampered with the bad elbow, scored only six points. The injury-riddled Tar Heels (Tommy La Garde did not play after February 11 when he suffered a severe knee sprain in practice) finished 2nd with an outstanding 28–5 record and Dean Smith was voted Coach of the Year.

Meanwhile, Wake Forest was invited to the Midwest Regionals and placed second. The Deacons beat Arkansas 86–80 and Southern Illinois 86–81, before bowing to Marquette 82–68. The Deacons were led by ACC Player of the Year Rod Griffin, Skip Brown, and Jerry Schellenberg. Wake Forest under Coach Carl Tacy finished the year with a fine 22–8 record.

In May, the Conference rejected Virginia Tech's application for membership in the ACC. Virginia Tech had applied for admission back in February, and a committee of Conference representatives had visited the Blacksburg campus to review its athletic policies and facilities. Virginia Tech had been mentioned as a possible member back in 1953 when the Conference was being formed, and their name had come up periodically ever since. VPI was reportedly sponsored by Virginia, Clemson, and Duke, but needed the votes of five of the seven members for approval. This was the first formal vote in league history. Virginia Tech had withdrawn from the Southern Conference in 1965 to become an independent. Commissioner James said, "this does not bind the conference at any time in the future to a seven-member limit or to consider applications such as Virginia Tech's again. But I would certainly say that for the present time this is it."

At the Spring meeting, the Conference approved a recommendation by the Athletic Directors that would establish Conference championships for women in basketball and tennis. The tennis tournament would be held at Wake Forest on October 7 and 8, and the basketball tournament would be held at Virginia on February 9–11, 1978.

North Carolina won the 16th annual Carmichael Cup for excellence in all sports during the 1976–77 season. The Tar Heels won the basketball, fencing, tennis and golf championships to finish with 75 points. Maryland won five championships: football, cross-country, indoor track, outdoor track, and lacrosse to finish second with 71 points. No other member of the league, besides these two, has ever won the Cup.

On August 1, Tom Butters was named as Acting Athletic Director at Duke. Butters came to Duke in 1968 as Director of Special Events and Head Baseball Coach. In 1971 he assumed the duties of Director of the Iron Dukes (the athletic fund-raising organization) and Assistant Athletic Director. He was replaced as baseball coach by ex-St. Louis Cardinal and N.Y. Yankee star Enos (Country) Slaughter. In November of 1976 he became an assistant to the Chancellor, and one year later was officially named as Athletic Director.

In the fall it was announced that the ABC television network had signed an agreement with the ACC to televise the 1978 ACC Championship game live on ABC's "Wide World of Sports." As a result, the format for the Tournament was changed so that the first round games would be played a day earlier, on Wednesday, with the semifinals on Thursday. Friday would be a rest day as the Championship game would be played a day earlier, on Wednesday, with the semifinals on Thursday. Friday would be a rest day as the Championship game would be played on Saturday afternoon at 4:30 instead of Saturday evening. Roone Arledge, President of ABC News and Sports said: incorporate basketball—through this outstanding game—into our roster of standout events in 1978." The C.D. Chesley Company, which televised ACC basketball games during the regular season, would televise the first two rounds of the Tournament.

The ACC also announced that they would use three referees for all Conference basketball games and non-Conference games that did not call for an outside official. The new three-man system was developed to keep up with the accelerated pace of the game, since most teams were employing a fast break offense and full court pressure defenses. The new rule, which the ACC basketball coaches had approved two years earlier, but which had been held back by the athletic directors because of the cost involved, would go into effect for the 1977–1978 season. It was also agreed to try the alternate handshaking during the player introductions similar to that which is done during the NCAA Basketball Finals.

The first ACC Women's Tennis Tournament was held at Wake Forest on October 6–8, and North Carolina captured the team title with 62 points. Clemson was the runner-up with 56 points, followed by Virginia, 55 points; Duke, 53 points; Wake Forest, 38 points; Maryland, 27 points; and North Carolina State, 22 points. Susan Hill (seeded third from Clemson) upset Cindy Johnson (seeded first from Duke) 6–1 and 6–0 in the First Flight Singles Championship.

On Tuesday, November 8, Charles (Chuck) Erickson, age 70, died at North Carolina Memorial Hospital in Chapel Hill, after suffering a heart attack. Erickson was Athletic Director at the University of North Carolina from 1952 until 1968, and continued to serve as a consultant after his retirement. Erickson had graduated from North Carolina in 1931 and returned in 1933 as a member of the athletic staff. When Bob Fetzer retired in 1952, Erickson replaced him, and during his 16 year tenure as Athletic Director he built one of the leading athletic programs in the country. Erickson played a key role in the formation of the ACC, and was active on a national level with the NCAA. Consolidated University President William Friday spoke for many when he said:

Chuck Erickson served the university with utter unselfishness and with total personal dedication. Intercollegiate sports at Chapel Hill and in the Atlantic Coast Conference grew and developed in the best tradition under his leadership as athletic director. He was also a national figure, especially in the development of the television policies of the NCAA.

The eighth annual "Big Four" Tournament was held the first weekend in December. This year each team had the opportunity to play two games before squaring off with each other, and their combined record was 8–0. Wake Forest and North Carolina State had each won three tournaments and North Carolina had won the other one. Overall State was 9–5, Wake Forest was 8–6, North Carolina was 7–7, and Duke was 4–10 in tournament games. In the opening game, the Tar Heels beat Duke 79–66 behind Mike O'Koren and Phil Ford, and in the nightcap, Kenny Matthews' 15 foot shot at the buzzer gave the Wolfpack a 79–77 victory over the Deacons. The next night Duke beat Wake Forest 97–84 behind freshmen Gene Banks and Kenny Dennard for third place. In two games Deacon star Rod Griffin had scored 63 points—2 points shy of the record set by Kenny Carr of North Carolina State in 1976. In the Championship game, North Carolina beat State 87–82 behind Phil Ford's 30 points and his "four corners" leadership. For his outstanding performance, Ford was the recipient of the Eddie Cameron award as the Most Valuable Player in the tournament.

In football that fall, North Carolina broke Maryland's three-year monopoly by winning the ACC Championship with a 5–0–1 record. The tie was with Clemson, 13–13, who finished second in the Conference. Over all, both North Carolina and Clemson were 8–2–1, while Maryland and North Carolina State were both 7–4. For the first time in ACC history, four teams were selected for postseason bowl games. The previous high was three teams selected at the end of the 1974 season. In 25 years, 29 Conference teams have been selected for bowl games. There has been at least one Conference team in a bowl game every year since 1969, and 11 teams in the last four years.

North Carolina was invited to the Liberty Bowl in Memphis, Tennessee on December 19; Maryland to the Inaugural Hall of Fame Classic in Birmingham, Alabama on December 22; Clemson to the Gator Bowl in Jacksonville, Florida on December 30; and North Carolina State to the Peach Bowl in Atlanta, Georgia on December 31. This was the tenth bowl game each for North Carolina and Maryland and the eighth bowl game each for North Carolina State and Clemson.

North Carolina's opponent in the 19th annual Liberty Bowl was Nebraska, runner-up in the Big 8 Conference with an 8–3 record. The Cornhuskers were ranked 13th by the UPI, and the Tar Heels, led by freshman sensation "Famous Amos" Lawrence who rushed for a single game record of 286 yards against Virginia, were ranked 11th by the UPI. In Memphis Memorial Stadium, 49,456 fans watched North Carolina take a 14–7 half-time lead behind two touchdown passes by quarterback Matt Kupec, younger brother of former North Carolina star Chris Kupec. Tom Biddle kicked a record 47 yard field goal in the third quarter to up Carolina's lead to 17–7. However, reserve quarterback Randy Garcia entered the game in the last period and threw three passes, two for touchdowns, to lift Nebraska to a 21–17 victory. Tailback Lawrence and All-ACC defensive tackle Rod Broadway missed most of the game with injuries. Matt Kupec was selected as the Outstanding Player. This was Coach Bill Dooley's last game as the Tar Heel mentor, for in January he resigned from North Carolina to accept the position as Head Coach and Athletic Director at Virginia Tech. Dooley had taken North Carolina to six bowls, more bowl games than any other coach in ACC history.

Maryland faced Big 10 opponent Minnesota with 7–4 record in the Hall of Fame Classic. A crowd of 47,000 watched this inaugural game in Birmingham on a cold night with temperatures in the thirties. The Gophers scored on their first possession to take a 7–0 lead, but Mike Sochko cut the lead with a 32 yard field goal for Maryland. In the second quarter George Scott scored two touchdowns within a three minute span to give the Terrapins a 17–7 halftime lead. Neither team scored in the second half as Maryland's defense was led by Charlie Johnson, later named the game's Outstanding Defensive Player. Quarterback Larry Dick threw for 211 yards, and receiver Chuck White caught eight passes for 126 yards to pace the Terrapins. White was named the Outstanding Offensive Player. This was Maryland's fifth consecutive bowl game under Head Coach Jerry Claiborne, tying him with the late Jim Tatum who had also taken Maryland to five bowl appearances (although not in succession).

Clemson was making its first bowl trip in 18 years (1959) when it faced Pittsburgh in the 33rd annual Gator Bowl. Clemson was led by quarterback Steve Fuller, who led the Conference in total offense with 1900 yards, and was selected ACC Player of the Year. Head Coach Charlie Pell, who directed Clemson to its best football record since 1950, was selected as the ACC Coach of the Year in his first year at the helm. Pitt, ranked No. 1 in 1976 and 10th-ranked this year, came into the game with an 8–2–1 record, identical to that of Clemson, who was ranked 11th. The Gator Bowl matchup drew a record crowd of 72,289 fans, of which over 25,000 were orange-clad Clemson supporters. However, the Panthers dominated the game as their quarterback Matt Cavanaugh set a new Gator Bowl record by completing 23 of 37 passes for 387 yards. Clemson's only score in the 34–3 defeat came on a record 49 yard field goal by Obed Ariri, who had been a star soccer player for the Tigers.

North Carolina State was making its fifth bowl appearance in the last six years when it faced Iowa State in the 10th annual Peach Bowl. The Cyclones, with an 8–3 record, tied for second in the Big 8 Conference, and were ranked 14th. The Wolfpack were led by running back Ted Brown who rushed for a State record of 1261 yards breaking the old mark of 1169 yards set by Stan Fritts in 1974. A crowd of 36,733 turned out on New Year's Eve and saw Johnny Evans put on a triple-threat performance that set a Peach Bowl record of 265 yards total offense. The Wolfpack quarterback passed for 202 yards and two touchdowns, ran for 62 yards and one touchdown, and punted six times for a 44.6 yard average. Evans was named the game's Outstanding Player, and teammate Richard Carter was named the Outstanding Defensive Player. The Wolfpack jumped out to a 21–0 lead at half-time, and scored a record 42 yard field goal by Jay Sherrill in the fourth quarter to win 24–14. The Cyclone's only points were scored in the final period although both teams amassed over 400 yards total offense in the game. Ted Brown rushed for 114 yards and threw two passes for 47 yards, as Coach Bo Rein led the Wolfpack to an 8–4 record in his second season.

This was a fitting climax to the 1977 season in which the ACC surpassed all other conferences in the percentage of bowl appearances, four teams out of a seven-member conference. The Conference also set a new all-time high in total attendance and average attendance at football games. A total of 1,396,742 fans witnessed 38 home games making 1977 the sixth straight year and ninth time that the Conference had drawn over a million fans in one season. The average attendance also set a new record with 36,756 per game. The Atlantic Coast Conference entered 1978 on a high note in its Silver Jubilee

Year.

As the new year started, two Conference schools announced changes in their head football coaches on approximately the same dates. On January 3, Bill Dooley visited Virginia Tech to discuss the vacant football coaching and athletic director positions. Five days later on January 8, the rumors were confirmed when Virginia Tech announced that Dooley had signed a five-year contract as Head Football Coach and Athletic Director. In 11 years at North Carolina, the 43-year-old Dooley had won more games than any other Tar Heel football coach, compiling a 69–53–2 record. He won three ACC Championships and took North Carolina to six bowl games in the preceding eight years.

There was much speculation in the following two weeks as to who Dooley's successor would be. Approximately 15 candidates had been interviewed for the job when it was announced on January 21 that Dick Crum, Head Football Coach at Miami University in Ohio, had been tapped. The 43-year-old Crum had a four year record of 34–10–1 at Miami, which included three Mid-American Conference Championships and two Tangerine Bowl victories.

On the same day Bill Dooley was visiting Virginia Tech, Wake Forest was informing Chuck Mills that he had been relieved as Head Football Coach. Mills came to Wake Forest from Utah State and in five years his overall record was 11–43–1. Two weeks later, on January 20, it was announced that John Mackovic, offensive coordinator at Purdue, would be the new Head Coach. Mackovic, 34, had played quarterback for the Deacons and was the ACC leader in total offense in 1964, his senior year.

Meanwhile, at its 72nd annual convention, in Atlanta, the NCAA created a new "Super Division." After four years of discussion, the controversial decision to split the current 144 major schools in Division I into Division I-A and I-AA was approved. In a rare roll-call vote, the restructuring plan passed by an 82–73 margin with one abstention (12 conferences also voted). The ACC voted 6–1 in favor with North Carolina opposed. The so-called "super football conference" had been advocated by the major football schools ever since the three-division arrangement was adopted in 1973. They desired their own autonomy in order to be able to pass legislation that was pertinent to their philosophical and economic positions. However they had often been thwarted by schools with smaller programs who were more numerous and could outvote them. It was Dr. Edwin Cady, the Faculty Representative from Duke, who finally took the floor to sum up the feelings of the major football schools.

In the past 10 or 15 years we have not had freedom to address ourselves effectively to the solutions of our problems…I have grown weary of the notion that somehow, if you belong to what is now a Division III school or a Division II school, you are more moral or you are more interested in matters intellectual.

The restructuring in Division I would be based on a formula that involved scheduling, football attendance, size of stadium, and number of varsity sports. The last criteria was an amendment sponsored by the Ivy League which made the original proposal less exclusive.

On the last weekend in January, Phil Ford scored 17 points in a 98–64 triumph over Clemson to break Lennie Rosenbluth's all-time scoring record at North Carolina. Rosenbluth, who led the Tar Heels to the National Championship in 1957, scored 2,045 points in his three year varsity career. Ford's 17 points pushed his four year total to 2,051, placing him fifth on the all-time ACC scoring list which was led by Wake Forest's Dickie Hemric (2,587 points in four years). By the end of the season Ford had moved up to third place on the ACC scoring list with a four year total of 2,299 points. David Thompson was the second leading scorer with 2,309 points in three years.

At their Winter meeting in February the Conference returned to the Sedgefield Inn in Greensboro to celebrate their Silver Anniversary. It was the site where 25 years earlier, on May 8, 1953, the Atlantic Coast Conference had been formed. Only Eddie Cameron, past Athletic Director at Duke, and Frank Howard, past Athletic Director at Clemson, of those faculty chairmen and athletic directors who had been at the original meeting in 1953, were able to return for the Jubilee dinner on February 8.

In their business meeting the Conference agreed to donate $10,000 to the University of Evansville whose entire basketball team had been killed in an airplane crash on December 13. Other colleges and conferences were also donating money to help Evansville rebuild their basketball program. The Conference formed a Women's Sports Liaison Committee and added three women's championships in volleyball, swimming, and cross-country to begin in 1978–79. The Conference had already held a tennis championship back in October and would hold a basketball championship that same week.

The first ACC Women's Basketball Tournament was held at the University of Virginia on February 9–11. The three-day affair was structured like the men's tournament with three first round games on Thursday, the semifinals on Friday and the championship game on Saturday afternoon. Top-seeded North Carolina State, ranked No. 2 in the nation, drew a bye on the first day. In the opening round, all the favorites won as 2nd-seeded Maryland, ranked No. 8 in the nation, beat 7th-seeded Duke 103–39; 3rd-seeded Clemson beat

6th-seeded Virginia 73–59; and 4th-seeded North Carolina beat 5th seeded Wake Forest 79–52. In the semifinals, State beat North Carolina 89–58 and Maryland beat Clemson 98–75. On Saturday, Maryland upset North Carolina State 89–82 to win the Championship. The Terrapins were led by the Tournament's Most Valuable Player Tara Heiss, who scored 30 points.

The recruiting controversy surrounding Darrell Nicholson, the all-star linebacker from North Carolina Forsyth High School in Winston-Salem, was settled when he signed a national letter-of-intent scholarship with the University of North Carolina. Earlier Nicholson had signed an institutional letter-of-intent with North Carolina A & T and an ACC letter-of-intent with North Carolina. He then asked to be released from the Carolina agreement in order to sign with another conference institution but Commissioner James refused the request after meeting with Nicholson and his parents.

It was then announced that the NCAA had ruled reserve center Geof Crompton of North Carolina ineligible for the remaining four games of the regular basketball season. Crompton had played in four recreational league games in his hometown during December 1976 while he was out of school and this violated an NCAA rule barring organized competition outside of school games. A similar ruling had caused Clyde Austin of North Carolina State to miss the first two games of the season. Ironically the NCAA had just relaxed its rules against off-season competition at their January convention. Crompton would be eligible for the ACC Tournament, but not for North Carolina's season-ending game with arch-rival Duke.

The regular season championship was decided in Chapel Hill on Saturday, February 25. North Carolina, selected Number One in preseason polls, entered the game with a 22–6 record overall and an 8–3 Conference record. Duke, rebounding from a 14–13 and 2–10 Conference record in 1977, entered the game 20–5 overall and with an identical Conference mark of 8–3. This was a renewal of the old battles between two traditional giants. The Tar Heels were not at full strength as Crompton had been ruled ineligible, Phil Ford had a sprained wrist, Mike O'Koren was playing his first game in two weeks on a sprained ankle, and Al Wood was coming off a month of the flu. The Blue Devils, however, had not won in Carmichael Auditorium since 1966 (88–77), the year they finished third in the NCAA Tournament, although they had beaten the Tar Heels earlier in the season 92–84 in Durham. Before a packed crowd of 10,000 cheering fans the Blue Devils jumped out to an early 10 point lead only to see the Tar Heels close it to one at the half 37–36. In the second half the lead seesawed back and fourth until with 26 seconds to go and Duke behind

84–83, Jim Spanarkel missed the second shot of a one and one which would have tied the score. Three subsequent foul shots increased the final margin to 87–83 in North Carolina's favor. For Duke, freshman Gene Banks had 25 points; Jim Spanarkel, 23 points; and center Mike Gminski, 21 points. The man of the hour, however, was Phil Ford, the senior guard who was playing his last game in Carmichael Auditorium before an emotional crowd. Ford rose to the occasion, as he had done so many times in the past, by scoring a career high of 34 points. He hit a sensational 13 of 19 shots from the floor, added 8 of 11 free throws and five assists in an unforgettable performance. Al Wood had 19 points for his career high, and Mike O'Koren had 14 points. The victory gave North Carolina the regular season championship, the bye in the Tournament, and an NCAA spot in the playoffs.

As the 25th Annual ACC Basketball Tournament got underway in Greensboro there were some changes in the usual format. The Tournament was spread over four days instead of the usual three days—the first round was on Wednesday, March 1, the semifinals on Thursday, March 2, and the finals on Saturday, March 4 (Friday was an off-day); and for the first time the finals would be on national television (ABC's Wide World of Sports, Saturday afternoon at 4:30 P.M.). The biggest and most controversial change however, was the decision to use nonconference officials for the Tournament. This was a change that had been discussed at Conference meetings for a number of years before the final decision was made. In announcing the decision, Commissioner James emphasized that:

Under no circumstances should this be concluded as dissatisfaction with the conference officiating staff or the performance of their duties.

Rather, it has been to respond to the concerns of many that when ACC teams enter post-season play, the philosophy of officiating used by some officials assigned to those contests might well vary from ours and prove disadvantageous to our teams.

If our experiment is successful, we plan to seek an agreement with conferences holding end-of-season tournaments, whereby we would exchange officials with them for assignment to our respective tournaments.

In explaining the change from the three-man officiating crew used in the ACC this year for the first time back to the traditional two-man crew, James said,

Until the NCAA adopts a three-official rule, we feel it might be desirable to start using two men in the tournament games, since our post-season representatives will be playing under those conditions in NCAA and/or NIT competition.

As was expected, the ACC Officials were upset with this decision, but the Conference said that they would evaluate this experiment after the 1978 Tournament was completed to determine if they would continue this policy in the future. The officials used in the Tournament were drawn from the Southeastern Conference.

The ACC was the only major college conference in the country in which every team in the league had a winning record during the 1977–78 season, and the combined record of the seven Conference members against outside competition was an outstanding 81–12 for an .871 percentage. This was far above the Big Ten Conference in second place with a .643 percentage. Every team, at one time or another during the season, had been ranked in the Top 20.

The first round pairings were the same as in the 1977 Tournament, but the seedings were different. The opening game was on Wednesday afternoon at 3:00 and it pitted the Duke Blue Devils against the Clemson Tigers. Duke had defeated Clemson twice during the regular season. Clemson got the opening tap and held the ball, forcing Duke to come out of their 2–3 zone. The Blue Devils then stole the ball and scored, and from then on built up a 40–28 halftime lead by playing almost flawless basketball. The Blue Devils scored the first eight points of the second half to increase their margin to 20 points, and coasted home to an 83–72 victory. Duke was led by freshman Kenny Dennard who scored a career high 22 points, mostly from the corners. Mike Gminski added 20 points and 12 rebounds.

The second game at 7:00 P.M. Wednesday evening had North Carolina State against Maryland. The Wolfpack had won both regular season games, and had beaten the Terrapins eight times in Tournament games. This game turned into a 2 1/2 hour marathon before Maryland won in the third overtime, the ACC's longest game ever. The Wolfpack were behind 48–36 at the half, but a shot by "Tiny" Pinder tied the game 84–84 at the end of the regulation game. In the first overtime, State had a two point lead with 15 seconds to play when "Jo Jo" Hunter tied it with a jump shot at the buzzer 92–92. In the second overtime, "Hawkeye" Whitney missed a foul shot and a last second shot that would have broken the 98–98 tie for State. In the third overtime, Craig Davis scored State's first eight points, but Albert King hit the winning free throws for Maryland as they squeaked out a 109–108 thriller. This game was reminiscent of the final game in 1974 in which State beat Maryland 103–100 in overtime. Larry Gibson of Maryland played all 55 minutes and led both teams with 27 points and 18 rebounds.

It was almost 10:00 P.M. before Wake Forest and Virginia squared off in the third game of the opening round. Both teams had won at home during the regular season. The Deacons raced out to a 20–5 lead in the first 10 minutes and took a 33–19 lead into the locker room

149

at half-time. Wake's tight man-to-man defense held the Cavaliers to only three field goals in the first half. The Deacons upped their lead to 23 points during the second half and then cruised in with a 72–61 victory. Frank Johnson led the Deacons with 23 points, 22 coming in the second half.

In the first game of the semifinals on Thursday, Duke faced Maryland at 7:00 P.M. Duke had won both games against the Terrapins during the regular season. Duke struggled to a first half lead of 37–31 as the cold-shooting Blue Devils hit only 40 percent of their shots, and their All-ACC center Mike Gminski was only 1 for 10 from the field. However in the second half, Gminski made five of seven and the Blue Devils upped their shooting to 50% as they pulled away to a 81–69 victory. The Blue Devils had balanced scoring as all five starters hit in double figures, led by Jim Spanarkel's 21 points and Gene Banks' 17 points. Larry Boston led Maryland with 21 points, but the Terrapins missed the services of their highly recruited freshman Albert King who had back spasms and only played four minutes.

In the 9:00 P.M. game Wake Forest faced league champion North Carolina. The two teams had each won at home during the regular season. The Deacons fell behind by 11 points in the first half before coming back to a 38–32 deficit at half-time. In the second half the Deacons methodically fought back, as they took advantage of Tar Heel turnovers and missed shots, to take the lead with 11 minutes to go. The Deacons protected the lead down the stretch as subs Ed Thurman and Dave Morris sank seven free throws in the last three minutes to give Wake Forest an 82–77 upset victory over 10th-ranked North Carolina. The Deacons were led by Leroy McDonald who scored 21 points and Rod Griffin who scored 18 points. Phil Ford, the ACC Player of the Year, tried to carry the Tar Heels alone as he scored 30 points, but it was to no avail.

For the first time, the final game was in the afternoon on Saturday instead of in the evening; for the first time since 1964, Wake Forest was in the finals; and for the first time since 1969, Duke was in the finals. Both teams had won at home during the regular season (Gminski was hurt and did not play at Wake Forest). Wake's upset of North Carolina had put extra pressure on Duke in a must-win contest for both teams. If North Carolina had beaten Wake Forest, then the winner of the championship game would receive an automatic bid to the NCAA Tournament and the loser an at-large bid. Now North Carolina as the regular season winner would receive the at-large bid, and the Duke-Wake Forest winner the automatic bid. The loser could only hope for an NIT bid.

The tip off for the 1978 ACC Championship came at 4:30 Saturday

Left: Jim Spanarkel, Duke, basketball star; Below: Rod Griffin, Wake Forest, basketball star; Bottom left: Phil Ford, North Carolina, basketball star

afternoon before 15,836 fans in the Greensboro Coliseum and a nationwide television audience. It pitted the inside strength of the Blue Devils against the quickness of the Demon Deacons. Wake Forest controlled the first half behind Rod Griffin's 14 points and six rebounds and took a 42–37 lead at half-time. The Blue Devils came roaring out of the locker room to outscore the Deacons 12–4 in the first 3 1/2 minutes of the second half, and with 13 minutes to go had upped their lead to 57–50. Then Duke's strength began to tell as Gminski had 18 points and 10 rebounds in the second half and Griffin was held to one rebound. The Blue Devils' aggressiveness inside on offense and in their 2–3 zone defense was too much for the Deacons, and they rolled to an 85–77 victory. Mike Gminski led the Blue Devils with 25 points and 16 rebounds, followed closely by Gene Banks with 22 points and 10 rebounds, and Jim Spanarkel's 20 points. For the valiant Deacons, Rod Griffin had 25 points and 7 rebounds and Leroy McDonald had 22 points and 14 rebounds. Gminski, Banks, Spanarkel, Griffin, and McDonald swept the First Team places on the All-Tournament team, and Spanarkel won the Everett Case Award as the Tournament's Most Valuable Player. Bill Foster, who in his fourth year at Duke had rebuilt the Blue Devils into a national contender, was selected as the ACC Coach of the Year, and freshman sensation Gene Banks won the Rookie of the Year Award.

Duke had won their first ACC Championship since 1966, and received a bid to the NCAA Tournament. The Blue Devils' (23–6) first round opponent in the East at Charlotte was Rhode Island (24–6). North Carolina, the regular season champion, received an at-large bid to the NCAA Tournament, and the Tar Heels (23–7) first round opponent in the West, in Tempe, Arizona, was San Francisco (22–5). North Carolina State (18–9) and Virginia (20–7) both received bids to the NIT. The Cavaliers hosted Georgetown (21–6) in Charlottesville in the opening round, and the Wolfpack hosted South Carolina (16–11) in Reynolds Coliseum in another first round game. The last time these two teams met was in the ACC semifinals in 1971, when the Gamecocks won 69–56 on their way to the ACC title.

The National Invitation Tournament made its selections shortly after the NCAA had competed its 32-team field, and in a new format, the first round and quarterfinal games were held at regional sites. Virginia, making its third NIT appearance, opened the 41st NIT by hosting Georgetown. The Cavaliers had lost to CCNY 64–35 in 1941, and Lafayette 72–71 in 1972. Virginia rallied from a 39–34 deficit at half-time to tie the regulation game at 58–58, but the Hoyas hit two free throws in the final ten seconds of the overtime to win 70–68. Steve Castellan had 20 points and Jeff Lamp had 18 points for the

Cavaliers as they ended the season 20–8.

North Carolina State played their opening round NIT game in Raleigh where they faced the Gamecocks of South Carolina. The Wolfpack were making their fifth NIT appearance, losing in the first round in 1948 and 1951, and finishing third in 1947 and 1976. State was aggressive from the opening tip-off and jumped out to a 35–25 halftime lead. In the second half, State increased their margin to 19 after only six minutes, and the outcome was never in doubt as they coasted to an 82–70 victory. State overpowered the Gamecocks by outrebounding them 36–19, and received balanced scoring from Pinder, Warren, Austin, and Whitney who were all in double figures. The quarterfinal game was also played in Reynolds Coliseum, and State's opponent was the University of Detroit, with a 25–3 record. State took a 44–38 halftime lead as both teams raced up and down the court, and the Wolfpack, relying again on their height and depth, went on to win 84–77. "Tiny" Pinder paced the Wolfpack with 18 points and 21 rebounds, and "Hawkeye" Whitney followed with 17 points and 14 rebounds. State had a big rebounding edge over the Titans 64–33 which spelled the difference.

The semifinals and finals of the NIT were held in Madison Square Garden, and North Carolina State faced Georgetown, with a 23–6 record, in the first semifinal game. The Hoyas moved out to a 42–35 half-time lead, and increased their margin to 12 points before the Wolfpack started their comeback. State eventually caught up and then went ahead by six points in the closing minutes before the Hoyas came back to tie it 78–78 with 20 seconds to go. Georgetown had the lead in overtime 85–84 with six seconds left when Clyde Austin brought the ball up court and hit a desperation 35 foot shot at the buzzer to give State a dramatic 86–85 victory. "Tiny" Pinder and "Hawkeye" Whitney each had another big game as they accounted for 25 points and 11 rebounds, and 26 points and 7 rebounds respectively. The Wolfpack's opponent in the Championship game of the NIT was the Texas Longhorns with a 25–5 record. The Longhorns raced to a 54–39 lead at halftime behind a well-executed fast break and numerous floor length passes. The second half margin rose to 24 points before State slowly chipped away to the final 8 point deficit, 101–9 . Jim Krivacs scored 33 points and Ron Baxter had 26 points to pace the Longhorns, as they shared the Most Valuable Player Award. State was again lead by Whitney - 22 points, Pinder - 21 points, and Austin - 17 points. North Carolina State finished with a fine 21–10 record (the sixth 20-win season for Coach Norm Sloan) and second place in the National Invitation Tournament.

In the National Collegiate Athletic Association Tournament, North

Carolina faced the University of San Francisco in a first round game in Tempe, Arizona. San Francisco had won back-to-back NCAA titles in 1955 and 1956, while North Carolina captured the national crown in 1957. The Tar Heels fell behind 21–8 at the start of the game before pulling up to a 32–32 tie at halftime. Five minutes into the second half North Carolina was ahead by six points, but a cold streak hit the Tar Heels, and they fell behind the Dons by nine points. The Tar Heels rallied furiously in the closing minutes and pulled within two points with five seconds to go. However, two final free throws gave San Francisco the four point margin of victory, 68–64. Phil Ford struggled for only 14 points as he ended his career by becoming the first player in ACC history to participate in four NCAA Tournaments. North Carolina, beset by injuries throughout the year, still finished the season with a fine 23–8 record.

The Duke University Blue Devils opened their NCAA Tournament quest with a first round game against Rhode Island in Charlotte. The Blue Devils' sluggish play in the first half found them behind 31–30 at the break. In the second half, Duke pulled ahead 42–38 with 12 ½ minutes to play, but poor shooting by the Devils enabled the Rams to take a 62–59 lead with 41 seconds to go. Mike Gminski hit a jumper to close the gap to one and then sank both ends of a one-and-one to put the Blue Devils up 6 –62. Three last second shots failed to drop for the Rams, as Gminski batted the third one away at the buzzer to preserve the Duke victory. Gminski had 25 points and 10 rebounds to pace the Blue Devils, who shot only 42.6 percent from the floor. Freshman sharp-shooter "Sly" Williams had 27 points for the Rams before fouling out with 17 seconds to go.

Duke, ranked 7th in the final Associated Press poll, moved to the Eastern Regionals in Providence, Rhode Island, to face 20th-ranked Pennsylvania with a 20–7 record. The tempo picked up in this game, and both teams traded baskets on their way to a 40–40 tie just before the first half ended. Penn missed a last-second shot and Gminski was fouled on the rebound. He sank both free throws and Bob Bender then stole the inbounds pass and sank an 18 footer at the buzzer to put the Blue Devils up by four. After intermission, Duke upped its lead to 48–44 before Penn scored 12 in a row to take the lead with eight minutes to go. Then the game turned around. Mike Gminski blocked three straight lay-up attempts by the Quakers, which were converted by the Blue Devils who continued their surge to regain the lead. In the closing minutes the Blue Devils led by as many as 10 points before winning 84–80. Jim Spanarkel had 21 points for the Blue Devils, including 9 for 9 from the foul line, and Gene Banks also had 21 points plus 10 rebounds.

In the Eastern Regional finals, Duke's opponent was the Villanova Wildcats with a 22–8 record. The Blue Devils had been stung by criticism for their lackadaisical performance against Rhode Island and Penn, and their team quickness had been questioned. Determined to show their true capabilities, the Blue Devils came out running and ran up a 15-point lead after only eight minutes had elapsed. Playing with aggressiveness and intensity, the Blue Devils caused the Wildcats to turn the ball over five out of their first six trips down the court, and built up a 46–32 halftime lead. Executing the fast break and outlet pass to perfection, the Blue Devils coasted to a 90–72 victory. Duke's passing game netted them 26 assists on 39 field goals, and they controlled the boards. Jim Spanarkel led the Blue Devils with 22 points, followed by Gminski with 21 points and 10 rebounds, Banks with 17 points and 10 rebounds, and Dennard with 16 points. Spanarkel won his second straight Most Valuable Player Award, and he was joined on the All-Tournament Team by Gminski and Banks. Duke's impressive victory dispelled any doubts about the quality of ACC basketball.

Duke now advanced to the NCAA Final Four for the fourth time (1963, 1964, 1966). The NCAA Tournament was held in the Checkerdome in St. Louis, and Duke was joined by Notre Dame (23–6), Kentucky (28–2), and Arkansas (31–3). The combined record of the four teams was an outstanding 108–17, with each having a 52 percent or better field goal average and a 70 percent or better free throw average. Duke's opponent in the first semifinal game on Saturday afternoon at 2:15 was the Fighting Irish of Notre Dame, ranked 6th by the Associated Press, and a slight favorite in this game. The Blue Devils started the game where they left off against Villanova, and raced out to a 4 – 29 advantage at half-time. Duke continued to dominate the game in the second half and held a 14 point lead, 80–66 with less than four minutes to go. All of a sudden the Irish started to hit from the outside, and coupled with some costly ball handling errors by the Blue Devils, the Irish pulled to within two points with 18 seconds left to play. However, Notre Dame missed the tying shot and Duke got the rebound. John Harrell then sank two free throws in the final nine seconds to ice the victory for the Blue Devils, 90–86. Mike Gminski dominated the inside as he hit 13 of 17 shots from the floor and three free throws to finish with 29 points. Gene Banks had 22 points and 12 rebounds, and Jim Spanarkel, with 12 for 12 from the foul line, had 20 points.

The Championship game was held on Monday night, March 27, and the Blue Devils were confronted with the Number 1 ranked team in the country, the Kentucky Wildcats. Kentucky had beaten

Right: Billy Packer and Dick Enberg, Broadcasters for 1978 NCAA Basketball Championships
Below: Bill Foster, Duke, Head Basketball Coach, with 1978 ACC and Eastern Regionals Champions

Arkansas 64–59 in the other semifinal game and was the favorite. Before 18,721 fans and a nationwide television audience, the veteran Kentucky team opened up a 45–38 half-time margin. Duke made only 9 of 23 shots from the field for a poor 39% in the first half, while Jack Givens was scoring 23 points for the Wildcats. Kentucky increased their lead to 16 points in the second half, before the Blue Devils started a gallant comeback. With 1 1/2 minutes to go Duke had cut the margin to 8 points, and with 25 seconds to play the lead was down to 4 points. However Kentucky got the last basket to win their fifth National Championship, 94–88. The Wildcats were led by the amazing performance of Jack Givens who scored 41 points (three short of the record 44 points Bill Walton scored for UCLA in the 1973 championship game). Gene Banks had 22 points, Jim Spanarkel, 21 points, and Mike Gminski, 20 points and 12 rebounds for the Blue Devils. Gminski and Spanarkel joined Givens, who won the Most Valuable Player Award, his teammate Rick Robey, and Ron Brewer of Arkansas on the All-Tournament Team. Brewer's last second shot had beaten Notre Dame 71–69 in the first game to give the Razorbacks 3rd place. Duke finished an incredible season with an outstanding 27–7 record under Bill Foster, who was selected as Coach of the Year along with Abe Lemons of Texas by the National Association of Basketball Coaches.

Three days after the NCAA Championship, Georgia Tech's Athletic Board voted unanimously to apply for admission to the Atlantic Coast Conference. The Board issued a formal statement on Thursday, March 30, which read:

Georgia Tech Athletic Director Doug Weaver this morning made a presentation regarding Tech and the Atlantic Coast Conference to the Tech Athletic Board of Trustees.

The board voted unanimously to affiliate with the ACC under mutually agreeable terms and has invited the conference's executive committee to meet with Tech representatives Monday in Atlanta for final discussions.

It is expected that the formal conditions of membership will be adopted at that time.

Following the meeting, Dr. Joseph Pettit, President of Georgia Tech, explained some of the reasons for Tech's desire to join the ACC.

Geographically the ACC is quite compatible with our student body . . . Each game has a special significance in a conference whether you're battling for second or third or whatever . . . Also, being in a conference tends to stabilize the finances of that group. Television revenue is a big factor. You share and pool. One team has good fortune one year, another the next . . . And you have a championship. Championships can become very lively. The ACC basketball tournament is a very significant thing . . . We feel this is an extremely important step for Georgia Tech and hopefully for the ACC.

Discussions concerning Georgia Tech's admission had been going on since January after the Southeastern Conference had voted not to expand, a decision which, if affirmative, would have allowed Georgia Tech to be readmitted. Georgia Tech had been an original member when the Southern Intercollegiate Athletic Association was formed in 1894. In 1921 it was one of 14 institutions that broke away from the SIAA and formed the Southern Conference. Then in 1932 it joined with twelve other schools that "split" from the Southern Conference to form the Southeastern Conference. Georgia Tech dropped out of the Southeastern Conference in January 1964 to become an independent. In 1975 it became a charter member of the Metro Seven Conference for basketball primarily, but including other sports except football.

On Monday morning, April 3, the Executive Board of the ACC, comprised of Dr. John Sawyer of Wake Forest, President; Dr. Robert Bryan of North Carolina State, Vice-President; Dr. Alan Williams of Virginia, Secretary-Treasurer; and Dr. Ken Vickery of Clemson, past-President, along with Commissioner Bob James met with the Georgia Tech Athletic Board of Trustees in Atlanta. Representing Georgia Tech were: Dr. Joseph Pettit, President; Dr. William Sangster, Faculty Representative; Professor William Schaffer, faculty member; Sam Flax, editor of the student newspaper; and Doug Weaver, Athletic Director.

After a brief meeting, in which there were no major obstacles, the Executive Committee of the Conference voted unanimously to accept Georgia Tech. The official statement read:

The Executive Committee of the Atlantic Coast Conference, meeting in Atlanta on April 3, 1978, having determined that Georgia Tech has fulfilled the requirements for membership, and that the Conference members have unanimously voted in favor of Georgia Tech's application is pleased on behalf of the Conference to accept Georgia Tech as a member.

The Executive Committee invited representatives from Georgia Tech to attend the annual spring meeting of the Conference in Myrtle Beach, on May 16, 1978 for formal induction into the Atlantic Coast Conference. Tech would participate in league business during the spring meeting, and would become a playing member of the Conference on July 1, 1979. According to Conference rules, three members must sponsor an institution's application, and five of the seven members must vote affirmatively for approval. However, according to Commissioner James, "I guess you could say all seven schools did, because it was a unanimous decision to bring them into the conference. I would look at it very seriously as seven schools serving as sponsors." James went on to say, "This represents the most

158

dramatic change in the ACC since South Carolina withdrew from the conference June 30, 1971."

The athletic directors at the Conference schools had gone on record in favor of adding Georgia Tech, and their reaction to Tech's admission was one of happiness and satisfaction. Tom Butters, Athletic Director at Duke, said he was pleased for several reasons:

First, Georgia Tech is a fine academic institution with a great athletic heritage. And they will broaden the scope of the ACC to two major metropolitan areas and open up our conference to an additional two million fans. There is no doubt that they will strengthen the conference.

Bill Cobey, Athletic Director at North Carolina, earlier had said:

This is an answer to a personal dream I've had for the ACC...Georgia Tech opens up Atlanta and the southeastern United States to the ACC. And they bring a great tradition in football to the conference. They're committed to a program of overall excellence.

Their basketball has improved in recent years and definitely will be able to stand next to ours. And I think it's excellent that we will again have four institutions from outside of North Carolina for balance.

Gene Hooks, Athletic Director at Wake Forest, said:

I'm very pleased that it has been worked out. Both the ACC and Georgia Tech wil profit by their membership, and I look forward to Wake Forest developing a competitive relationship with Georgia Tech as a conference member.

Willis Casey, Athletic Director at North Carolina State, seemed to sum it up for everyone when he said:

I'm just delighted they're going to be able to join the conference. I think everybody in the conference is glad to have Georgia Tech.

Speaking for Georgia Tech, and its "marriage" with the ACC, Athletic Director Doug Weaver said:

The courtship has been exciting and fascinating . . . The only hard thing about the whole thing is our relationship with the Metro Seven Conference. That conference was good for Tech and they are good people. But once in a while, you just have to do what you think is best.

Head Football Coach Pepper Rodgers expressed satisfaction with the affiliation and said:

From a Tech standpoint, I think it will be marvelous to be in the ACC. There are so many obvious advantages. It's great to be in a conference for a lot of reasons. Just think how much it will help the basketball program and the minor sports . . . And it will also help football tremendously when a schedule can be worked out.

Bobby Dodd, the retired head football coach and athletic director at Georgia Tech voiced his support in these words:

I would very much endorse it. Things have changed in the last 10 years. The ACC has gotten much better in football and they have always been the best conference in the country in basketball . . . I feel the ACC schools and Georgia Tech have a lot in common. The move should give both Tech and the ACC a lot of prestige.

Football scheduling seemed to be the only serious problem that remained to be worked out since most schools' schedules were already completed into the 1980's. Georgia Tech will continue to play its traditional rivals like Georgia, Auburn, Tennessee, and Alabama, and some of those games will probably be designated to count as "ACC games" until a full Conference schedule can be played around 1985. Duke is the only ACC team on Tech's schedule in 1978 and 1979, and in 1980 North Carolina joins Duke on their schedule.

Georgia Tech will compete in Conference championships in all sports beginning with the 1979–1980 school year. They will participate in the 1980 ACC Basketball Tournament, and their ticket allotment will be a three stage affair in which they will be allotted an increasing number of tickets the first two years until the third year when they will receive a full share. The prospects of playing the ACC Tournament in The Omni (15,389 seats), whose President and General Manager is Bob Kent, former General Manager of the Greensboro Coliseum, is very appealing to Conference members. It would enable the Conference to rotate the Tournament between the Capital Centre in the North (for Maryland and Virginia), the Greensboro Coliseum in the Center (for the four North Carolina schools), and The Omni in the South (for Clemson and Georgia Tech).

Neither the ACC or Georgia Tech would specify the amount of the Conference initiation fee, but speculation placed the figure considerably less than the $400,000 quoted in other years, and closer to a $100,000 fee. Commissioner James said that, "In our way of thinking each member holds an equal share in the conference. When our audit is complete July 1, then Tech will pay that part." James went on to make the following remarks concerning Georgia Tech's entry into the ACC:

Georgia Tech's past relationships with various ACC schools enhanced its opportunity, no question about it. It is one of those very natural things. I think it will be a very compatible conference of eight doggone fine educational institutions.

The University of North Carolina won the Carmichael Cup for the second consecutive year in 1977–78. This was the seventh time that the Tar Heels had won this coveted award in the 17th annual competition for overall sports achievement in the ACC. North Carolina finished with 71½ points; followed by North Carolina State, 65 points; Maryland, 59 points; Clemson, 55 points; Duke, 43 points; Virginia, 43 points; and Wake Forest, 21½ points.

At the Spring meeting of the Conference, Jim Kehoe, Athletic Director at Maryland since 1969, announced he would retire in September. The 59-year-old Kehoe had been at Maryland nearly 40 years as an athlete, professor, coach and administrator. He inherited an athletic program that operated on a 1½ million dollar budget with 12 varsity sports, and built it up to one of the leading programs in the country with a three million dollar budget and 23 varsity teams.

The Conference was well represented in postseason NCAA competition. ACC Champion Maryland and Virginia were both selected for the NCAA Lacrosse Tournament. The Terrapins beat the Cavaliers 15–10 in the first round, and then lost in the semifinals to Johns Hopkins 17–11, the eventual national champions. ACC co-champions North Carolina State and North Carolina were invited to the NCAA Tennis Tournament. Although both teams lost in the first round (the Tar Heels to 2nd-seeded UCLA 7–2, and the Wolfpack to 4th-seeded SMU 8–1) John Sadri, ACC singles champion, made it to the finals. Then, in what many considered to be one of the greatest NCAA championship tennis matches ever, the Wolfpack's John Sadri lost to top-seeded John McEnroe of Stanford 6–7, 6–7, 7–5, 6–7 in a four-hour marathon. In the NCAA Track and Field Championships, freshman sensation Renaldo Nehemiah of Maryland was edged out of first place at the tape in the 110 meter high hurdles while teammate Brian Melly also captured a second place in the high jump. Stewart Ralph of Clemson was second in the javelin, and Ralph King of North Carolina finished fifth in the 5000 meters. In the team standings, Maryland tied for ninth place.

In baseball, both Clemson, the ACC Champion, and North Carolina, the runner-up, were invited to NCAA postseason play. The Tigers, 38–12 on the season were selected for the Atlantic Regionals and the Tar Heels 33–14 on the season were selected for the South Atlantic Regionals. Clemson beat the University of Miami (Fla.) 8–5 in the opening round at Miami, and then lost to Marshall 9–3 and was beaten in a return game with Miami 7–5 to be eliminated.

At Auburn, in the opening round, North Carolina beat East Tennessee 15–1 behind their ace pitcher Greg Norris. The Tar Heels won their second in a row by defeating Auburn 3–2, but then lost to consolation winner Memphis State 8–6. This forced a second game between North Carolina and Memphis State in the double elimination tournament. In the championship game for the South Atlantic Regionals, the Tar Heels trailed 8–3 before coming from behind to win 11–9. Greg Norris improved his record to 14–0 which made him the winningest pitcher going into the College World Series in Omaha. The Tar Heels were making their first trip since 1966 to the eight team double elimination tournament that determines the NCAA Champion. In 1960 and 1966, under Coach Walter Rabb, the Tar Heels were eliminated after only two games.

In the opening round, Oral Roberts handed Greg Norris his first defeat as the Titans shut out North Carolina 11–0. Now in the losers' bracket, the Tar Heels won their first College World Series baseball game in 30 years eliminating St. John's 9–5. Greg Robinson then hit a three-run homer in the bottom of the eighth inning to give North Carolina a comeback victory over Michigan 7–6. The Tar Heels now advanced to the final four with Southern Cal, Arizona State, and Miami. Their next opponent was Southern Cal, the school with the most World Series titles, 10, and the most World Series victories, 63. The Tar Heels, behind Greg Norris, shut out the Trojans through the first seven innings, and were leading 2–0, before disaster struck. In the eighth, two passed balls, a walk and a single gave Southern Cal two runs, and the Trojans scored the winning run in the ninth on a single, a wild pitch, a stolen base, and a sacrifice. North Carolina finished an outstanding season with a 38–17 record behind first year coach Mike Roberts, and Greg Norris, the ACC Baseball Player of the Year, was selected for the All-American team.

Finally, in the NCAA Golf Championships in Eugene, Oregon, the Conference was represented by ACC Champion Wake Forest and North Carolina. In individual play, the Tar Heels' John McGough tied for fourth place with a 54-hole total of 213. This was the best finish for a North Carolina golfer since Harvie Ward won the individual crown in 1949. In team play, the Tar Heels finished fifth and Wake Forest finished seventh.

The NCAA achievements were a fitting climax to the Silver Anniversary of the Atlantic Coast Conference. The Conference had started the year off in grand style by sending four football teams: North Carolina, Maryland, Clemson, and North Carolina State to postseason Bowl Games, where Maryland and North Carolina State were victorious. The ACC had also sent four basketball teams: Virginia, North Carolina State, North Carolina, and Duke to postseason tournaments, where North Carolina State was second in the NIT and Duke was second in the NCAA Tournament. The Conference, by admitting Georgia Tech, had made its first expansion since adding Virginia back in 1953, thus becoming an eight member league again. In 25 years, the ACC has made its mark as one of the outstanding athletic conferences in the United States, and if the past is any indication of the future, the Atlantic Coast Conference will continue its role as a national leader in intercollegiate athletics.

1st row, left to right: Robert C. (Bob) James, Atlantic Coast Conference Commissioner; Bill Dooley, North Carolina, Head Football Coach 1967–1978; Dean Smith, North Carolina, Head Basketball Coach 1962 to present

2nd row, left to right: Lou Holtz, North Carolna State, Head Football Coach 1972–1975; Norm Sloan, North Carolina State, Head Basketball Coach, 1967 to present

163

1st row, left to right: Wayne (Tree) Rollins, Clemson, basketball star; John Lucas, Maryland, basketball star; John Roche, South Carolina, basketball star

2nd row, left to right: Tony Waldrop, North Carolina, track star; Wally Walker, Virginia, basketball star; Steve Fuller, Clemson, football star

Above: Damon Ogunsuyi, Clemson, soccer star

Right: Godwin Ogbueze, Clemson, soccer star

Below: Dave Buckey, North Carolina State, football star

Part III

Member Institutions in the ACC

(Including ex-member South Carolina)

12

Member Institutions in the Atlantic Coast Conference

(Including ex-member South Carolina)

CLEMSON UNIVERSITY

Clemson University, located in Clemson, South Carolina, was founded in 1889 as Clemson Agricultural and Mechanical College. The name was changed to Clemson University on July 1, 1964. Clemson is a land-grant, state-supported university, fully accredited by the Southern Association of Colleges and Schools. Its enrollment has grown from 446 students at the opening of the University in 1893 to 11,383 students for the school year 1977–78. This figure includes 5,531 undergraduate men, 3,089 undergraduate women, 1,043 graduate men, and 626 graduate women. The major academic divisions in the University are the Colleges of Agriculture Sciences, Liberal Arts, Forest and Recreation Resources, Engineering, Architecture, Education, Industrial Management and Textile Science, Nursing Sciences, and the Graduate School.

The university is located on the shores of Hartwell Lake in the northwestern corner of South Carolina. The campus of over 25,000 acres is located on the site of the old Fort Hill Estate which Thomas Green Clemson gave to the state of South Carolina for the establishment of an agricultural and mechanical college. Clemson, a distinguished scientist, was the first Secretary of Agriculture (then called Superintendent) of the United States. His father-in-law was the famous Southern statesman, John C. Calhoun, and the restored home of the Calhouns is on the Clemson campus today.

The school colors are purple and burnt orange, the team nickname is "Tigers," the mascot is a Tiger, and the school song is "Tiger Rag." The home football games are played in Clemson Memorial Stadium (Frank Howard Field) with 43,451 permanent seats, with the largest crowd being 54,129. Remodelling in 1978 will increase the capacity to 53,000 permanent seats. The stadium, completed in 1942, is known throughout the South as "Death Valley." In each end zone are the letters IPTAY—"I Pay Thirty A Year." This club was organized by Dr. Rupert Fike in 1934 to finance athletic scholarships at Clemson.

Clemson played its first intercollegiate football season in 1896, winning two games and losing one, under Coach Walter M. Riggs, later to become President of Clemson. In 82 consecutive seasons, under 20 head coaches, the Tigers have won 387 games, lost 313 games, and there have been 40 ties. The famous Heisman Trophy, awarded each year to the outstanding football player in the nation, is named after a former Clemson football coach, John Heisman. Heisman had an outstanding record of 19 wins and only 3 losses as head coach from 1900 to 1903 before moving on to Georgia Tech. Jess Neely, before becoming Head Coach and Athletic Director at Rice Unversity, took Clemson to its first bowl in 1940 and beat Boston College 6 to 3 in the Cotton Bowl.

Frank Howard, a 1931 graduate of Alabama and a line coach under Neely, became Head Coach and Athletic Director at Clemson in 1940. In 30 seasons under Howard, Clemson won 165 games, lost 118 games, and went to six bowl games with the following results: 1949 Gator Bowl—Clemson 24, Missouri 23; 1951 Orange Bowl—Clemson 14, Miami (Fla.) 14; 1952 Gator Bowl—Miami (Fla.) 14, Clemson 0; 1957 Orange Bowl—Colorado 27, Clemson 21; 1959 Sugar Bowl—Louisiana State 7, Clemson 0; 1959 Bluebonnet Bowl—Clemson 23, Texas Christian 7. Howard, who had one of the longest tenures of any major football coach in the nation, was honored as the ACC Coach of the Year in 1958 and 1966. Hootie Ingram replaced Frank Howard and coached three years, 1970–72. Red Parker followed Ingram and coached four years, 1973–76. Parker was selected as ACC Coach of the Year in 1974. Charlie Pell was named Clemson's 20th Head Football Coach on December 1, 1976, and in 1977 he was selected the ACC Coach of the Year. In his first season he took Clemson to the Gator Bowl where they lost to Pittsburgh 34–3. Buddy Gore was selected as the Football Player of the Year in 1967, and Steve Fuller won this award in 1977. Clemson has won six ACC football championships, including a tie in 1965.

Frank Dobson was the first Clemson basketball coach in 1912, and in 67 seasons, under 17 head coaches, Clemson has won 587 games and lost 731 games, including one Southern Conference championship in 1939. For 12 consecutive years (1959–1970) the Tigers were led by the four Mahaffey brothers, Tommy, Donnie, Randy, and Richie. Banks McFadden had the longest tenure of any coach (10 years) and he was succeeded by Press Maravich in 1957. When Maravich left Clemson in 1962 to become Assistant Coach at North Carolina State, he was succeeded by Bobby Roberts. Tates Locke coached from 1971–75, and the present Head Coach, Bill Foster was appointed on April 9, 1975. In his first year, Foster took Clemson to the NIT where they lost in the first round to Providence 91–86, and in 1977 the Tigers had their best year ever, 22–6. The Tigers play their home basketball games in Littlejohn Coliseum which was opened in 1968, and has 9,720 permanent seats and 830 portable seats on the floor.

Clemson has won six ACC baseball championships, and the records date back to 1900. Track was started by F.H. Calhoun in 1905, and although the exact starting date of tennis cannot be ascertained, the 1913 Constitution and Bylaws of the Athletic Association said, "For the present there shall be five organized departments of sport, viz: Baseball, Football, Basketball, Track and Tennis." Cross-country became a varsity sport in 1921, golf began in 1921, and swimming in 1924. Soccer gained varsity status in 1967, and since that time Clemson has won six ACC Championships (1972–77); six consecutive NCAA play-off bids (including the final four twice—1973 and 1976); and has an 11-year record of 129 wins, 32 losses, and 7 ties. This outstanding record has been achieved by Head Coach Ibrahim M. Ibrahim who first organized the sport at Clemson back in 1967. Clemson competed in the Conference Fencing Tournament in 1971, and awarded their first varsity letters in 1973. The first wrestling team was begun during the 1975-76 season. Clemson competes in 12 of the Carmichael Cup sports, having only a club team in lacrosse.

Clemson was a charter member of the Southern Intercollegiate Athletic Association in 1894, joined the National Collegiate Athletic Association in December 1912, resigned in 1915, and was readmitted in 1919. Clemson was a charter member of the Southern Intercollegiate Conference in 1921, and a founder of the Atlantic Coast Conference in 1953. At the founding of the ACC, Robert F. Poole was President of the University, Lee W. Milford was Faculty Chairman, and Frank Howard was Athletic Director. As of September 1977, Robert C. Edwards was President of the University, Kenneth N. Vickery was Faculty Representative, and Bill McLellan was Athletic Director.

Clemson

Above: Clyde Brown, soccer star
Right: Craig White, baseball star
Below: Joel Wells, football star

Right: Harry Olszewski, football star
Far right: George (Butch) Zatezalo, basketball star
Bottom: Bennie Cunningham, football star

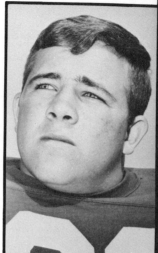

Duke University, located in Durham, North Carolina, was founded as Union Institute in 1839. In 1851 the name was changed to Normal College, and in 1859 it became Trinity College. In 1924 it took on its present name, Duke University.

Methodist and Quaker farmers in 1838 opened the doors of Brown's Schoolhouse, an elementary subscription school in Randolph County. A year later they met to organize an educational society for the support of a private academy, and took the name Union Institute. In 1851 the Institute became a state-affiliated training school for teachers, and was known as Normal College. The North Carolina Conference of the Methodist Episcopal Church took control of Normal College in 1859 and changed the name to Trinity College. Under the leadership and financial backing of Washington Duke and his oldest son Benjamin, Trinity College was moved to Durham in 1892. In 1924 the youngest son, James Buchanan Duke, signed the $40,000,000 Duke indenture which provided funds to develop Trinity College, now Duke University.

Six years later the University moved into newly constructed Gothic buildings on the West Campus, and the original Trinity College site on the East Campus became the Women's College. Today, on the 8,000 acre campus, the major academic divisions of the university are: Trinity College of Arts and Sciences; School of Engineering; School of Nursing; and the Graduate Schools of Arts and Sciences, Law, Divinity, Medicine, Forestry, and Business Administration. Forty Duke alumni are now serving as college presidents; and the former President of the United States, Richard M. Nixon, graduated from the Duke Law School in 1937. The enrollment at Duke University is composed of 3,283 undergraduate men, 2,499 undergraduate women, and 3,544 graduate and professional students for a total enrollment of 9,326 students.

The school colors are royal blue and white, the team nickname is the "Blue Devils," and the team mascot is a student dressed as a Blue Devil. The school songs are "Dear Old Duke" and "Blue and White." The home football games are played in Wade Stadium, built in 1929, but renamed in honor of Wallace Wade in 1967. The Stadium has 44,000 permanent seats with the largest crowd being 57,000. It was in Wade Stadium on January 1, 1942, that the only Rose Bowl game ever played outside of Pasadena, California was held.

Intercollegiate football began at Duke on Thanksgiving Day in 1888 when Trinity College beat North Carolina 16 to 0 in Raleigh. This is considered by many to be the first football game of modern day style

173

(oval ball) below the Mason-Dixon Line. That first team was organized by the Trinity President, John Franklin Crowell. In 1891 Trinity claimed the Southern championship by beating Furman, North Carolina, and defending champion Virginia. In 1895 the Trinity faculty banned intercollegiate football because of the fear of professionalism. It was not until 25 years later, in 1920, that the ban was lifted and intercollegiate football was reinstated.

Wallace Wade came to Duke in 1931 as Head Football Coach and Athletic Director after a highly successful tenure at Alabama. In 16 seasons, Wade's teams won 110 games, lost 36 games, and tied 7 games. During this time Duke won six Southern Conference championships, including an undefeated and unscored-upon regular season schedule in 1938, earning the nickname, "Iron Dukes." At the end of that season they went to the Rose Bowl and suffered their first loss, 7 to 3, to Southern California. On January 1, 1942, Duke lost to Oregon State 20 to 16 in the transplanted Rose Bowl Game in Durham before 56,000 fans. That spring Wade received his commission in the Army, and served as a lieutenant colonel until the end of World War II.

Eddie Cameron, backfield coach for Wade, guided the Blue Devils for the next four years, winning three Southern Conference championships, and taking them to the Sugar Bowl in 1945 where they beat Alabama 29 to 26. Wade returned to Duke in 1946 and remained as Head Football Coach and Athletic Director until 1951 when he was selected as the first Commissioner of the Southern Conference. Cameron became Athletic Director in 1951 and Bill Murray was named as Head Football Coach. Murray took the Blue Devils to three more bowl games, beating Nebraska 34 to 7 in the Orange Bowl in 1955, losing to Oklahoma 48 to 21 in the Orange Bowl in 1958, and beating Arkansas 7 to 6 in the Cotton Bowl in 1961. Murray resigned after the 1965 season to become Executive Secretary of the American Football Coaches Association. He was succeeded by Tom Harp, who in turn was succeeded by Mike McGee in 1971. In 66 seasons, under 13 head coaches, Duke has won 348 games, lost 213 games, and tied 28 games.

Duke has won four ACC championships and tied for two others. Bill Murray was selected as the ACC Football Coach of the Year in 1954, 1960, and 1962. Jerry Barger was selected as the ACC Football Player of the Year in 1954 and Mike McGee won this honor in 1959 as well as that of ACC Athlete of the Year in 1960. Jay Wilkinson won the Football Player of the Year Award in 1963, Ernie Jackson won it in 1971, and Steve Jones won it in 1972. Eight men from Duke— William Wallace Wade, Clarence "Ace" Parker, George McAfee, Dan Hill, Jr., Eric Tipton, Fred Crawford, William D. Murray, and

174

E.M. Cameron are enshrined in the National Football Foundation's Hall of Fame.

W.W. "Cap" Card organized the first basketball team at Trinity College in 1906, and that year the first intercollegiate basketball games in North Carolina were played between Trinity and Wake Forest. It was a home and home series, and Wake Forest won both games, 24–10 and 15–5. Eddie Cameron had the longest tenure of any coach, 14 years (1929–1942), and in that period Duke won 226 games and lost only 99 games. During that time they won three Southern Conference championships. Gerry Gerard succeeded Cameron and won two Southern Conference championships in his eight years as head coach. Harold Bradley continued the tradition of consecutive winning seasons (since 1940) for the next nine years, and during his tenure the Blue Devils were led by All-American and Player of the Year, Dick Groat. Groat went on to have an outstanding career as a professional baseball player with the Pittsburgh Pirates and the St. Louis Cardinals.

In 1959, Vic Bubas, an assistant to Everett Case at North Carolina State, came to Duke. In his first year as Head Basketball Coach, Bubas won the ACC Championship, and then added three more ACC Championships before retiring in 1969. Bubas won three NCAA regional titles, and was named ACC Basketball Coach of the Year in 1963, 1964, and 1966. In ten years Bubas had a 213–67 coaching record at Duke. In the spring of 1969, Bubas was named Director of Public Relations at Duke, and in 1976 he resigned to become Commissioner of the Sun Belt Conference. He was succeeded as Head Coach by Raymond (Bucky) Waters. Waters had been an assistant to Bubas for six years before leaving Duke to become Head Coach at West Virginia in 1965. Waters took the Blue Devils to two NIT appearances before he resigned in 1973. His assistant, Neil McGeachy, coached one year and under him Duke won its 100th game. Bill Foster was hired in March of 1974 as the new Head Coach after successful coaching stints at Rutgers and Utah. In 1978, Foster won the ACC Championship, the Eastern Regional Championship, and finished 2nd for the National Championship. Foster was selected as the ACC Basketball Coach of the Year, and National Coach of the Year (with Abe Lemons) that season.

In 1963 Art Heyman was selected as the ACC Basketball Player of the Year and the ACC Athlete of the Year. In 1964 Jeff Mullins won the same two awards. In 1966 Steve Vacendak was selected as the ACC Basketball Player of the Year and also won the Everett Case Award. Tate Armstrong was a member of the 1976 U.S. Olympic Team which won the Gold Medal. The ACC Rookie of the Year

Award was won by Jim Spanarkel in 1976. Mike Gminski shared this award with "Hawkeye" Whitney of North Carolina State in 1977, and Gene Banks won this award in 1978. Jim Spanarkel won the Everett Case Award and the Most Valuable Player Award in the Eastern Regionals in 1978. Duke has had 10 All-American selections (first or second team). The home basketball games are played in Cameron Indoor Stadium (1940) which has a capacity of 8,542. In 73 years, under 17 head coaches, the Blue Devils have won 1,069 games and lost 567 games.

There were five athletic teams at Trinity College before it became Duke University. In addition to football and basketball, Trinity played its first baseball game in 1889, organized a track team in 1902, and started a tennis club in 1904. Cross-country became a varsity team in 1926, wrestling and swimming in 1927, and boxing and golf in 1928. The first official year for soccer was 1935, and lacrosse was started in 1938. In 1940 boxing was dropped from the intercollegiate athletic program by the Athletic Council and lacrosse was substituted as an official sport. There was a varsity gymnastics team from 1951 to 1955, and fencing became a varsity sport in 1968. Duke University competes in all 13 of the Carmichael Cup sports.

Duke has hosted four track meets of world acclaim: the Pan Africa-USA meet in 1971, the Martin Luther King games in 1973, the USSR -USA meet in 1974, and the Pan Africa-USA-West Germany meet in 1975. The meets were under the direction of Head Coach Al Buehler, who has won six ACC Cross-country Championships, and Dr. Leroy Walker of North Carolina Central University. In 1978 Duke hosted the 9th Annual AIAW National Swimming and Diving Championships. (Association of Intercollegiate Athletics for Women.)

Duke University joined the National Collegiate Athletic Association in December 1925, joined the Southern Conference in December 1928, and was a founder of the Atlantic Coast Conference in 1953. At the founding of the ACC, Hollis Edens was President of the University, Charles E. Jordan was Faculty Chairman, and Edmund M. Cameron was Athletic Director. As of September 1977, Terry Sanford was President of the University, Edwin H. Cady was Faculty Representative, and Tom Butters was Athletic Director.

Duke

Above right: Bill Murray, Head Football Coach 1951–1965 and Mike McGee, football star and present Head Football Coach

Above: Ernie Jackson, football star

Right: Jack Marin and Mike Lewis, basketball stars

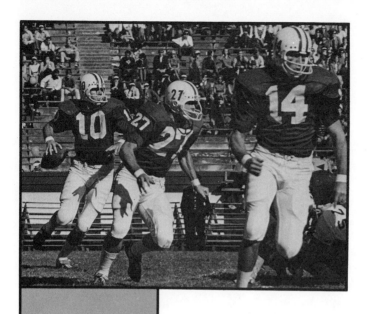

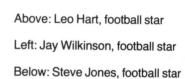

Above: Leo Hart, football star

Left: Jay Wilkinson, football star

Below: Steve Jones, football star

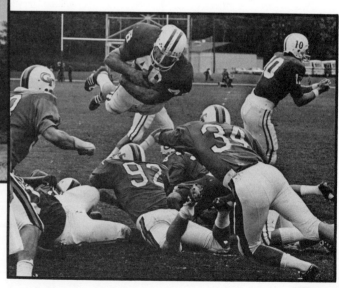

The Georgia Institute of Technology, located in Atlanta, Georgia, was chartered by the state of Georgia in 1885. Opening ceremonies were held on October 7, 1888, under the name the Georgia School of Technology. In 1948, the present name, Georgia Institute of Technology, was adopted and fans and alumni know it best as Georgia Tech.

The college is located in downtown Atlanta on a 280 acre campus containing more than 120 buildings. In the past 20 years over 45 new buildings have been constructed, including the recently opened Fuller E. Callaway III Student Athletic Complex. The four buildings that make up this $5 million complex include a commons buildings, an exercise gym, a swimming pool, and a multipurpose gymnasium. The complex houses the Department of Physical Education and Recreation, and is the center for Intramural Athletics.

For the first eight years the only curriculum at Georgia Tech led to a bachelor's degree in mechanical engineering. Then in 1896, courses were added that led to degrees in electrical engineering and civil engineering. In 1925 the first master's degree was awarded, and in 1950 the first doctor's degree was granted. There are now 18 schools in the University contained in four colleges: the College of Engineering, the College of Sciences and Liberal Studies, the College of Industrial Management, and the College of Architecture. The enrollment at Georgia Tech consists of 8,549 men and 1,564 women, including 1,608 graduate students for a total enrollment of 10,113.

The school colors are old gold and white; the team nicknames are the "Yellow Jackets," "Ramblin' Wrecks," and "Engineers"; and the school song is the popular, "I'm a Ramblin' Reck from Georgia Tech." The home football games are played in famous Grant Field. It was named Hugh Inman Grant Field in 1914 at the request of John W. Grant. Grant was a member of the Board of Trustees, and gave $50,000 to start a building fund in memory of his late son. The original stands which held 5,600 were built largely by students. By 1925, seating capacity had been increased to 30,000, and continued improvements have brought the seating in Grant Field to 55,853 permanent seats and 2,268 temporary bleacher seats. The largest crowd was 60,316 against Georgia in 1973.

Georgia Tech played its first football game in 1892, and during the next ten years the football team was coached by volunteers. Tech's 11-year record during this period was 8–32–5. John W. Heisman became Head Coach in 1904, after a successful coaching stint at Clemson. In 16 years, Heisman had an outstanding record of 102–29

179

–6, and was undefeated (9–0) in 1917 when Tech was declared National Champions. William A. Alexander coached for the next 25 years with a record of 134–95–15. In 1928 Tech was undefeated (9-0), and then beat California in the Rose Bowl, 8-7, to win again the National Championship. Alexander was also Director of Athletics from 1932 until his death in 1950. Robert "Bobby" Dodd took over as Head Coach in 1945, and in his 22 years he had an outstanding record of 165-64-8. In 1952 Tech again went undefeated (11-0) and defeated Mississippi 24-7 in the Sugar Bowl to be ranked No. 2 in the country. Dodd took the Yellow Jackets to 12 postseason bowl games and won 9 of them. He also served as Athletic Director from 1950 until his retirement on June 1, 1976. Dodd was succeeded by Leon "Bud" Carson in 1967 and his five-year record was 27 wins and 27 losses. Bill Fulcher had a 12-10-1 record in the next two years, and he was followed by the present Head Coach, Franklin "Pepper" Rodgers, who took over in 1974. Rodgers, a 1955 alumnus, has a record of 23-20-1.

Georgia Tech's six full-time football coaches have all had winning or break-even records. Operating as an independent from 1892 to 1921, Tech's record was 126-63-11. As a member of the Southern Conference from 1922 to 1933, the record was 53-39-10. As a member of the Southeastern Conference from 1933 to 1963, the record was 196-105-12. Then again as an independent from 1964 to 1977, the record was 82-63-3. In addition, Georgia Tech has won 14 Bowl games (third on the list for most bowl victories behind Alabama's 15 victories and Southern Cal's 16 victories) and has lost 7. From 1951 to 1956, the Yellow Jackets won six straight Bowl games, a record that was later tied by Nebraska after the 1974 season. John Heisman, William Alexander, and Bobby Dodd are all members of the National Football Foundation and Helms Athletic Foundation Hall of Fame. Some of the outstanding football players in the last twenty-five years have included: Leon Hardeman, Don Stephenson, Maxie Baughan, Billy Lothridge, Eddie McAshan, and Randy Rhino.

Georgia Tech beat Georgia twice during the 1905–06 basketball season, and lost twice to Georgia during the 1908–09 season. However it wasn't until the 1909–10 season that the Yellow Jackets had a full-time coach and were a regular varsity team. That year they had a 1-5 record under John Heisman. There was no team for the next three years, but Heisman coached again in 1914 and 1915. Then basketball was dropped until William Alexander took over in 1920. Roy Mundorff coached 17 seasons winning 164 games and losing 129. John (Whack) Hyder had the longest tenure of any coach, 22 years, and his record showed 292 victories and 271 losses. Dwane Morrison, the present coach, replaced Hyder on March 14, 1973. In five years,

Morrison's record is 62 wins and 72 losses. In 62 seasons, under eight head coaches, Georgia Tech has won 663 and lost 635 basketball games. The all-time leading scorer for the Yellow Jackets was center Rich Yunkus who scored 2,232 points for a 26.6 average during his career, 1969–71. He was followed by All-American guard Roger Kaiser, who scored 1,628 points for a 20.4 average during his career, 1958–61.

Georgia Tech appeared in the NCAA Mid East Regional in 1960, beating Ohio University 57–54, and losing to Ohio State 86–69. In 1970, the Yellow Jackets played in the NIT, beating Duquesne 78–68 and losing to St. John's 56–55. In 1971, Georgia Tech had an outstanding 23-9 record and was invited back to the NIT. They beat La Salle 70-67, Michigan 78-70, and St. Bonaventure 76-71 in double overtime before losing to North Carolina 91-62 in the finals. All three postseason teams were coached by "Whack" Hyder. The Yellow Jackets play their home games in Alexander Memorial Coliseum which seats 6,966. The largest home game attendance was 7,769 in 1970 against Jacksonville.

Georgia Tech competes in 11 varsity sports. The approximate years each of the sports became varsity are as follows: football, 1892; baseball, 1905; track, 1905; cross-country, 1908; basketball (men), 1910; tennis, 1915; golf, 1918; swimming, 1919; gymnastics, 1947; wrestling, 1964; and basketball (women), 1977. There is also a club lacrosse team.

George Tech was a charter member of the Southern Intercollegiate Athletic Association in 1894, and joined the National Collegiate Athletic Association in 1916. It was also a charter member of the Southern Intercollegiate Conference in 1921 and a charter member of the Southeastern Conference in 1932. In 1964, Georgia Tech resigned from the Southeastern Conference to become an independent. It became a charter member of the Metropolitan College Athletic Conference (Metro Seven) in June 1975, and in 1978 it was admitted to the Atlantic Coast Conference. At the time Georgia Tech joined the ACC, Joseph M. Pettit was President of the University, William M. Sangster was Faculty Chairman, and Douglas W. Weaver was Athletic Director.

The University of Maryland, located in College Park, Maryland, was founded in 1807 as the College of Medicine of Maryland in Baltimore. In 1812 the Faculties of Divinity, Law, and Arts and Sciences were added, and these four colleges became known as the University of Maryland. In 1856 an agricultural college was established at College Park, and with the passage of the Morrill Act in 1862, it became the Land-Grant College of Maryland. In 1920 the two institutions were combined as the University of Maryland under a single Board of Regents. Maryland State College became a division of the University of Maryland in 1948. A new campus, opened at Catonsville in September 1966, was known as the University of Maryland, Baltimore County. Both colleges operate autonomous athletic programs.

The major academic divisions in the University are the Colleges of Agriculture; Arts and Sciences; Business and Public Administration; Education; Engineering; Home Economics; Physical Education, Recreation, and Health; University College; and the Graduate School on the campus at College Park. The six professional schools of Dentistry, Law, Medicine, Nursing, Pharmacy, and Social Work, are in Baltimore. Courses are also offered in 178 centers overseas and 60 centers in this country through the University College. The enrollment at Maryland, the largest in the ACC, is 35,890 students. This figure includes 13,136 undergraduate men, 10,796 undergraduate women, and 11,958 graduate students.

The school colors are red and white and black and gold; the team nickname is "Terrapins" or "Terps," and the mascot is a Terrapin. The school songs are "Maryland, My Maryland" and "Hail, Alma Mater." The home football games are played in Byrd Stadium with 45,000 permanent seats, with the largest crowd being 58,973. There is a six-lane tartan track around the field.

Maryland played its first intercollegiate football season in 1892, losing all three games, under team captain W.W. Skinner. The football teams through 1901, with the exception of 1895 when there was no team, were coached by the team captains. D.J. Markey was the first coach in 1902. In 85 seasons, under 20 head coaches (not counting the team captains), Maryland has won 413 games, lost 351 games, and there have been 38 ties.

H.C. Byrd, for whom Byrd Stadium is named, had the longest tenure of any Head Coach at Maryland and in his 23 seasons (1912–1934) his record showed 177 wins, 81 losses, and 15 ties. Byrd later became President of Maryland, and was a leader in the "split" from the Southern Conference. From 1947 through 1955, Maryland was a national powerhouse under the late Jim Tatum. In Tatum's nine seasons as Head Coach, the Terrapins won 73 games against only 15 losses and 4 ties. During that period Maryland won the National Championship in 1953, tied for two ACC Championships, and participated in five bowl games. Their first bowl game was a 20 to 20 tie with Georgia in the 1948 Gator Bowl in Tatum's first season as Head Coach. They returned to the Gator Bowl in 1950 and beat Missouri 20 to 7. After an undefeated season in 1951, they beat Tennessee 28 to 13 in the 1952 Sugar Bowl. They lost to Oklahoma in the 1954 Orange Bowl 7 to 0 after another undefeated season, and again to Oklahoma in the 1956 Orange Bowl 20 to 6. Jim Tatum won National Coach of the Year honors in 1953, as well as ACC Coach of the Year in 1953 and 1955. Bernie Faloney was selected as the ACC Football Player of the Year in 1953, and Bob Pellegrini won the same award in 1955.

Jerry Claiborne, the present Head Coach, took over in 1972 and has returned Maryland to national prominence in football. Maryland won the ACC football championship in 1974, 1975, and 1976 and entered the 1977 season with a record 20-game winning streak. Claiborne was voted ACC Coach of the Year in 1973, 1975, and 1976, and he took the Terrapins to five straight bowl games during this period. Maryland lost the 1973 Peach Bowl to Georgia 17-16; lost the 1974 Liberty Bowl to Tennessee 7-3; beat Florida in the 1975 Gator Bowl 13-0; lost the 1977 Cotton Bowl to Houston 30-21; and beat Minnesota in the inaugural Hall of Fame Classic 17-7 in 1977. Randy White won the ACC Football Player of the Year Award in 1974 as well as the Outland Trophy as the outstanding lineman in the country.

H. Burton Shipley was the first Maryland basketball coach in 1923. He was Head Coach for 24 years compiling a record of 243 victories and 199 losses, and he won the Southern Conference Championship in 1931. Shipley also coached the baseball team for 37 years where he won 363 games and the Southern Conference Championship in 1936. Bud Millikan was Head Coach for 17 years before resigning in 1968, and he led Maryland to their only ACC basketball championship in 1958. The present Head Coach is Charles (Lefty) Drisell, a Duke graduate who came to Maryland in 1969 from Davidson. In eight seasons Drisell's teams have won 165 games and lost 61. In 1972, the Terrapins won the NIT Championship and in 1973 and 1975 they were second in the Eastern and Midwest NCAA Regionals respectively. In 1975 Maryland won the ACC regular season championship, and Drisell was voted ACC Coach of the Year. Maryland has been ranked in the Top 20 five years in a row (1972–76), and these outstanding teams were led by

All-American Tom McMillen, a Rhodes Scholar; Len Elmore; and John Lucas, ACC Athlete of the Year in 1976. In 55 seasons, under five head coaches, Maryland has won 718 games and lost 545 games. The home games are played in Cole Field House, with a seating capacity of 14,500.

Maryland has completely dominated the ACC in the number of championships won in all sports. In 25 years Maryland had won 127 championships and shared 7 others. Included in this record are: 20 wrestling championships, 16 soccer championships (co-champions in 1966), 24 indoor and 24 outdoor track championships, and 18 lacrosse championships. Present Athletic Director Jim Kehoe instituted the winning tradition in track by compiling a 92-11 dual meet record in 2 years as Head Coach. In wrestling, "Sully" Krause's teams have not only dominated the ACC Tournament, but also had a 73 consecutive Conference match winning streak during his 32 years at the helm. In 1968 Maryland tied for the National Soccer Championship under Doyle Royall. Maryland won the National Lacrosse Championship in 1955 and 1956 under Jack Faber and Al Heagy, and shared the title in 1959 and 1967. Since the NCAA Play-offs started in 1971, Maryland has won the Championship in 1973 and 1975, and finished second in 1971, '74, and '76. Those great teams were led by Frank Urso, a four-time first team All-American, and were coached by "Bud" Beardmore. In 1978 Maryland finished second in the Seventh Annual AIAW Basketball Championship.

Since the Carmichael Cup was inaugurated in 1962 for excellence in all sports in the ACC, Maryland has won the Cup 10 times, fielding varsity teams in all 13 conference sports. The years the present sports gained varsity status are as follows: football, 1892; baseball, 1893; tennis, 1914; track (indoor and outdoor), 1921; cross-country, 1922; basketball, 1923–1924; lacrosse, 1924; boxing, 1931 (dropped in 1956); soccer, 1946; wrestling, 1947–1948; golf, 1948; swimming, 1956–1957; and fencing, 1971.

Maryland joined the National Collegiate Athletic Association in December 1919, was a charter member of the Southern Intercollegiate Conference in 1921, and was a founder of the Atlantic Coast Conference in 1953. At the founding of the ACC, H.C. Byrd was President of the University, Geary F. Eppley was Faculty Chairman, and James M. Tatum was Athletic Director. As of September 1977, Wilson H. Elkins was President of the University, Robert L. Gluckstern was Chancellor, Charles Taff was Faculty Representative, and James Kehoe was Athletic Director.

Maryland

Top: Jim Kehoe, Athletic Director 1969–1978 and Chris Weller, Assistant Athletic Director for Women's Sports 1976 to present
Above right: Charles (Lefty) Drisell, Head Basketball Coach 1970 to present
Left: Deane Beman, golf star

185

Left: Gary Collins, football star

Below: Frank Urso, lacrosse star

Bottom left: Randy White, football star and Jerry Claiborne, Head Football Coach 1972 to present

The University of North Carolina, located in Chapel Hill, North Carolina, was chartered by the General Assembly in 1789, and first admitted students in 1795. It is the oldest state university in the United States and its first students were enrolled during the presidency of George Washington. In 1931, the University of North Carolina at Chapel Hill, the North Carolina College for Women at Greensboro, and the North Carolina State College of Agriculture and Engineering at Raleigh were consolidated into the University of North Carolina system. Each institution is headed by a Chancellor, who in turn is responsible to the President and a single Board of Trustees of the University.

Chapel Hill, the town called by many "The Southern Part of Heaven," is unique in that it and the University are often referred to as one. James Knox Polk, the eleventh President of the United States, was a graduate of the class of 1818. Thirty-one of North Carolina's 50 governors have been graduates of the University at Chapel Hill. The Morehead Planetarium was the first planetarium on a university campus and it has been active in training the U.S. astronauts.

The major academic divisions in the University at Chapel Hill are: the General College; the College of Arts and Sciences; the Graduate School; and the Schools of Business Administration, Education, Journalism, Law, Library Science, Social Work, Dentistry, Medicine, Nursing, Pharmacy, and Public Health. The enrollment at North Carolina is composed of 8,900 undergraduate men, 4,400 under-graduate women, and 6,100 graduate students for a total of 18,400 students.

The School colors are Carolina blue and white; the team nickname is "Tar Heels," and the team mascot is a Ram. The school songs are "Hark the Sound," "Here Comes Carolina," "Carolina Victory," and "Tar Heels on Hand." The home football games are played in Kenan Memorial Stadium with 48,000 permanent seats, with the largest crowd being 50,200. The stadium was built in 1927, and enlarged in 1963 by William Rand Kenan, Jr. as a memorial to his parents.

North Carolina played in the first two intercollegiate football games in the state of North Carolina in 1888, losing to Trinity College (now Duke University) and Wake Forest. Football was banned by the faculty for the 1890 season, but has been played ever since, with the exception of two years during World War I, 1917 and 1918. In 88 seasons, under 28 head coaches, the Tar Heels have won 441 games, lost 320 and there have been 50 ties.

Carl Snavely, Head Coach for 10 years, took North Carolina to its

187

first three bowl games. They lost to Georgia 20 to 10 in the 1947 Sugar Bowl; to Oklahoma 14 to 6 in the 1949 Sugar Bowl (after an undefeated season marred by only one tie); and to Rice 27 to 13 in the 1950 Cotton Bowl. This was during the era of Charlie Justice, an All-American who is now in the Football Hall of Fame along with Coach Carl Snavely. Jim Tatum, who had brought national prominence to the football teams at Maryland and had been a key figure in the formation of the ACC, returned to his alma mater, North Carolina, in 1956. After only three years as Head Coach, Tatum died suddenly in 1959.

It was Jim Hickey who brought North Carolina its first bowl victory in 1963 by beating the Air Force Academy 35 to 0 in the Gator Bowl. That year Hickey shared ACC Coach of the Year honors with Earle Edwards of North Carolina State. In 1965 Danny Talbott was selected as the ACC Football Player of the Year, and the ACC Athlete of the Year in 1966. Hickey resigned in 1966 to become Athletic Director at the University of Connecticut and was replaced by Bill Dooley.

In 11 years as Head Coach, Dooley won more games than any other North Carolina coach with a record of 69-53-2. The Tar Heels won back-to-back ACC championships in 1971 and 1972 (going undefeated both years in league play) and also won the 1977 Championship. The 1972 team was 11-1 overall, and extended its win streak to 15 in a row against Conference competition. Don McCauley, the All-American halfback, was voted ACC Football Player of the Year in 1969 and 1970, and ACC Athlete of the Year in 1971. Bill Dooley was ACC Coach of the Year in 1971. Mike Voight, the Tar Heel's all-time leading rusher and scorer won the ACC Football Player of the Year award in 1975 and 1976. Amos Lawrence rushed for 286 yards against Virginia to establish an NCAA record for freshmen, and was selected as the Rookie of the Year in 1977. During Dooley's reign North Carolina appeared in six bowl games in eight years. They lost to Arizona State 48–26 in the Peach Bowl in 1970; lost to Georgia 7–3 in the Gator Bowl in 1971; beat Texas Tech 32–28 in the Sun Bowl in 1972; lost to Mississippi State 26-24 in the Sun Bowl in 1974; lost to Kentucky 21-0 in the Peach Bowl in 1976; and lost to Nebraska 21-17 in the Liberty Bowl in 1977. A month later Dooley resigned to become Head Football Coach and Athletic Director at Virginia Tech. He was replaced by Dick Crum, Head Coach at Miami University (Ohio). Crum's four-year record at Miami was 34-10-1 including three Mid-American Conference Championships and two Tangerine Bowl victories.

North Carolina started intercollegiate basketball in 1911, and in 68 consecutive years, under 15 head coaches, the Tar Heels have won

1,152 games while losing 457 games. The 1924 team was undefeated in 23 games under Coach Norman Shepard and the 1957 team was undefeated in 32 games and won the National Championship under Coach Frank McGuire. That year McGuire was selected as the ACC Coach of the Year, and Lennie Rosenbluth was honored as the ACC Athlete of the Year and Basketball Player of the Year. Other ACC Basketball Player of the Year Awards have been won by Pete Brennan in 1958, Lee Shaffer in 1960, Billy Cunningham in 1965, Larry Miller in 1967 and 1968, Mitch Kupchak in 1976, and Phil Ford in 1978. In 1968, Miller won the ACC Athlete of the Year Award; Charlie Scott won this award in 1970; and Phil Ford was the winner in 1977 and 1978. Ford was also selected as the Player of the Year by the Basketball Writers Association and the Basketball Coaches Association in 1978.

North Carolina has won seven NCAA Regional Championships, seven ACC Championships, and eight Southern Conference Championships in addition to the NCAA Championship in 1957 and the NIT Championship in 1971. The Tar Heels under Frank McGuire, won 164 games and lost only 58 from 1953 to 1961. Dean Smith, the present coach, who was an assistant to McGuire and succeeded him as Head Coach, has won 363 games and lost only 121 in 17 seasons, and was selected ACC Coach of the Year in 1967, 1968, 1971, 1976, and 1977. North Carolina has had at least one player on the last four U.S. Olympic teams: Larry Brown in 1964; Charlie Scott in 1968; Bobby Jones in 1972; and Phil Ford, Walter Davis, Mitch Kupchak, and Tom La Garde in 1976. Dean Smith was the winning U.S. Olympic Coach in 1976. The home basketball games are played in the William D. Carmichael, Jr. Auditorium ("Blue Heaven" as it is known by Tar Heel fans) which was opened in 1965 and seats 10,000.

North Carolina has won the Carmichael Cup seven times, the only other school in the ACC to win it besides Maryland. North Carolina fields varsity teams in all 13 conference sports, and has won 57 championships and 8 co-championships. Most outstanding have been the 20 championships and two co-championships in tennis, the 7 championships in cross-country and the 7 championships in fencing. Under John Kenfield and Don Skakle, the Tar Heels have built a dynasty in tennis that shows an amazing overall record of 919 wins against only 98 losses and 9 ties. In present Coach Skakle's 20 years at the helm, the Tar Heels have an outstanding record of 378 wins and 38 losses and 18 of 20 ACC Championships. Two of the many outstanding players have been Vic Seixas (in the 40s) and Freddie McNair (in the 70s). The years the present sports gained varsity status are as follows: football, 1889; baseball, 1891–1892; track, 1898–1899; tennis, 1907–1908; basketball, 1910–1911; wrestling, 1922–1923;

cross-country, 1925–1926; golf, 1930; swimming, 1939; soccer, 1947; lacrosse, 1949; fencing, 1968–1969; and gymnastics, 1969–1970.

North Carolina was a charter member of the Southern Intercollegiate Athletic Association in 1894, a charter member of the National Collegiate Athletic Association in 1906, a charter member of the Southern Intercollegiate Conference in 1921, and a founder of the Atlantic Coast Conference in 1953. At the founding of the ACC Gordon Gray was President of the University, Robert B. House was Chancellor, Allan W. Hobbs was Faculty Chairman, Oliver K. Cornwell was Chairman of the Department of Physical Education and Athletics, and Charles P. Erickson was Director of Athletics. As of September, 1977, William Friday was President of the University, Ferebee Taylor was Chancellor, Benson Wilcox was Faculty Representative, and Bill Cobey was Athletic Director.

North Carolina

Above: Thompson Mann (right), swimming star

Left: Jim Beatty, track star

191

Top: Mike Voight, football star

Left: Larry Miller, basketball star

Above right: Don McCauley, football star

North Carolina State University, located in Raleigh, North Carolina, was founded in 1887 as a land-grant institution. In 1889 when the first students enrolled, it was known as the North Carolina College of Agriculture and Mechanic Arts. In 1931 it was consolidated into the University of North Carolina system, and in 1965 the present name, North Carolina State University at Raleigh, was adopted.

The main University campus is located in the capital city of Raleigh on 2,500 acres. The University conducts educational extension and research programs on campus and throughout North Carolina. The major academic divisions in the University are the Schools of Agriculture and Life Sciences, Design (including architecture and landscape architecture), Education, Engineering, Forestry, Liberal Arts, Physical Sciences and Applied Mathematics, and Textiles. State also has a Graduate School, a Division of Continuing Education, 17 branch agricultural experiment stations, and agents in each of North Carolina's 100 counties. The enrollment at North Carolina State is composed of 9,900 undergraduate men, 4,205 undergraduate women, and 3,625 graduate and special students for a total of 17,730 students.

The school's colors are red and white, the team nickname is the "Wolfpack," and the team mascot is a Wolf. The school songs are "State College Keeps Fighting Along," and "Alma Mater." The home football games are played in Carter Stadium which has 44,000 permanent seats, with the largest crowd being 50,500. The stadium, named after W.J. and Harry Carter, textile executives and alumni, was opened in 1966 and is lighted. It replaced old Riddick Stadium which was developed in several stages, beginning in 1916 and finally completed in 1939. North Carolina State played its first intercollegiate football game in 1892, beating Raleigh Academy 14 to 6. In 86 consecutive seasons, under 27 head coaches, the Wolfpack have won 334 games, lost 351 games, and tied 57 games.

Gus Tebell, past Athletic Director at Virginia, was Head Football Coach and Head Basketball Coach at North Carolina State from 1925 through 1929. Earle Edwards who came to State in 1954 had the longest tenure, 17 seasons, in State's history. He was ACC Coach of the Year in 1957, 1965, and 1967. In 1963 Edwards shared this honor with Jim Hickey of North Carolina. During that time, North Carolina State went to the Liberty Bowl twice, losing to Mississippi State 16 to 12 in 1963, and beating Georgia 14 to 7 in 1967. They also played in the 1947 Gator Bowl under Head Coach Beattie Feathers, losing 34 to 13 to Oklahoma. Al Michaels took over as interim coach in 1971 and Lou Holtz was named Head Coach in 1972. Under Holtz, who was ACC Coach of the Year in 1972, the Wolfpack went to four bowls: beating West Virginia 49-13 in the 1972 Peach Bowl; beating Kansas 31-18 in the 1973 Liberty Bowl; tying Houston 31-31 in the 1974 Astro-Bluebonnet Bowl; and losing to West Virginia 13-10 in the 1975 Peach Bowl. Holtz became Head Coach of the New York Jets in 1976, and then returned to the college ranks in 1977 at Arkansas. Bo Rein replaced Holtz in 1976, and in his second year he took the Wolfpack to the 1977 Peach Bowl where they beat Iowa State 24-12.

North Carolina State has won four ACC football championships and tied for two others. Dick Christy was selected as the Football Player of the Year in 1957, and the ACC Athlete of the Year in 1958. Roman Gabriel was selected as the Football Player of the Year in 1960 and again in 1961, as well as winning the Athlete of the Year award in 1961. Willie Burden won the Football Player of the Year award in 1973. In 1975, Ted Brown won the Rookie of the Year award, and in 1978 Johnny Evans was honored as the national collegiate male Athlete of the Year by the Fellowship of Christian Athletes.

Basketball began at North Carolina State in 1911 under Coach E.V. Freeman, but the won and lost records are not complete for that year. In 1913, the first recorded season, the Wolfpack won 3 games and lost 7 games. In 68 seasons, under 14 head coaches, North Carolina State has won 969 games and lost 518 games. The home basketball games are played in William Neal Reynolds Coliseum which was completed in 1949, with a seating capacity of 12,400. It was the site of the Southern Conference basketball tournament from 1933 through 1953, with the exception of four years (1947 to 1950) when the tournament was held at Duke. It was also the site of the ACC Basketball Tournament from 1953 through 1966.

The most notable of all the coaches has been Everett Case, "Mr. Basketball of North Carolina." Case arrived in Raleigh in 1946 after a highly successful coaching career in Indiana high schools where his record for 23 years was 726 games won and only 75 games lost. Case won the Southern Conference championship his first year at State, and in his 19 years as Head Coach, North Carolina State won 379 games and lost only 134. They won the Southern Conference championship six consecutive years (1947–1952), the ACC Championship four times (1954, 1955, 1956, 1959), and the Dixie Classic seven out of twelve years. Case was ACC Coach of the Year in 1954, 1955, and 1958. Ronnie Shavlik was ACC Basketball Player of the Year in 1956, and Lou Pucillo was the ACC Athlete of the Year and the Basketball Player of the Year in 1959.

Everett Case was forced to retire after the first two games of the

1964–65 season because of poor health, but State went on to win the ACC Championship under Press Maravich. That year Maravich was selected as ACC Coach of the Year. He resigned in 1966 to become Head Coach at Louisiana State University, and Norman Sloan, the present coach, replaced him. Sloan was selected as ACC Coach of the Year in 1970, 1973, and 1974. In 1973 the Wolfpack finished undefeated with a 27–0 record and in 1974 they won the National Championship with a 30–1 record. These great teams were led by the amazing David Thompson who was Player of the Year in 1973, '74, and '75; National Basketball Player of the Year in 1974 and '75; and ACC Athlete of the Year in 1973 and '75. North Carolina State has won eight ACC basketball championships, and finished 2nd in the NIT in 1978.

North Carolina State has won 14 ACC swimming championships, including 12 in the last 13 years, and shared three others. In 22 seasons under present Athletic Director Willis Casey, the Wolfpack won 183 meets and lost only 29. The present coach, Don Easterling, has continued the winning tradition with a record of 73–10 in his eight seasons. In the 1968 Olympic Games, Steve Rerych won two gold medals in the 400 and 800 meter free style relay; and in the 1976 Olympics, Steve Gregg won a silver medal in the 200 meter butterfly and Don Harrigan won a bronze medal in the 200 meter backstroke. The modern Carmichael Gymnasium and Natatorium were planned and developed under the leadership of the late Paul Derr. Derr served as Chairman of the Physical Education Department from 1951 until his retirement in 1976, and he also served as Head Cross-Country and Track Coach during that time. The Wolfpack have also won four ACC baseball championships. State competes in all 13 of the Carmichael Cup sports and has won 33 championships and 6 co-championships. The years the present sports gained recognition are: football, 1892; baseball, 1903; track, 1910; basketball, 1913; cross-country, 1923; wrestling, 1924; swimming, 1933; golf, 1933; tennis, 1934; soccer, 1955; rifle, 1961; fencing, 1965; and lacrosse, 1973.

North Carolina State joined the National Collegiate Athletic Association in 1908, was a charter member of the Southern Intercollegiate Conference in 1921, and a founder of the Atlantic Coast Conference in 1953. At the founding of the ACC, Gordon Gray was President of the University, Carey H. Bostian was Chancellor, Hilbert A. Fisher was Faculty Chairman, and Roy B. Clogston was Athletic Director. As of September 1977, William Friday was President of the University, Joab L. Thomas was Chancellor, Robert S. Bryan was Faculty Representative, and Willis Casey was Athletic Director.

North Carolina State

Top left: Willis R. Casey, Athletic Director 1969 to present; Center left: Earle Edwards, Head Football Coach 1954–1970; Above: David Thompson, basketball star; Bottom left: Steve Rerych, swimming star

196

Top: Ted Brown, football star

Bottom: Willie Burden, football star

197

The University of Virginia, located in Charlottesville, Virginia, was chartered under the sponsorship of Thomas Jefferson in 1819. The University opened its doors in March of 1825 to 125 students, one of whom was Edgar Allen Poe. On the tombstone of Thomas Jefferson, located in the family cemetery at Monticello, are these words written by Thomas Jefferson himself:

Here was buried Thomas Jefferson, Author of the Declaration of American Independence, of the Statute of Virginia for Religious Freedom, and Father of the University of Virginia, Born April 2, 1743 O.S. died July 4, 1826.

Jefferson selected the site, designed the original buildings and landscaping, supervised the construction, directed the selection of the faculty, and outlined the courses of instruction. Jefferson adapted the classic design of ancient Rome for his "academic village"; and the Rotunda, the dominating building which was formerly the library, was scaled down from the Roman Pantheon. The policy-making body of the University is the Board of Visitors, with an elected Rector as chairman. Jefferson was the first Rector of the University and James Madison and James Monroe were members of the first Board of Visitors. Another United States President, Woodrow Wilson, studied law at Virginia from 1878 to 1880.

The major academic divisions of the University are: the College of Arts and Sciences; Graduate School of Arts and Sciences; Graduate School of Business Administration; McIntire School of Commerce; and the Schools of Architecture, Education, Engineering and Applied Science, General Studies, Law, Medicine, and Nursing. The University of Virginia confers no honorary degrees.

The enrollment at Virginia is composed of 5,619 undergraduate men, 4,711 undergraduate women and 5,573 graduate and professional students for a total of 15,903 students. Virginia was one of the first American universities to establish an Honor System and it has been completely student controlled and administered since 1842.

The school colors are orange and blue, the team nickname is the "Cavaliers," the team mascot is a student dressed as a Cavalier, and the school song is "Good Old Song." The home football games are played in Scott Stadium, which has 25,000 permanent seats, with the largest crowd being 34,200. The stadium was the gift of the late Fredrick W. Scott as a memorial to his parents, and was dedicated in 1931. A major renovation program was undertaken in 1974 with the installation of an astro-turf playing surface (the only one in the Conference) and new aluminum seating. Double decking of the stadium with two 6,000 seat sections is scheduled for completion in 1978.

Virginia played its first intercollegiate football schedule in 1888, beating two prep schools and losing to Johns Hopkins University. That was the year that football was first played south of the Potomac. John Poe was appointed as the first Head Football Coach in 1893, and in two years Poe won 16 games and lost only five. In 1907 Virginia turned to an alumni coaching system (usually a graduate student) for the next fifteen years. In the years 1913, 1914, and 1915, three different alumni coaches went undefeated in the South and won 23 out of 26 games. Virginia returned to a full-time coach in 1923 with the appointment of Earle A. (Greasy) Neale. Gus Tebell, a nominee for the first ACC Commissioner, was Head Football Coach from 1934 to 1936, and Head Basketball Coach from 1931 to 1951. Tebell retired as Athletic Director in 1962, and died seven years later. The 1908 team was the only undefeated team, winning 7 games and tying one, but the 1941 team, which lost only one game (21-19 to Yale) is considered to be the most outstanding. It was led by All-American Bill Dudley who is in the Football Hall of Fame. In 87 seasons (no teams in 1917 and 1918 due to the war), under 36 head coaches, Virginia has won 408 games, lost 372 games, and tied 45 games.

Bill Elias was selected as the ACC Football Coach of the Year in 1961, and George Blackburn won the same honor in 1968. Dick Bestwick, the present Head Coach was hired in 1976. In 1966 Bob Davis was selected as the ACC Football Player of the Year, and in 1968 Frank Quayle earned this same honor, as well as that of Athlete of the Year in 1969. Virginia is the only team in the ACC that has never played in a bowl game.

Intercollegiate basketball was first played at Virginia in 1906 under Head Coach Henry Lannigan. In 24 years, the longest tenure of any coach to date, Lannigan won 240 games and lost only 89, including an undefeated season in 1915. In 73 seasons, under seven head coaches, the Cavaliers have won 763 games and lost 681 games. In 1955 All-American Richard "Buzz" Wilkinson was one of the first three college basketball players who averaged more than 30 points per game for a full season. In 1972 Bill Gibson won the ACC Coach of the Year award and Barry Parkhill won the ACC Basketball Player of the Year award. The present Head Coach, Terry Holland, came to Virginia in 1975, and in 1976 Virginia won its first ACC Basketball Championship. The home basketball games are played in University Hall, completed in 1965, with a seating capacity of 9,486 for convocations and 8,250 for basketball games.

Baseball was given official recognition as an intercollegiate sport in 1888, and track, wrestling, boxing, swimming, lacrosse, tennis, golf, soccer, and cross-country were added and developed during the

199

'teens and twenties. Virginia won the 1938 Boxing Championship, but boxing was dropped as a varsity sport in 1966. Virginia competes in all 13 Carmichael Cup sports. The lacrosse team has won six ACC Championships, including the NCAA Championship in 1972, and the wrestling team has won three ACC Championships.

Virginia was a charter member of the Southern Intercollegiate Athletic Association in 1894, joined the National Collegiate Athletic Association in December 1907, was a charter member of the Southern Intercollegiate Conference in 1921, and resigned from the Southern Conference in 1936. Virginia joined the Atlantic Coast Conference in December 1953. At the time Virginia joined the ACC, Colgate W. Darden was President of the University, L.G. Moffat was Faculty Chairman, and Gus K. Tebell was Athletic Director. As of September 1977, Frank L. Hereford, Jr. was President of the University, D. Alan Williams was Faculty Representative, and Gene Corrigan was Athletic Director.

Virginia

Above: Jim Bakhtier, football star

Top right: Bob Davis, football star

Lower right: Keith Witherspoon, track star

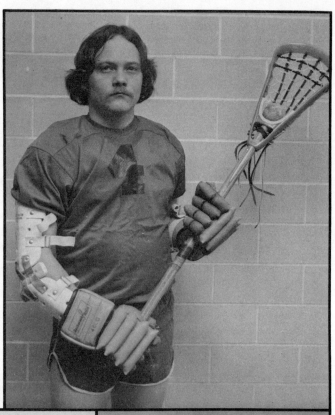

Top right: Jay Connor, lacrosse star

Bottom right: Evan J. (Bus) Male, Director of Facilities and Finance 1956 to present

Bottom left: Barry Parkhill, basketball star

202

Wake Forest University, located in Winston-Salem, North Carolina, was founded in 1834 as Wake Forest Institute in the town of Wake Forest. In 1838 the school was rechartered as Wake Forest College. The Trustees of the College and the Baptist State Convention accepted an offer made in 1946 by the Z. Smith Reynolds Foundation of an annual grant of $350,000. In return the College agreed to move the campus to Winston-Salem if other friends would provide a campus and buildings. The Charles H. Babcock family contributed part of the Reynolds Estate for the new campus, and the ground-breaking ceremonies were held in 1951. In 1955 the Z. Smith Reynolds Foundation increased its annual contribution to the College to $500,000 and the actual move took place in the spring of 1956. The old buildings in Wake Forest were sold to the Southeastern Baptist Theological Seminary.

The College which became Wake Forest University in 1967, consists of the following academic divisions: School of Arts and Sciences, School of Law, Babcock School of Management, Division of Graduate Studies, and the Bowman Gray School of Medicine. The enrollment at Wake Forest is composed of 1,790 undergraduate men, 747 undergraduate women, 289 graduate students, 200 business school students, 389 medical students, and 475 law students for a total of 4,496 students. This is the smallest enrollment of any institution in the Atlantic Coast Conference.

The school colors are old gold and black, the team nickname is the "Deamon Deacons," and the team mascot is a student dressed as a Deacon. The school songs are "Dear Old Wake Forest" and "Oh, Here's to Wake Forest." The home football games are played in Groves Stadium which opened in 1968 with 30,057 permanent seats, with the largest crowd being 30,150. The stadium is lighted.

Wake Forest beat North Carolina 6 to 4 in a "football" game in Raleigh on October 18, 1888. Although this was the first intercollegiate game in the state, it was patterned after rugby and a round ball was used. Duke and North Carolina, employing more rushing than kicking and using an oval ball, met on November 29, 1888, in what is considered to be the first real game of football in North Carolina and the South. The Head Football Coach at Wake Forest in 1889 was W.C. Riddick, who later became Head Football Coach and then President at North Carolina State University. In 1892 Wake Forest tied Virginia Military Institute, and beat Washington and Lee, Richmond, and Tennessee in a period of four days. The trustees banned football for the 1890 and 1894 seasons, and then abolished it altogether from 1896 until 1908. Football was restored by the trustees in 1908, and in 77 seasons, under 27 head coaches, the Deacons have won 255 games, lost 382 games, and tied 31 games.

In "Big Four" competition, Wake Forest has played North Carolina since 1888, and North Carolina State since 1895, with but few interruptions. Wake Forest played Trinity College (now Duke University) in 1889 and 1893 and then, since Duke abandoned football for 25 years, did not resume the rivalry until 1921.

Wake Forest had its greatest success during the 14-year reign (1937–1950) of Head Football Coach Douglas C. (Peahead) Walker. During that period, the Deacons won 77 games, lost 51 games, and tied 6 games. They beat South Carolina 26 to 14 in the first annual Gator Bowl in 1946, and lost to Baylor 20 to 7 in the 1949 Dixie Bowl. Jim Weaver was Head Football Coach at Wake Forest from 1933 until 1937, when he became Athletic Director, a position he held until his election in 1954 as the first Commissioner of the Atlantic Coast Conference. Paul Amen was selected as the ACC Football Coach of the Year in 1956 and 1959. Bill Tate won this award in 1964 and Cal Stoll won it in 1970. Bill Barnes was selected as the ACC Football Player of the Year in 1956, and Brian Piccolo achieved this same honor in 1964, as well as being selected the ACC Athlete of the Year in 1965. Norm Snead was an outstanding quarterback from 1958–60, and went on to a long career in professional football. James McDougald was selected as the Rookie of the Year in 1976, and was only the fourth runner in NCAA history to rush for more that 1,000 yards (1,018) in his freshman year. Chuck Mills coached from 1973–1977, and was replaced by John Mackovic, offensive coordinator at Purdue and a Wake Forest alumnus ('65), in January 1978.

J. Richard Crozier introduced intercollegiate basketball in the state of North Carolina in 1906. As Head Coach at Wake Forest, Crozier won three games and lost three games in that initial spring schedule. The highlights of the season were home and away victories over Trinity College (now Duke University), 24 to 10 and 15 to 5. Crozier coached 12 years at Wake Forest, and later served as Head Basketball Coach at North Carolina State for three years. Murray Greason, a member of the Helms Hall of Fame, had the longest tenure, 23 seasons as Head Coach, and in 1956, was selected as the ACC Basketball Coach of Year. During that period Dickie Hemric was selected as the ACC Basketball Player of the Year in 1954 and in 1955, as well as the ACC Athlete of the Year in 1955. Horace "Bones" McKinney succeeded Greason in 1957 and led Wake Forest to the ACC Basketball Championship in 1961 and 1962, advancing to third place in the Nationals in 1962. McKinney was selected as the ACC Basketball Coach of the Year in 1960 and 1961, while All-American Len Chappell was selected as the ACC Basketball Player of the Year in 1961 and 1962. Chappell was also the ACC Athlete of the Year in 1962. Charlie Davis won the Basketball Player of the Year award in 1971 and Rod Griffin won this award in 1977. Skip Brown was an outstanding guard for four years (1974–1977), holds every school assist record, and is the third leading scorer in school history. The present Head Coach, Carl Tacy, came to Wake Forest in April of 1972. In 72 years, under 16 head coaches, the Deacons have won 829 games and lost 689 games. The home basketball games are played in Memorial Coliseum, completed in 1955, with a seating capacity of 8,200.

Wake Forest played its first intercollegiate baseball game in 1891 against the University of North Carolina. The game was played at Raleigh, and the Deacons won 10 to 7 in 11 innings. In 1951 Wake Forest represented the United States in the Pan American Games, and in 1955, under Taylor Sanford (Coach of the Year), they won the NCAA Championship. The annual state meet in Greensboro in 1909 was the first intercollegiate track meet in which Wake Forest participated. Tennis was introduced back in 1886, but the first six-man team was organized in 1929. Golf became a part of the intercollegiate program in 1933, and since then Wake Forest has won 15 ACC Championships and two NCAA Championships (1974 and 1975). In 1974 Curtis Strange was NCAA Champion and Player of the Year, and in 1975 Jay Haas won the same two honors. The legendary Arnold Palmer and Lanny Wadkins were two other outstanding Deacon golfers. Jesse Haddock was selected as Golf Coach of the Year in 1974 and 1975, and since he became the head coach in 1960, his teams have won 90 of 110 dual matches.

The first official records for cross-country were started in 1954. There was no team between 1949 and 1953, and prior to 1949, the records are incomplete. Wrestling was discontinued in 1960, and the records prior to 1954 are incomplete. Swimming became part of the intercollegiate program in 1956, after the college moved to Winston-Salem. Wake Forest competes in nine of the Carmichael Cup sports, having no teams in soccer, wrestling, lacrosse, or fencing.

Wake Forest joined the Southern Conference in February 1936, the National Collegiate Athletic Association in December 1936, and was a founder of the Atlantic Coast Conference in 1953. At the founding of the ACC, Harold W. Tribble was President of the University, F. W. Clonts was Faculty Chairman, and James H. Weaver was Athletic Director. As of September 1977, James R. Scales was

President of the University, John W. Sawyer was Faculty Representative, and Gene Hooks was Athletic Director.

Wake Forest

Left: Bill Armstrong, football star
Middle left: Lanny Wadkins, golf star
Middle right: Jesse Haddock, Head Golf Coach 1960 to present
Bottom right: Norm Snead, football star

Above: Charlie Davis, basketball star; Left: Skip Brown, basketball star; Below: Murray Greason, Head Basketball Coach 1934–1957

The University of South Carolina, located in Columbia, South Carolina, was founded in 1801, and first opened its doors in 1805 as the oldest fully state-supported institution of higher learning. At the time of the Civil War, it was one of the leading colleges in the South, but when war came the students left en masse to join the Confederate ranks. By March 1862, only nine students remained on campus, and in June, the college closed down. The buildings were used as a Confederate hospital, and the presence of wounded troops from both armies probably saved the campus from being burned in General Sherman's march in 1865. After the war, the University was reopened and reorganized along the lines of the University of Virginia. The main campus of approximately 130 acres is located downtown in the state capital of Columbia. The major academic divisions of the University are: the College of Arts and Science, the College of Business Administration, the College of Engineering, the College of General Studies, the School of Education, the School of Journalism, the School of Law, the School of Nursing, the School of Pharmacy, and a Graduate School. The enrollment at South Carolina is 23,577 students. This figure includes 8,202 undergraduate men, 6,877 undergraduate women, 1,402 two-year students, 7,096 graduate (including law and medicine) students, and plus more than 10,000 on the regional campuses.

The school colors are garnet and black, the team nickname is the "Fighting Gamecocks," and the team mascot is a Gamecock. The school songs are, "Carolina Fight Song," and "We Hail Thee Carolina." The home football games are played in Williams-Brice Stadium, (formally named Carolina Stadium). Built in 1934, the stadium has been enlarged over the years until it now has 54,406 permanent seats. The stadium is lighted and has an astro-turf surface.

South Carolina played its first intercollegiate football schedule in 1894, losing both games, although there was some evidence of a "pick up" game between South Carolina and Furman in 1892. However it was not until 1899 that more than three games were played in any one season. In 1906 the Trustees abolished football for that season. In 82 seasons, under 25 head coaches, the Gamecocks have won 350 games, lost 352 games, and tied 37 games. Rex Enright, a prime mover in the formation of the Atlantic Coast Conference, was Head Football Coach from 1938 through 1955, with the exception of the war years 1943–1945. Enright also served as Athletic Director from 1938 until his death in 1960. Johnnie McMillan took South Carolina to its first bowl game in 1946, and the Gamecocks lost to Wake Forest 26 to 14 in the first annual Gator Bowl. Alex Hawkins was selected as the ACC Football Player of the Year in 1958, and Billy Gambrell won the same award in 1962. Bobby Bryant was selected as the ACC Athlete of the Year in 1967, and Paul Dietzel was the ACC Coach of the Year in 1969. Dietzel came to South Carolina in 1966 as Head Football Coach and Athletic Director. In his nine years as Head Coach the Gamecocks won 42 games, lost 53, and tied one. His 1969 team won the ACC Championship with an undefeated Conference record (6-0) and was 7-3 overall. The Gamecocks lost to West Virginia in the Peach Bowl that year 14-3. Jim Carlen replaced Dietzel in 1975 as Head Football Coach and Athletic Director, and in his first year he took the Gamecocks to the Tangerine Bowl where they lost to Miami (Ohio) 20-7.

Basketball began with the 1908–09 season and the Gamecocks dropped three decisions. Under Head Coach Billy Laval, the Gamecocks won 18 games, lost only 2 games, and won the Southern Conference championship in 1933. Frank Johnson had the longest tenure of any head coach, 16 years between 1941 and 1958, missing only 1944 and 1945. In 1962 Bob Stevens was selected as the ACC Coach of the Year. In 70 seasons, under 24 head coaches, South Carolina has won 743 games and lost 653 games. South Carolina plays its home basketball games in the Carolina Coliseum (The Frank McGuire Arena) which was opened in 1968 with a seating capacity of 12,401. The coliseum has a tartan playing surface in the arena. Also opening in the fall of 1968 was "The Roost," a five-building dormitory-dining hall complex at the Rex Enright Athletic Center which houses 166 student athletes.

The present Head Coach, Frank McGuire, came to South Carolina in 1964. McGuire has twice been named National Coach of the Year, and has twice been honored as ACC Basketball Coach of the Year. The first ACC honor was in 1957 when he won the National Championship at North Carolina with an undefeated team (32-0). The second time was in 1969 at South Carolina. John Roche was selected as the ACC Basketball Player of the Year in 1969 and 1970. In 1970, South Carolina won the ACC regular season championship with an undefeated, 14-0, record and in 1971 they won the ACC Tournament and placed fourth in the Eastern Regionals. Both years the Gamecocks were ranked 6th in the country. In five years at St. John's, McGuire's record was an impressive 103 victories and 35 losses. In 1953 he went to North Carolina as Head Coach and in nine seasons, the Tar Heels won 164 games and lost only 58 games. During the 1961–1962 season, McGuire coached the Philadelphia Warriors in the National Basketball Association. In 29 years as a Head Coach,

McGuire has won 519 games and lost only 212, including a 14 year record at South Carolina of 252 wins and 119 losses.

South Carolina tied for the ACC golf championship in 1964 and tied for the ACC tennis championship in 1968. South Carolina competed in nine of the Carmichael Cup sports, having no teams in soccer, wrestling, lacrosse, or fencing. Baseball began in 1895, but the dates the other sports gained varsity recognition were unavail- from the Sports Information Office at the time of this writing.

South Carolina joined the Southern Intercollegiate Conference in 1922, the National College Athletic Association in December 1936, and was a founder of the Atlantic Coast Conference in 1953. South Carolina withdrew from the ACC on July 1, 1971. At the founding of the ACC, Donald Russell was President of the University, James T. Penney was Faculty Chairman, and Rex Enright was Athletic Director. As of September 1977, James B. Holderman was President of the University, William F. Putnam was the NCAA Delegate, and Jim Carlen was Athletic Director.

South Carolina

Top right: Frank McGuire, Associate Director of Athletics and Head Basketball Coach 1965 to present
Top left: Bobby Bryant, football star
Bottom right: Billy Gambrell, football star
Bottom left: Paul Dietzel, Atheltic Director and Head Football Coach 1966–1974

212

Alex Hawkins, football star

Part IV

Record Section

Atlantic Coast Conference Constitution

Purpose

It is the purpose and function of this Conference to promote intercollegiate athletics, to keep it in proper bounds by making it an incidental and not the principal feature of college and university life, and to regulate it by wise and prudent measures in order that it may improve the physical condition, strengthen the moral fibre of students, and form a constituent part of the education for which universities and colleges were established and are maintained.

Voting Delegates

The members of this conference shall be entitled to one vote each. The voting delegate shall be the representative of the member institution, appointed by the president, or by the duly constituted authority of the college, and shall be a regular full-time member of the faculty with voting power, or an administrative officer in that institution. The voting delegate shall be one whose primary duty is not in athletics.

Institutional Control

There shall be institutional responsibility and control of intercollegiate athletics by member institutions.

Atlantic Coast Conference
NCAA Champions

Sport	Year	College	Coach
Baseball	1955	Wake Forest	Taylor Sanford
Basketball	1957	North Carolina	Frank McGuire
	1974	North Carolina State	Norm Sloan
Boxing*	1938	Virginia	John LaRowe
Golf	1974	Wake Forest	Jesse Haddock
	1975	Wake Forest	Jesse Haddock
Lacrosse	1972	Virginia	Glenn Thiel
	1973	Maryland	Bud Beardmore
	1975	Maryland	Bud Beardmore
Soccer	1968	Maryland (Co-Champions)	Doyle Royal

*Tied for unofficial championship—team points were not officially awarded prior to 1948. The boxing championships were discontinued in 1961.

Left, 1st row: Norvall Neve, Administrative Assistant and Supervisor of Officials 1969 to present; Marvin (Skeeter) Francis, Administrative Assistant and Service Bureau Director 1969 to present

2nd row: Mrs. Nancy Thompson, Administrative Assistant and Secretary 1954 to present; Mrs. Jean M. Patton, Secretary 1968 to present

Below, left to right: Smith Barrier, Service Bureau Director 1954–1967; Irwin Smallwood, Assistant Director of Service Bureau 1954–1966; Eugene (Gene) Corrigan, Administrative Assistant and Director of Service Bureau 1967–1969

Top: H.C. (Joby) Hawn, Supervisor of Football Officials 1956–1968
Center: Lou Bello, ACC Basketball Official 1953–1971
Right: Merrill P. (Footsie) Knight, Supervisor of Basketball Officials 1957–1968.

Champions By Years

Champions of the conference since its inauguration are as follows:

Football

1953—Duke and Maryland, tied	1962—Duke	1969—South Carolina
1954—Duke	1963—North Carolina and	1970—Wake Forest
1955—Maryland and Duke, tied	N. C. State, tied	1971—North Carolina
1956—Clemson	1964—N. C. State	1972—North Carolina
1957—N. C. State	1965—Clemson and	1973—N. C. State
1958—Clemson	N. C. State, tied	1974—Maryland
1959—Clemson	1966—Clemson	1975—Maryland
1960—Duke	1967—Clemson	1976—Maryland
1961—Duke	1968—N. C. State	

Cross Country

1953—N. C. State	1961—North Carolina	1969—Maryland
1954—Maryland	1962—North Carolina	1970—Duke
1955—Maryland	1963—North Carolina	1971—North Carolina
1956—North Carolina	1964—Maryland	1972—Maryland
1957—North Carolina	1965—Maryland	1973—Duke
1958—Duke	1966—Maryland	1974—Maryland
1959—Duke	1967—Maryland	1975—Duke
1960—North Carolina	1968—Maryland	1976—Maryland

Soccer

1953—Maryland	1962—Maryland	1969—Virginia
1954—Maryland	1963—Maryland	1970—Virginia
1955—Maryland	1964—Maryland	1971—Maryland
1956—Maryland	1965—Maryland	1972—Clemson
1957—Maryland	1966—Maryland and	1973—Clemson
1958—Maryland	North Carolina, tied	1974—Clemson
1959—Maryland	1967—Maryland	1975—Clemson
1960—Maryland	1968—Maryland	1976—Clemson
1961—Maryland		

Basketball

1954—N. C. State	1962—Wake Forest	1970—N. C. State
1955—N. C. State	1963—Duke	1971—South Carolina
1956—N. C. State	1964—Duke	1972—North Carolina
1957—North Carolina	1965—N. C. State	1973—N. C. State
1958—Maryland	1966—Duke	1974—N. C. State
1959—N. C. State	1967—North Carolina	1975—North Carolina
1960—Duke	1968—North Carolina	1976—Virginia
1961—Wake Forest	1969—North Carolina	1977—North Carolina

Swimming

1954—N. C. State	1962—Maryland	1969—N. C. State
1955—N. C. State	1963—Maryland, N. Carolina	1970—Maryland
1956—North Carolina and	N. C. State, tied	1971—N. C. State
N. C. State, tied	1964—Maryland and	1972—N. C. State
1957—North Carolina	North Carolina, tied	1973—N. C. State
1958—North Carolina	1965—Maryland	1974—N. C. State
1959—North Carolina	1966—N. C. State	1975—N. C. State
1960—Maryland	1967—N. C. State	1976—N. C. State
1961—Maryland, N. Carolina,	1968—N. C. State	1977—N. C. State
N. C. State, tied		

Indoor Track

1954—Maryland	1962—Maryland	1970—Maryland
1955—North Carolina	1963—Maryland	1971—Maryland
1956—Maryland	1964—Maryland	1972—Maryland
1957—Maryland	1965—Maryland	1973—Maryland
1958—Maryland	1966—Maryland	1974—Maryland
1959—Maryland	1967—Maryland	1975—Maryland
1960—Maryland	1968—Maryland	1976—Maryland
1961—Maryland	1969—Maryland	1977—Maryland

Wrestling

1954—Maryland	1962—Maryland	1970—Maryland
1955—Maryland	1963—Maryland	1971—Maryland
1956—Maryland	1964—Maryland	1972—Maryland
1957—Maryland	1965—Maryland	1973—Maryland
1958—Maryland	1966—Maryland	1974—Virginia
1959—Maryland	1967—Maryland	1975—Virginia
1960—Maryland	1968—Maryland	1976—N. C. State
1961—Maryland	1969—Maryland	1977—Virginia

Fencing

1971—North Carolina
1972—North Carolina
1973—North Carolina

1974—North Carolina
1975—North Carolina

1976—North Carolina
1977—North Carolina

Baseball

1954—Clemson
1955—Wake Forest
1956—Duke
1957—Duke
1958—Clemson
1959—Clemson
1960—North Carolina
1961—Duke

1962—Wake Forest
1963—Wake Forest
1964—North Carolina
1965—Maryland
1966—North Carolina
1967—Clemson
1968—N. C. State
1969—North Carolina

1970—Maryland
1971—Maryland
1972—Virginia
1973—N. C. State
1974—N. C. State
1975—N. C. State
1976—Clemson
1977—Wake Forest

Golf

1954—Duke
1955—Wake Forest
1956—North Carolina
1957—Wake Forest
1958—Wake Forest
1959—Duke
1960—North Carolina
1961—Duke
1962—Duke

1963—Wake Forest
1964—Maryland and South Carolina, tied
1965—North Carolina
1966—Duke
1967—Wake Forest
1968—Wake Forest
1969—Wake Forest

1970—Wake Forest
1971—Wake Forest
1972—Wake Forest
1973—Wake Forest
1974—Wake Forest
1975—Wake Forest
1976—Wake Forest
1977—North Carolina

Tennis

1954—North Carolina
1955—North Carolina
1956—North Carolina
1957—Maryland
1958—North Carolina
1959—North Carolina
1960—North Carolina
1961—North Carolina
1962—North Carolina

1963—North Carolina
1964—Maryland
1965—North Carolina
1966—North Carolina
1967—North Carolina
1968—North Carolina and South Carolina, tied
1969—Clemson

1970—North Carolina
1971—North Carolina
1972—North Carolina
1973—North Carolina
1974—North Carolina
1975—North Carolina
1976—North Carolina
1977—North Carolina

Track & Field

1954—Maryland
1955—North Carolina
1956—Maryland
1957—Maryland
1958—Maryland
1959—Maryland
1960—Maryland
1961—Maryland

1962—Maryland
1963—Maryland
1964—Maryland
1965—Maryland
1966—Maryland
1967—Maryland
1968—Maryland
1969—Maryland

1970—Maryland
1971—Maryland
1972—Maryland
1973—Maryland
1974—Maryland
1975—Maryland
1976—Maryland
1977—Maryland

Lacrosse

1954—Duke
1955—Maryland
1956—Maryland
1957—Maryland
1958—Maryland
1959—Maryland
1960—Maryland
1961—Maryland

1962—Virginia
1963—Maryland
1964—Virginia
1965—Maryland
1966—Maryland
1967—Maryland
1968—Maryland
1969—Virginia

1970—Virginia
1971—Virginia
1972—Maryland
1973—Maryland
1974—Maryland
1975—Virginia
1976—Maryland
1977—Maryland

All-Time Championship Competition
(As of September, 1977)

	Clemson	Duke	Maryland	N. Carolina	N. C. State	Virginia	W. Forest
BASEBALL							
Championship	5	3	3	4	4	1	4
Co-Champion	—	—	—	—	—	—	—
BASKETBALL							
Championship	—	4	1	7	8	1	2
Co-Champion	—	—	—	—	—	—	—
CR. COUNTRY							
Championship	—	5	11	7	1	—	—
Co-Champion	—	—	—	—	—	—	—
FENCING							
Championship	—	—	—	7	—	—	—
Co-Champion	—	—	—	—	—	—	—
FOOTBALL							
Championship	5	4	3	2	4	—	1
Co-Champion	1	2	2	1	2	—	—
GOLF							
Championship	—	5	—	4	—	—	14
Co-Champion	—	—	1	—	—	—	—
LACROSSE							
Championship	—	1	17	—	—	6	—
Co-Champion	—	—	—	—	—	—	—
SOCCER							
Championship	5	—	16	—	—	2	—
Co-Champion	—	—	1	1	—	—	—
SWIMMING							
Championship	—	—	4	3	13	—	—
Co-Champion	—	—	3	4	3	—	—
TENNIS							
Championship	1	—	2	20	—	—	—
Co-Champion	—	—	—	1	—	—	—
TRACK (IN.)							
Championship	—	—	23	1	—	—	—
Co-Champion	—	—	—	—	—	—	—
TRACK (OUT.)							
Championship	—	—	23	1	—	—	—
Co-Champion	—	—	—	—	—	—	—
WRESTLING							
Championship	—	—	20	—	1	3	—
Co-Champion	—	—	—	—	—	—	—
Championship	16	22	123	56	31	13	21
Co-Champions	1	2	7	7	5	0	0

(The University of South Carolina won one football championship, one basketball championship, and co-championships in golf and tennis before resigning from the conference in June, 1971.)

Bowl Records

CLEMSON (4-3-0)

1/1/40	COTTON BOWL (won over Boston College 6-3).
1/1/49	GATOR BOWL (won over Missouri 24-23).
1/1/51	ORANGE BOWL (won over Miami 15-14).
1/1/52	GATOR BOWL (lost to Miami 0-14).
1/1/57	ORANGE BOWL (lost to Colorado 21-27).
1/1/59	SUGAR BOWL (lost to L. S. U. 0-7).
12/19/59	BLUEBONNET BOWL (won over T. C. U. 23-7).

DUKE (3-3-0)

1/2/39	ROSE BOWL (lost to Southern California 3-7).
1/1/42	ROSE BOWL (lost to Oregon State 16-20), (game transferred to Durham, N. C.).
1/1/45	SUGAR BOWL (won over Alabama 29-26).
1/1/55	ORANGE BOWL (won over Nebraska 34-7).
1/1/58	ORANGE BOWL (lost to Oklahoma 21-48).
1/1/61	COTTON BOWL (won over Arkansas 7-6).

MARYLAND (3-5-1)

1/1/48	GATOR BOWL (tied with Georgia 20-20).
1/2/50	GATOR BOWL (won over Missouri 20-7).
1/1/52	SUGAR BOWL (won over Tennessee 28-13).
1/1/54	ORANGE BOWL (lost to Oklahoma 0-7).
1/2/56	ORANGE BOWL (lost to Oklahoma 6-20).
12/28/73	PEACH BOWL (lost to Georgia 16-17)
12/16/74	LIBERTY BOWL (lost to Tennessee 3-7)
12/29/75	GATOR BOWL (won over Florida 13-0)
1/1/77	COTTON BOWL (lost to Houston 21-30)

NORTH CAROLINA (2-7-0)

1/1/47	SUGAR BOWL (lost to Georgia 10-20).
1/1/49	SUGAR BOWL (lost to Oklahoma 6-14).
1/2/50	COTTON BOWL (lost to Rice 13-27).
12/28/63	GATOR BOWL (won over Air Force 35-0).
12/30/70	PEACH BOWL (lost to Arizona State 26-48)
12/31/71	GATOR BOWL (lost to Georgia 3-7)
12/30/72	SUN BOWL (won over Texas Tech, 32-28)
12/28/74	SUN BOWL (lost to Mississippi State 24-26)
12/31/76	PEACH BOWL (lost to Kentucky 0-21)

NORTH CAROLINA STATE (3-3-1)

1/1/47	GATOR BOWL (lost to Oklahoma 13-34).
12/21/63	LIBERTY BOWL (lost to Mississippi State 12-16).
12/16/67	LIBERTY BOWL (won over Georgia 14-7).
12/29/72	PEACH BOWL (won over West Virginia 49-13)
12/17/73	LIBERTY BOWL (won over Kansas 31-18)
12/23/74	BLUEBONNET BOWL (tied with Houston 31-31)
12/31/75	PEACH BOWL (lost to West Virginia 10-13)

VIRGINIA (no bowl games played)

WAKE FOREST (1-1-0)

1/1/46	GATOR BOWL (won over South Carolina 26-14).
1/1/49	DIXIE BOWL (lost to Baylor 7-20).

(South Carolina while a member of the ACC lost to Wake Forest in the 1946 Gator Bowl and to West Virginia in the 1969 Peach Bowl).

Bluebonnet
(1-0-1)

Cotton Bowl
(2-2-0)

Dixie Bowl
(0-1-0)

Gator Bowl
(5-4-1)

Liberty Bowl
(2-2-0)

Orange Bowl
(2-4-0)

Peach Bowl
(1-4-0)

Rose Bowl
(0-2-0)

Sugar Bowl
(2-3-0)

Sun Bowl
(1-1-0)

Composite ACC Football Standings 1953-1976

(Bowl Games Not Included)

Team	Conference Games						All Games					
	Won	Lost	Tied	Pct.	Points	Opp.	Won	Lost	Tied	Pct.	Points	Opp.
Duke	82	48	7	.624	2677	1942	128	106	13	.545	4345	3964
Clemson	84	51	3	.620	2491	2065	124	115	7	.518	4327	4291
Maryland	81	56	3	.589	2649	2063	127	115	4	.524	4513	3934
N.C. State	75	60	7	.553	2533	2222	114	122	11	.484	4172	4252
North Carolina	80	70	2	.533	2808	2411	121	123	3	.496	4424	4441
Wake Forest	47	100	5	.326	1987	3094	72	167	8	.308	3109	5323
*Virginia	28	94	1	.232	1643	3036	73	161	2	.314	3506	5413
(Former Member)												
South Carolina	56	54	4	.509	1832	1787	82	92	6	.472	2987	3032

*Virginia not counted in first ACC football standings (1953) since it did not become Conference member until December 1953.

Series Standings Between ACC Teams

(Conference Games Only 1953-1976)

Team	Clemson	Duke	Maryland	N. Car.	N.C. St.	S. Car.*	Virginia	W. For.	Total
Duke	8-9-1	——	8-5-0	11-12-1	13-8-3	11-5-1	14-4-0	17-5-1	= 82-48-7
Clemson	——	9-8-1	10-13-1	12-8-0	8-10-0	9-9-0	16-0-0	20-3-1	= 84-51-3
Maryland	13-10-1	5-8-0	——	12-9-0	10-11-1	12-6-0	14-6-0	15-6-1	= 81-56-3
N.C. State	10-8-0	8-13-3	11-10-1	12-12-0	——	6-6-2	15-1-0	13-10-1	= 75-60-7
North Carolina	8-12-0	12-11-1	9-12-0	———	12-12-0	9-7-0	16-7-0	14-9-1	= 80-70-2
Wake Forest	3-20-1	5-17-1	6-15-1	9-14-1	10-13-1	6-12-0	8-9-0	———	= 47-100-5
*Virginia	0-16-0	4-14-0	6-14-0	7-16-0	1-15-0	1-11-1	———	9-8-0	= 28-94-1

*In order to keep standings in balance the record of Conference games against South Carolina is included. South Carolina, a charter member, withdrew from the ACC on June 30, 1971.

**Since Virginia did not become a member of the ACC until December 1953 its losses to Duke, North Carolina and South Carolina during the 1953 season are not counted in the above Series Standings.

A total of 549 Conference games have been played since 1953. Sixteen have been ties. An average of 33.9 points have been scored in these league contests.

All-Time Series Through 1976

Team	Clemson	Duke	Maryland	N. Car.	N.C. St.	Virginia	W. For.	Total
Duke	11-9-1	——	14-6-0	29-29-4	33-15-4	19-9-0	40-15-2	= 146-83-11
Clemson	——	9-11-1	10-14-1	14-11-0	28-16-1	16-0-0	30-11-1	= 107-63-4
North Carolina	11-14-0	29-29-4	22-17-1	——	43-17-6	45-33-3	47-24-2	= 197-134-16
Maryland	14-10-1	6-14-0	——	17-22-1	14-15-4	24-15-2	17-7-1	= 92-83-9
N.C. State	16-28-1	15-33-4	15-14-4	17-43-6	——	19-6-1	38-26-6	= 120-150-22
Virginia	0-16-0	9-19-0	15-24-2	33-45-3	6-19-1	——	11-8-0	= 74-131-6
Wake Forest	11-30-1	15-40-2	7-17-1	24-47-2	26-38-6	8-11-0	——	= 91-183-12

First game between ACC members on October 18, 1888, when Wake Forest defeated North Carolina, 6-4, at Raleigh, N. C.

Longest series between Conference members is 81 games, North Carolina vs. Virginia. The first game in this series was played in 1892.

The Carmichael Cup

The Carmichael Cup, inaugurated by the Atlantic Coast Conference in 1961-62, is a memorial to the late William Donald Carmichael, Jr., of Chapel Hill, N. C., and the University of North Carolina. It is awarded annually for excellence in all sports, a so-called "power rating" in ACC competition. Each of the 13 sports counts equally with the winner of each championship receiving seven points, the second place team six, etc.

Only two schools have captured the coveted trophy. Maryland has won it ten times while North Carolina has won it six times.

1977 Carmichael Cup Standings

School	Football	Cross Country	Soccer	Basketball	Swimming	Indoor Track	Wrestling	Fencing	Baseball	Golf	Track & Field	Tennis	Lacrosse	Total
North Carolina	6	6	3½	7	5	6	6	7	3½	7	6	7	5	75
Maryland	7	7	6	4	2	7	5	6	6	6	7	1	7	71
N.C. State	3	3	3½	3	7	5	4	4	3½	4	5	6	4	55
Clemson	1	4	7	5½	6	4	2	5	7	3	3	3	x	50½
Virginia	2	2	5	1½	3	2	7	2	1	2	2	4	6	39½
Duke	4	5	2	1½	4	3	3	3	1	2	2	4	3	37½
Wake Forest	5	1	X	5½	1	1	X	X	5	5	1	5	X	29½

(X—Did Not Field Team)

Past Carmichael Cup Standings

1962
Maryland	72
Duke	70½
North Carolina	67½
Virginia	46
Clemson	43
N. C. State	39
Wake Forest	37½
South Carolina	32½

1963
Maryland	78
Duke	72
North Carolina	69
Virginia	48
Clemson	40½
Wake Forest	39
N. C. State	37
South Carolina	21½

1964
North Carolina	81
Maryland	80½
Duke	58½
Virginia	43½
N. C. State	39½
Clemson	38
Wake Forest	36
South Carolina	33

1965
Maryland	85½
North Carolina	75½
Duke	52
N. C. State	49
Virginia	41½
Wake Forest	37
South Carolina	34
Clemson	33½

1966
North Carolina	75
Maryland	72½
Duke	57½
N. C. State	53½
South Carolina	45
Virginia	41
Clemson	31
Wake Forest	29½

1972
North Carolina	74½
Maryland	68½
Virginia	54

1967
Maryland	76
North Carolina	71½
N. C. State	48
Duke	46½
Clemson	44
South Carolina	43
Virginia	41
Wake Forest	35

1968
Maryland	75½
North Carolina	72½
N. C. State	54½
Duke	51½
South Carolina	49½
Virginia	43½
Clemson	37½
Wake Forest	28½

1969
Maryland	73½
North Carolina	70
Duke	56½
Virginia	50½
N. C. State	46
Clemson	45
South Carolina	40½
Wake Forest	31

1970
Maryland	81
North Carolina	67½
Virginia	52
Duke	51½
N. C. State	49½
South Carolina	48
Clemson	37½
Wake Forest	26

1971
North Carolina	81
Maryland	74½
Duke	67½
Virginia	58½
N. C. State	49½
Clemson	39½
South Carolina	39½
Wake Forest	33

1975
Maryland	78
North Carolina	67
N. C. State	58½

Duke	51½	Virginia	47½
N. C. State	44	Duke	43
Clemson	33½	Clemson	40½
Wake Forest	27	Wake Forest	21½

<table>
<tr><td colspan="2">1973</td><td colspan="2">1976</td></tr>
<tr><td>North Carolina</td><td>68½</td><td>Maryland</td><td>69</td></tr>
<tr><td>Maryland</td><td>66</td><td>North Carolina</td><td>68½</td></tr>
<tr><td>N. C. State</td><td>59</td><td>N. C. State</td><td>65½</td></tr>
<tr><td>Duke</td><td>55</td><td>Duke</td><td>46</td></tr>
<tr><td>Virginia</td><td>43½</td><td>Clemson</td><td>45½</td></tr>
<tr><td>Clemson</td><td>39</td><td>Virginia</td><td>35½</td></tr>
<tr><td>Wake Forest</td><td>25</td><td>Wake Forest</td><td>28</td></tr>
<tr><td colspan="2">1974</td><td colspan="2">1977</td></tr>
<tr><td>Maryland</td><td>72</td><td>North Carolina</td><td>75</td></tr>
<tr><td>North Carolina</td><td>70½</td><td>Maryland</td><td>71</td></tr>
<tr><td>N. C. State</td><td>58½</td><td>N.C. State</td><td>55</td></tr>
<tr><td>Duke</td><td>48½</td><td>Clemson</td><td>50½</td></tr>
<tr><td>Virginia</td><td>46</td><td>Virginia</td><td>39½</td></tr>
<tr><td>Clemson</td><td>40½</td><td>Duke</td><td>37½</td></tr>
<tr><td>Wake Forest</td><td>20</td><td>Wake Forest</td><td>29½</td></tr>
</table>

ACC Basketball Tournament Champions

1954–1977

ACC AT RALEIGH (REYNOLDS COLISEUM)

1954	N. C. State (Everett Case)	Wake Forest	OT 82-80
1955	N. C. State (Everett Case)	Duke	87-77
1956	N. C. State (Everett Case)	Wake Forest	76-64
1957	North Carolina (Frank McGuire)	South Carolina	95-75
1958	Maryland (Bud Millikan)	North Carolina	86-74
1959	N. C. State (Everett Case)	North Carolina	80-56
1960	Duke (Vic Bubas)	Wake Forest	63-59
1961	Wake Forest (Bones McKinney)	Duke	96-81
1962	Wake Forest (Bones McKinney)	Clemson	77-66
1963	Duke (Vic Bubas)	Wake Forest	68-57
1964	Duke (Vic Bubas)	Wake Forest	80-59
1965	N. C. State (Press Maravich)	Duke	91-85
1966	Duke (Vic Bubas)	N. C. State	71-66

ACC AT GREENSBORO

1967	North Carolina (Dean Smith)	Duke	82-73

ACC AT CHARLOTTE

1968	North Carolina (Dean Smith)	N. C. State	87-50
1969	North Carolina (Dean Smith)	Duke	85-74
1970	N. C. State (Norman Sloan)	South Carolina	2 OT 42-39

ACC AT GREENSBORO

1971	South Carolina (Frank McGuire)	North Carolina	52-51
1972	North Carolina (Dean Smith)	Maryland	73-64
1973	N. C. State (Norman Sloan)	Maryland	76-74
1974	N. C. State (Norman Sloan)	Maryland	OT 103-100
1975	North Carolina (Dean Smith)	N. C. State	70-66

ACC AT LANDOVER, MARYLAND

1976	Virginia (Terry Holland)	North Carolina	67-62

ACC AT GREENSBORO

1977	North Carolina (Dean Smith)	Virginia	75-69

All-ACC Basketball Teams
1954–1977

1954
Dickie Hemric, Wake Forest
Gene Shue, Maryland
Mel Thompson, N. C. State
Rudy D'Emilio, Duke
Buzz Wilkinson, Virginia
PLAYER OF YEAR: Hemric

1955
Dickie Hemric, Wake Forest
Ronnie Shavlik, N. C. State
Buzz Wilkinson, Virginia
Lennie Rosenbluth, North Carolina
Ronnie Mayer, Duke
PLAYER OF YEAR: Hemric

1956
Ronnie Shavlik, N. C. State
Lennie Rosenbluth, North Carolina
Vic Molodet, N. C. State
Lowell Davis, Wake Forest
Joe Belmont, Duke
PLAYER OF YEAR: Shavlik

1957
Lennie Rosenbluth, North Carolina
Grady Wallace, South Carolina
Jack Murdock, Wake Forest
Tommy Kearns, North Carolina
Jack Williams, Wake Forest
PLAYER OF YEAR: Rosenbluth

1958
Pete Brennan, North Carolina
Lou Pucillo, N. C. State
Tommy Kearns, North Carolina
Jim Newcome, Duke
Herb Busch, Virginia
PLAYER OF YEAR: Brennan

1959
Lou Pucillo, N. C. State
York Larese, North Carolina
John Richter, N. C. State
Doug Moe, North Carolina
Carroll Youngkin, Duke
PLAYER OF YEAR: Pucillo

1960
Al Bunge, Maryland
Len Chappell, Wake Forest
Lee Shaffer, North Carolina
York Larese, North Carolina
Choppy Patterson, Clemson
PLAYER OF YEAR: Shaffer

1961
Len Chappell, Wake Forest
Art Heyman, Duke
York Larese, North Carolina
Doug Moe, North Carolina
Billy Packer, Wake Forest
PLAYER OF YEAR: Chappell

1962
Len Chappell, Wake Forest
Art Heyman, Duke
Jeff Mullins, Duke
Art Whisnant, South Carolina
Jon Speaks, N. C. State
PLAYER OF YEAR: Chappell

1963
Art Heyman, Duke
Billy Cunningham, North Carolina
Jeff Mullins, Duke
Dave Wiedeman, Wake Forest
Larry Brown, North Carolina
PLAYER OF YEAR: Heyman

1964
Billy Cunningham, North Carolina
Jeff Mullins, Duke
Ronnie Collins, South Carolina
Chip Conner, Virginia
Frank Christie, Wake Forest
PLAYER OF YEAR: Mullins

1965
Billy Cunningham, North Carolina
Larry Lakins, N. C. State
Jack Marin, Duke
Bob Verga, Duke
Bob Leonard, Wake Forest
PLAYER OF YEAR: Cunningham

1966
Bob Lewis, North Carolina
Jack Marin, Duke
Bob Verga, Duke
Eddie Biedenbach, N. C. State
Bob Leonard, Wake Forest
PLAYER OF YEAR:
  Steve Vacendak, Duke

1967
Larry Miller, North Carolina
Bob Verga, Duke
Bob Lewis, North Carolina
Paul Long, Wake Forest
Randy Mahaffey, Clemson
PLAYER OF YEAR: Miller

1968
Larry Miller, North Carolina
Mike Lewis, Duke
Charlie Scott, North Carolina
Skip Harlicka, South Carolina
Eddie Biedenbach, N. C. State
PLAYER OF YEAR: Miller

1969
John Roche, South Carolina
Charlie Davis, Wake Forest
Bill Bunting, North Carolina
Charlie Scott, North Carolina
Vann Williford, N. C. State
PLAYER OF YEAR: Roche

1970
John Roche, South Carolina
Charlie Scott, North Carolina
Vann Williford, N. C. State
Charlie Davis, Wake Forest
Tom Owens, South Carolina
PLAYER OF YEAR: Roche

1971
Charlie Davis, Wake Forest
John Roche, South Carolina
Dennis Wuycik, North Carolina
Randy Denton, Duke
Tom Owens, South Carolina
PLAYER OF YEAR: Davis

1972
Barry Parkhill, Virginia
Robert McAdoo, North Carolina
Tom McMillen, Maryland
Dennis Wuycik, North Carolina
Tom Burleson, N. C. State
PLAYER OF YEAR: Parkhill

1973
David Thompson, N. C. State
Tom Burleson, N. C. State
Tom McMillen, Maryland
George Karl, North Carolina
Gary Melchionni, Duke
PLAYER OF YEAR: Thompson

1974
David Thompson, N. C. State
Bobby Jones, North Carolina
Len Elmore, Maryland
Monte Towe, N. C. State
John Lucas, Maryland
PLAYER OF YEAR: Thompson

1975
David Thompson, N. C. State
Mitch Kupchak, North Carolina
John Lucas, Maryland
Skip Brown, Wake Forest
Skip Wise, Clemson
PLAYER OF YEAR: Thompson

1976
Mitch Kupchak. North Carolina
John Lucas, Maryland
Kenny Carr, N. C. State
Phil Ford, North Carolina
Tate Armstrong, Duke
PLAYER OF YEAR: Kupchak

1977
Rod Griffin, Wake Forest
Phil Ford, North Carolina
Skip Brown, Wake Forest
Kenny Carr, N. C. State
Walter Davis, North Carolina
PLAYER OF THE YEAR: Griffin

Selected by the Atlantic Coast Sports Writers Association

226

All-ACC Tournament Teams
1954–1977

1954
Dickie Hemric, Wake Forest
Gene Shue, Maryland
Mel Thompson, N. C. State
Ron Shavlik, N. C. State
Skip Winstead, North Carolina

1955
Buzz Wilkinson, Virginia
Ronnie Shavlik, N. C. State
Ronnie Mayer, Duke
Dickie Hemric, Wake Forest
Lowell Davis, Wake Forest

1956
Vic Molodet, N. C. State
Lennie Rosenbluth, North Carolina
Jack Murdock, Wake Forest
Jack Williams, Wake Forest
John Maglio, N. C. State

1957
Lennie Rosenbluth, North Carolina
Grady Wallace, South Carolina
Jack Williams, Wake Forest
Pete Brennan, North Carolina
Jack Murdock, Wake Forest

1958
Pete Brennan, North Carolina
Nick Davis, Maryland
Lou Pucillo, N. C. State
Charles McNeil, Maryland
Tommy Kearns, North Carolina

1959
Lou Pucillo, N. C. State
John Richter, N. C. State
Lee Shaffer, North Carolina
Paul Adkins, Virginia
George Stepanovich, N. C. State

1960
Len Chappell, Wake Forest
Doug Kistler, Duke
Howard Hurt, Duke
Lee Shaffer, North Carolina
York Larese, North Carolina

1961
Len Chappell, Wake Forest
Art Heyman, Duke
Billy Packer, Wake Forest
John Frye, Duke
Art Whisnant, South Carolina

1962
Len Chappell, Wake Forest
Jim Brennan, Clemson
Art Heyman, Duke
Jeff Mullins, Duke
Billy Packer, Wake Forest

1963
Art Heyman, Duke
Jeff Mullins, Duke
Dave Wiedeman, Wake Forest
Billy Cunningham, North Carolina
Ken Rohloff, N. C. State

1964
Jeff Mullins, Duke
Jay Buckley, Duke
Billy Cunningham, North Carolina
Frank Christie, Wake Forest
Bob Leonard, Wake Forest

1965
Bob Leonard, Wake Forest
Larry Worsley, N. C. State
Bob Verga, Duke
Steve Vacendak, Duke
Larry Lakins, N. C. State
CASE AWARD: Worsley
(Coaches began award for MVP in
tournament, named for late Everett
N. Case)

1966
Eddie Biedenbach, N. C. State
Steve Vacendak, Duke
Tommy Mattocks, N. C. State
Bob Verga, Duke
Mike Lewis, Duke
CASE AWARD: Vacendak

1967
Larry Miller, North Carolina
Bob Verga, Duke
Al Salvadori, South Carolina
Bob Lewis, North Carolina
Paul Long, Wake Forest
CASE AWARD: Miller

1968
Larry Miller, North Carolina
Gary Gregor, South Carolina
Dick Grubar, North Carolina
Jack Thompson, South Carolina
Skip Harlicka, South Carolina
CASE AWARD: Miller

1969
Charlie Scott, North Carolina
Charlie Davis, Wake Forest
Dick DeVenzio, Duke
Steve Vandenberg, Duke
John Roche, South Carolina
CASE AWARD: Scott

1970
Vann Williford, N. C. State
Charlie Davis, Wake Forest
Tom Owens, South Carolina
Chip Case, Virginia
Tom Riker, South Carolina
CASE AWARD: Williford

1971
Barry Parkhill, Virginia
Tom Owens, South Carolina
John Roche, South Carloina
Lee Dedmon, North Carolina
Paul Coder, N. C. State
CASE AWARD (Tie): Dedmon and Roche

1972
Barry Parkhill, Virginia
Dennis Wuycik, North Carolina
Robert McAdoo, North Carolina
George Karl, North Carolina
Tom McMillen, Maryland
CASE AWARD: McAdoo

1973
Tommy Burleson, N. C. State
David Thompson, N. C. State
Tom McMillen, Maryland
John Lucas, Maryland
Eddie Payne, Wake Forest
CASE AWARD: Burleson

1974
David Thompson, N. C. State
Tommy Burleson, N. C. State
Tom McMillen, Maryland
John Lucas, Maryland
Maurice Howard, Maryland
CASE AWARD: Burleson

1975
David Thompson, N. C. State
Mitch Kupchak, North Carolina
Kenny Carr, N. C. State
Phil Ford, North Carolina
Skip Wise, Clemson
CASE AWARD: Ford

1976
Wally Walker, Virginia
Billy Langloh, Virginia
Marc Iavaroni, Virginia
Mitch Kupchak, North Carolina
Tate Armstrong, Duke
Phil Ford, North Carolina
CASE AWARD: Walker

1977
Phil Ford, North Carolina
Mike O'Koren, North Carolina
Bobby Stokes, Virginia
Marc Iavaroni, Virginia
John Kuester, North Carolina
Kenny Carr, N. C. State
CASE AWARD: Kuester

Selected by the Atlantic Coast Sports Writers Association

Twenty-Five Year Composite on ACC Tournament
1953–1977

Team	Won	Lost	Pct.	Tourneys	Semis	Finals	Titles
N.C. State	33	17	.660	25	16	11	8
North Carolina*	32	17	.653	24	18	11	7
Duke	32	20	.615	25	17	10	5
Wake Forest	24	23	.511	25	15	8	2
South Carolina**	13	17	.433	18	9	3	1
Maryland	15	24	.385	25	11	4	1
Virginia	12	24	.333	25	9	2	1
Clemson	6	25	.193	25	5	1	0

*North Carolina did not participate in the 1961 Tournament.
**South Carolina withdrew from the Conference on June 30, 1971.

Composite Basketball Standings
1954–1978

Team	Conference Games			All Games		
	Won	Lost	Pct.	Won	Lost	Pct.
North Carolina	244	90	.709	510	169	.751
Duke	209	124	.628	458	226	.670
N.C. State	199	132	.601	456	209	.686
Maryland	166	167	.498	385	262	.601
Wake Forest	167	170	.496	368	310	.543
South Carolina*	101	145	.411	360	291	.553
Clemson	103	229	.310	270	366	.425
Virginia	98	230	.299	268	376	.416

*South Carolina withdrew from the Conference on June 30, 1971

ACC Basketball
The 25 Average Club 1954-1978

Player	School	Year	Games	FG	FT	Pts	Avg
Buzz Wilkinson	UVA	1955	28	308	382	898	32.1*
Grady Wallace	USC	1957	29	336	234	906	31.2
Buzz Wilkinson	UVA	1954	27	288	238	814	30.1
Len Chappell	WF	1962	31	327	278	932+	30.1
David Thompson	NCS	1975	28	347	144	838	29.9
Bill Yarborough	CLem.	1955	23	247	157	651	28.3
Len Rosenbluth	UNC	1957	32	305	285	895	28.0
Dickie Hemric	WF	1955	27	222	302	746	27.6
Bob Lewis	UNC	1966	27	259	222	740	27.4
Charlie Scott	UNC	1970	27	281	169	731	27.1
Len Rosenbluth	UNC	1956	23	227	160	614	26.7
Len Chappell	WF	1961	28	271	203	745	26.6

Kenny Carr	NCS	1976	30	322	154	798	26.6
Charlie Davis	WF	1971	26	251	188	690	26.5
Bob Verga	Duke	1967	27	283	139	705	26.1
David Thompson	NCS	1974	31	325	155	805	26.0
Bill Cunningham	UNC	1964	24	233	157	623	26.0
Butch Zatezalo	Clem.	1969	25	228	189	645	25.8
Len Rosenbluth	UNC	1955	21	189	158	536	25.5
Charlie Davis	WF	1970	26	234	196	664	25.5
Bill Cunningham	UNC	1965	24	237	135	609	25.4
Art Heyman	Duke	1962	24	219	170	608	25.3
Art Heyman	Duke	1961	25	229	171	629	25.2

*Record Scoring Average
+ Record Total Points

ACC Basketball
The 700–Point Club 1954–1978

Player	School	Year	Games	FG	FT	Pts	Avg
Len Chappell	WF	1962	31	327	278	932*	30.1
Grady Wallace	USC	1957	29	336	234	906	31.2
Buzz Wilkinson	UVA	1955	28	308	282	898	32.1+
Len Rosenbluth	UNC	1957	32	305	285	895	28.0
David Thompson	NCS	1975	28	347	144	838	29.9
Buzz Wilkinson	UVA	1954	27	288	238	814	30.1
David Thompson	NCS	1974	31	325	155	805	26.0
Kenny Carr	NCS	1976	30	322	154	798	26.6
Jeff Mullins	Duke	1964	31	300	150	750	24.2
Art Heyman	Duke	1963	30	265	217	747	24.9
Dickie Hemric	WF	1955	27	222	302	746	27.6
Len Chappell	WF	1961	28	271	203	745	26.5
Bob Lewis	UNC	1966	27	259	222	740	27.4
Charlie Scott	UNC	1970	27	281	169	731	27.1
Larry Miller	UNC	1968	32	268	181	717	22.4
Charlie Scott	UNC	1969	32	290	134	714	22.3
Vann Williford	NCS	1970	30	281	148	710	23.7
Ron Shavlik	NCS	1955	32	260	187	707	22.1
Bob Verga	Duke	1967	27	283	139	705	26.1
Larry Miller	UNC	1967	32	278	144	700	21.9

*Record Total Points
+ Record Scoring Average

ACC Basketball Player and Coach of the Year

Year	Player		Coach	
1954	Dick Hemric	WF	Everett Case	NCS
1955	Dick Hemric	WF	Everett Case	NCS

1956	Ronnie Shavlik	NCS	Murray Greason	WF
1957	Len Rosenbluth	UNC	Frank McGuire	UNC
1958	Pete Brennan	UNC	Everett Case	NCS
1959	Lou Pucillo	NCS	Harold Bradley	Duke
1960	Lee Shaffer	UNC	Horace McKinney	WF
1961	Len Chappell	WF	Horace McKinney	WF
1962	Len Chappell	WF	Bob Stevens	USC
1963	Art Heyman	Duke	Vic Bubas	Duke
1964	Jeff Mullins	Duke	Vic Bubas	Duke
1965	Bill Cunningham	UNC	Press Maravich	NCS
1966	Steve Vacendak	Duke	Vic Bubas	Duke
1967	Larry Miller	UNC	Dean Smith	UNC
1968	Larry Miller	UNC	Dean Smith	UNC
1969	John Roche	USC	Frank McGuire	USC
1970	John Roche	USC	Norm Sloan	NCS
1971	Charlie Davis	WF	Dean Smith	UNC
1972	Barry Parkhill	Va.	Bill Gibson	Va.
1973	David Thompson	NCS	Norm Sloan	NCS
1974	David Thompson	NCS	Norm Sloan	NCS
1975	David Thompson	NCS	Lefty Drisell	Md.
1976	Mitch Kupchak	UNC	Dean Smith	UNC
1977	Rod Griffin	WF	Dean Smith	UNC
1978	Phil Ford	UNC	Bill Foster	Duke

ACC Basketball Rookie of the Year

Year	Player	School
1976	Jim Spanarkel	Duke
1977	Mike Gminski	Duke
	Charles Whitney	NCS
1978	Gene Banks	Duke

Selected by the Atlantic Coast Sports Writers Association.

ACC Basketball All-Time Scoring Leaders
1954–1978

Player	School	Year Finished	Games	Points	Average
1. Dickie Hemric*	WF	1955	104	2587	24.87
2. David Thompson	NCS	1975	86	2309	26.84
3. Phil Ford*	UNC	1978	123	2290	18.61
4. Buzz Wilkinson	UVA	1955	78	2233	28.62+
5. Len Chappell	WF	1962	87	2165	24.88
6. Len Rosenbluth	UNC	1957	76	2045	26.90
7. Skip Brown*	WF	1977	108	2034	18.83
8. John Lucas*	Md.	1976	110	2015	18.31
9. Charlie Scott	UNC	1970	91	2007	22.05

10. Rod Griffin*	WF	1978	107	1985	18.55
11. Art Heyman	Duke	1963	79	1984	25.11
12. Larry Miller	UNC	1968	91	1982	21.78
13. Charlie Davis	WF	1971	79	1970	24.93
14. John Roche	USC	1971	85	1910	22.47
15. Jeff Mullins	Duke	1964	86	1888	21.85
16. Wally Walker*	UVA	1976	104	1849	17.77
17. Bob Lewis	UNC	1967	83	1836	22.12

* Indicates players who played four varsity seasons; all the others played only three.
\+ Record scoring average

Everett N. Case Award
ACC Basketball Tournament
Most Valuable Player

Year	Player	School
1965	Larry Worsley	NCS
1966	Steve Vacendak	Duke
1967	Larry Miller	UNC
1968	Larry Miller	UNC
1969	Charlie Scott	UNC
1970	Vann Williford	NCS
1971	John Roche and	USC
	Lee Dedmon	UNC
1972	Robert McAdoo	UNC
1973	Tommy Burleson	NCS
1974	Tommy Burleson	NCS
1975	Phil Ford	UNC
1976	Wally Walker	Va.
1977	John Kuester	UNC
1978	Jim Spanarkel	Duke

* Selected by the Head Coaches of the ACC Basketball Teams in honor of the late North Carolina State basketball coach Everett N. Case.

1978 All-ACC Basketball Team

First Team	Second Team
Phil Ford UNC (Sr.)	Gene Banks Duke (Fr.)
Rod Griffin WF (Sr.)	Jeff Lamp Va. (Fr.)
Mike Gminski Duke (So.)	Frank Johnson WF (So.)
Jim Spanarkel Duke (Jr.)	Charles Whitney NCS (So.)
Mike O'Koren UNC (So.)	Clyde Austin NCS (So.)

1978 All-ACC Tournament Team

First Team	Second Team
Mike Gminski Duke (So.)	Phil Ford UNC (Sr.)
Leroy McDonald WF (Sr.)	Frank Johnson WF (So.)
Rod Griffin WF (Sr.)	Kenny Dennard Duke (Fr.)
Jim Spanarkel Duke (Jr.)	Lawrence Boston Md. (Sr.)
Gene Banks Duke (Fr.)	Larry Gibson Md. (Jr.)

Selected by the Atlantic Coast Sports Writers Association.

ACC Record in NCAA Play

Six of the current members of the Atlantic Coast Conference have participated in the NCAA basketball playoffs since 1939. The ACC record stands at 64 victories and 37 losses for a .634 percentage.

ACC teams have captured two national championships, North Carolina in 1957 and North Carolina State in 1974, while finishing second five times, third five times and fourth twice.

The record is as follows:

Team (Years participated)	Years	Won	Lost	Pct.
Duke (1955-60-63-64-66-78)	6	15	6	.714
Wake Forest (1939-53-61-62-77)	5	9	5	.643
Maryland (1958-73-75)	3	5	3	.625
North Carolina (1941-46-47-57-59-67-68-69-72-75-76-77-78)	12	23	14	.621
N.C. State (1950-51-52-54-56-65-70-74	8	12	8	.600
Virginia (1976)	1	0	1	.000

ACC Players on NCAA All-Tournament Teams
(Final Round Only)

1957	Len Rosenbluth and Pete Brennan, North Carolina
1962	Len Chappell, Wake Forest
1963	Art Heymen, Duke (MVP)
1964	Jeff Mullins, Duke
1966	Jack Marin, Duke
1968	Larry Miller, North Carolina
1969	Charlie Scott, North Carolina
1972	Robert McAdoo, North Carolina
1974	David Thompson (MVP), Tommy Burleson, Monte Towe (All N.C. State)
1977	Mike O'Koren and Walter Davis, North Carolina
1978	Mike Gminski and Jim Spanarkel, Duke

ACC
SILVER ANNIVERSARY BASKETBALL TEAM
1954–1978

Player	School	Years Played	Position	Hgt	Wgt
Len Chappell	Wake Forest	1960-62	Center	6'8	240
Billy Cunningham	North Carolina	1963-65	Forward	6'6	218
Phil Ford	North Carolina	1975-78	Guard	6'2	171
Rod Griffin	Wake Forest	1975-78	Forward	6'6	225
Dickie Hemric	Wake Forest	1954-55	Center	6'6	227
Art Heyman	Duke	1961-63	Forward	6'5	205
John Lucas	Maryland	1973-76	Guard	6'4	170
Larry Miller	North Carolina	1966-68	Forward	6'3	210
Jeff Mullins	Duke	1962-64	Forward	6'4	185
John Roche	South Carolina	1969-71	Guard	6'3	175
Lennie Rosenbluth	North Carolna	1955-57	Center	6'5	195
Charlie Scott	North Carolina	1968-70	Forward	6'5	178
Ron Shavlik	North Carolina State	1954-56	Center	6'9	195
David Thompson	North Carolina State	1973-75	Forward	6'4	195
Bob Verga	Duke	1965-67	Forward	6'0	180

Selected by the Atlantic Coast Sports Writers Association

ACC
SILVER ANNIVERSARY FOOTBALL TEAM
1953-1977

OFFENSIVE TEAM

Position	Player	Hgt	Wgt	Last Season
End	Gary Collins (Md.)	6'3	200	1961
End	Claude (Tee) Moorman (Duke)	6'3	210	1960
Tackle	Mike Sandusky (Md.)	5'11	240	1956
Tackle	Stan Jones (Md.)	6'0	245	1953
Guard	Ken Huff (UNC)	6'3	261	1974
Guard	Harry Olszewski (Clem.)	5'11	237	1967
Center	Billy Bryan (Duke)	6'2	244	1976
Quarterback	Roman Gabriel (NCS)	6'3	218	1961
Running Back	Billy Barnes (WF)	5'11	181	1956
Running Back	Dick Christy (NCS)	5'10	180	1957
Running Back	Don McCauley (UNC)	6'0	198	1970
Placekicker	Steve Mike-Mayer (Md.)	6'0	180	1974

DEFENSIVE TEAM

Position	Player	Hgt	Wgt	Last Season
Lineman	Ron Carpenter (NCS)	6'6	250	1969
Lineman	Mike McGee (Duke)	6'1	213	1959

Lineman	Ed Meadows (Duke)	6'3	217	1953
Lineman	Randy White (Md.)	6'4	248	1974
Linebacker	Chris Hanburger (UNC)	6'0	195	1964
Linebacker	Bob Matheson (Duke)	6'3	227	1966
Linebacker	Bob Pellegrini (Md.)	6'2	215	1955
Back	Bill Armstrong (WF)	6'4	205	1976
Back	Bobby Bryant (USC)	6'0	174	1966
Back	Fred Combs (NCS)	5'10	180	1967
Back	Ernie Jackson (Duke)	5'10	165	1971
Punter	Johnny Evans (NCS)	6'2	200	1977

Selected by the Atlantic Coast Sports Writers Association

ACC Football Record vs. Non-Conference Foes
1953-1977
(Bowl Games Not Included)

Year	Won	lost	Tied	Pct.
1953	21	17	3	.549
1954	19	22	2	.465
1955	22	18	1	.549
1956	10	20	4	.353
1957	13	10	3	.558
1958	11	18	1	.383
1959	10	20	0	.333
1960	8	20	0	.286
1961	14	14	0	.500
1962	9	17	2	.375
1963	8	16	2	.346
1964	10	17	1	.375
1965	12	18	0	.400
1966	7	27	0	.206
1967	9	20	0	.310
1968	7	21	0	.250
1969	7	23	0	.233
1970	13	25	0	.342
1971	15	24	0	.385
1972	17	18	0	.486
1973	12	23	0	.343
1974	21	14	0	.600
1975	12	28	1	.305
1976	21	18	2	.537
1977	17	17	1	.500

ACC Football: The 1500–Yard Club
1954–1977

Player	School	Year	Plays	Yards	Avg.
Leo Hart	Duke	1968	403	2340	5.8
Leo Hart	Duke	1970	411	2315	5.6
Scott Gardner	Va.	1973	342	2120	6.2
Fred Summers	WF	1968	409	2103	5.1
Tommy Suggs	USC	1970	315	1948	6.2
Ken Pengitore	Clem.	1973	370	1941	5.2
Steve Fuller	Clem.	1977	347	1900	5.5
Mike Dunn	Duke	1976	344	1835	5.3
Mike Dunn	Duke	1977	352	1815	5.2
Bruce Shaw	NCS	1972	249	1763	7.1
Gene Arnette	Va.	1968	294	1755	6.0
Don McCauley	UNC	1970	327	1729	5.3
Gayle Bomar	UNC	1968	354	1724	4.9
Bob Avellini	Md.	1974	229	1689	7.4
Bob Davis	Va.	1966	309	1688	5.5
Tommy Suggs	USC	1968	278	1658	6.0
Norman Snead	WF	1960	312	1630	5.2
Dave Buckey	NCS	1974	262	1616	6.2
Leo Hart	Duke	1969	377	1612	4.3
Scott Gardner	Va.	1975	350	1593	4.6
Mark Manges	Md.	1976	264	1593	6.0
Chris Kupec	UNC	1974	222	1583	7.1
Scott Gardner	Va.	1974	276	1576	5.7
Johnny Evans	NCS	1977	327	1541	4.7
Dave Buckey	NCS	1975	298	1532	5.1
John Mackovic	WF	1964	267	1514	5.7

ACC Football: The 1,000 Yard Rushing Club

Player	School	Year	Carries	Yards	Average
Don McCauley	UNC	1970	324	1720	5.3
Mike Voight	UNC	1976	315	1407	4.5
Ted Brown	NCS	1977	218	1251	5.7
Mike Voight	UNC	1975	259	1250	4.8
Steve Jones	Duke	1972	287	1236	4.3
Larry Hopkins	WF	1971	249	1228	4.9
Frank Quayle	UVA	1968	175	1213	6.9
Amos Lawrence	UNC	1977	193	1211	6.3
Stan Fritts	NCS	1974	245	1169	4.8
Don McCauley	UNC	1969	204	1092	5.4
Ted Brown	NCS	1976	198	1088	5.5
James Betterson	UNC	1974	209	1082	5.2
Buddy Gore	Clem.	1967	230	1045	4.5

235

Brian Piccolo	WF	1964	252	1044	4.1
Mike Voight	UNC	1974	203	1033	5.1
James McDougald	WF	1976	232	1018	4.4
Willie Burden	NCS	1973	150	1014	6.8
Billy Barnes	WF	1956	168	1010	6.0
Sammy Johnson	UNC	1973	183	1006	5.5

ACC Football Player and Coach of the Year

Year	Player		Coach	
1953	Bernie Faloney	Md.	Jim Tatum	Md.
1954	Jerry Barger	Duke	Bill Murray	Duke
1955	Bob Pellegrini	Md.	Jim Tatum	Md.
1956	Bill Barnes	WF	Paul Amen	WF
1957	Dick Christy	NCS	Earle Edwards	NCS
1958	Alex Hawkins	USC	Frank Howard	Clem.
1959	Mike McGee	Duke	Paul Amen	WF
1960	Roman Gabriel	NCS	Bill Murray	Duke
1961	Roman Gabriel	NCS	Bill Elias	Va.
1962	Billy Gambrell	USC	Bill Murray	Duke
1963	Jay Wilkinson	Duke	Jim Hickey	UNC
			Earle Edwards	NCS
1964	Brian Piccolo	WF	Bill Tate	WF
1965	Danny Talbott	UNC	Earle Edwards	NCS
1966	Bob Davis	Va.	Frank Howard	Clem.
1967	Buddy Gore	Clem.	Earle Edwards	NCS
1968	Frank Quayle	Va.	George Blackburn	Va.
1969	Don McCauley	UNC	Paul Dietzel	USC
1970	Don McCauley	UNC	Cal Stoll	WF
1971	Ernie Jackson	Duke	Bill Dooley	UNC
1972	Steve Jones	Duke	Lou Holtz	NCS
1973	Willie Burden	NCS	Jerry Claiborne	Md.
1974	Randy White	Md.	Red Parker	Clem.
1975	Mike Voight	UNC	Jerry Claiborne	Md.
1976	Mike Voight	UNC	Jerry Claiborne	Md.
1977	Steve Fuller	Clem.	Charlie Pell	Clem.

ACC Football Rookie of the Year

Year	Player	School
1975	Ted Brown	NCS
1976	James McDouglad	WF
1977	Amos Lawrence	UNC

Selected by the Atlantic Coast Sports Writers Association.

Jacobs Blocking Trophy

Year	Name	School	Position
1953	Bill Wohrman	USC	Fullback
1954	Bill Wohrman	USC	Fullback
1955	Bob Pellegrini	Md.	Center
1956	Harold McElhaney	Duke	Fullback
1957	Harold McElhaney	Duke	Fullback
1958	John Saunders	USC	Fullback
1959	Doug Cline	Clem.	Fullback
1960	Dwight Bumgarner	Duke	Tackle
1961	Art Gregory	Duke	Tackle
	Jim LeCompte	UNC	Guard
1962	Art Gregory	Duke	Tackle
1963	Chuck Walker	Duke	Tackle
1964	Eddie Kesler	UNC	Fullback
1965	John McNabb	Duke	Guard
1966	Wayne Mass	Clem.	Tackle
1967	Harry Olszewski	Clem.	Guard
1968	Greg Shelly	Va.	Tackle
1969	Ralph Sonntag	Md.	Tackle
1970	Danny Ryczek	Va.	Center
1971	Geoff Hamlin	UNC	Fullback
1972	Ron Rusnak	UNC	Guard
1973	Bill Yoest	NCS	Guard
1974	Ken Huff	UNC	Guard
1975	Billy Bryan	Duke	Center
1976	Billy Bryan	Duke	Center
1977	Joe Bostic	Clem.	Guard

This trophy is awarded annually by William and Hugh Jacobs of Clinton, South Carolina, to the player voted the outstanding blocker in the ACC in a poll of the Head Football Coaches. The award is given in memory of William P. Jacobs, who served as President of Presbyterian College from 1935 until 1945, by his sons.

Jim Weaver
Postgraduate Scholarship

Year	Name	School	Sport
1971	Edward Kihm	Va.	Football & Baseball
1972	Bill Brafford	UNC	Football
1973	Ben Anderson	Clem.	Football
1974	Daniel Stroup	WF	Football
1975	David Wendell	Va.	Wrestling
1976	Kim Hoover	Md.	Football
	Darryl Jackson	NCS	Football

237

| 1977 | John Bryce | WF | Football |
| 1978 | Gary Friedman | Va. | Wrestling |

This scholarship is awarded annually to an outstanding ACC athlete who had distinguished himself by his academic record and leadership qualities. It is given in memory of the late James H. (Jim) Weaver, Commissioner of the ACC from 1954–1970, is valued at $1,000, and the recipient can represent any sports competition recognized by the ACC.

Brian Piccolo Award

Year	Name	School	Position
1970	Paul Miller	UNC	Quarterback
1971	Jim Webster	UNC	Linebacker
1972	Mark Johnson	Duke	Quarterback
1973	Al Neville	Md.	Quarterback
1974	David Visaggio	Md.	Defensive Guard
1975	Scott Gardner	Va.	Quarterback
1976	Jeff Green	Duke	Defensive End
1977	Ralph Stringer	NCS	Defensive Back

This award is given annually by the Greenville, South Carolina Touchdown Club in memory of the late Brian Piccolo. Piccolo was the 1964 winner of the ACC Player of the Year Award at Wake Forest, and a star running back for the Chicago Bears, who succumbed to cancer in 1970, at the age of 26. The award is made to the player, who in the opinion of the ACC Football Coaches, proves himself to be the most courageous in the Conference.

1977 ALL-ACC Football Team

Offensive Team		*Defensive Team*	
SE	Jerry Butler (Clem.)	L	Dee Hardison (UNC)
TE	Steve Young	L	Rod Broadway (UNC)
T	Lacy Brumley (Clem.)	L	Ken Sheets (UNC)
T	John Patterson (Duke)	L	Jonathan Brooks (Clem.)
G	Joe Bostic (Clem.)	L	Ted Klaube (Md.)
G	Mike Salzano (UNC)	LB	Randy Scott (Clem.)
C	Larry Tearry (WF)	LB	Buddy Curry (UNC)
QB	Steve Fuller (Clem.)	B	Alan Caldwell (UNC)
RB	Amos Lawrence (UNC)	B	Steve Ryan (Clem.)
RB	Ted Brown (NCS)	B	Richard Carter (NCS)
RB	James McDougald (WF)	B	Ralph Stringer (NCS)
K	Russ Henderson (Va.)		

Anthony J. McKevlin Award
ACC Athlete of the Year

Year	Athlete	School	Sport
1954	Joel Shankle	Duke	Olympic Track Performer
1955	Dick Hemrick	WF	All-American Basketball
1956	DaveSime	Duke	Olympic Track Performer
1957	Lennie Rosenbluth	UNC	All-American Basketball
1958	Dick Christy	NCS	All-American Football
1959	Lou Pucillo	NCS	All-American Basketball
1960	Mike McGee	Duke	All-American Football
1961	Roman Gabriel	NCS	All-American Football
1962	Len Chappell	WF	All-American Basketball
1963	ArtHeyman	Duke	All-American Basketball
1964	Jeff Mullins	Duke	All-American Basketball
1965	Brian Piccolo	WF	All-American Football
1966	Danny Talbott	UNC	All-ACC Football and Baseball
1967	Bobby Bryant	USC	All-ACC Football and Baseball
1968	Larry Miller	UNC	All-American Basketball
1969	Frank Quayle	Va.	All-ACC Football
1970	Charlie Scott	UNC	All-American Basketball
1971	Don McCauley	UNC	All-American Football
1972	BarryParkhill	Va.	All-American Basketball
1973	David Thompson	NCS	All-American Basketball
1974	Tony Waldrop	UNC	Outstanding Track Performer
1975	David Thompson	NCS	Basketball Player of the Year 1974& 1975
1976	John Lucas	Md.	All-American basketball and Tennis
1977	Phil Ford	UNC	All-American Basketball
1978	Phil Ford	UNC	All-American Basketball

This award is made by the Atlantic Coast Sports Writers Association in honor of the late Anthony J. McKevlin, Sports Editor of the Raleigh *News and Observer*, who died in 1946.

Atlantic Coast Sports Writers Association Presidents

1954	Merrill Whittlesey	The Star	Washington, D.C.
1955	Bob Quincy	Charlotte News	Charlotte, N.C.
1956	Add Penfield	WBIG Radio	Greensboro, N.C.
1957	Frank Spencer	Journal	Winston-Salem, N.C.
1958	Hugo Germino	Durham Sun	Durham, N.C.
1959	Jim Anderson	Greenville News	Greenville, S.C.
1960	Ray Reeve	WRAL–TV	Raleigh, N.C.
1961	Chris Cramer	Charlottesville Daily Progress	Charlottesville, Va.
1962	Jack Horner	Durham Morn. Herald	Durham, N.C.

1963	Whitney Kelley	Charlotte Observer	Charlotte, N.C.
1964	Shelley Rolfe	Richmond Times– Dispatch	Richomond, Va.
1965	Irwin Smallwood	Greensboro Daily News	Greensboro, N.C.
1966	Herman Helms	The State-Record	Columbia, S.C.
1967	Charlie Harville	WGHP–TV	High Point, N.C.
1968	Smith Barrier	Greensboro Daily News	Greensboro, N.C.
1969	Steve Guback	The Star	Washington, D.C.
1970	Leslie Timms	Herald	Spartanburg, S.C.
1971	Bill Jackson	WPTF Radio	Raleigh, N.C.
1972	John Stewart	Morning Sun	Baltimore, Md.
1973	Nick Mayo	Times–Herald	Newport News, Va.
1974	Woody Durham	WFMY–TV	Greensboro, N.C.
1975	Jennings Culley	News–Leader	Richmond, Va.
1976	Dan Daniels	WRC–TV	Washington, D.C.
1977	Mary Garber	Journal	Winston-Salem, N.C.

Executive Secretary: Dick Herbert, Public Relations Director, The American Football Coaches Association 1957–. Smith Barrier, Sports Editor, the Greensboro Daily News 1954–1957.

INDEX

241

Clogston, Roy B. 35, 37, 40, 95, 195
Clonts, Forrest W. 35, 38, 39, 40, 46, 205
Cobey, William W. (Bill) 67, 68, 95, 133
Cobey, William W. (Bill), Jr. 133, 150, 190
Coker, Don 62
Collins, Gary 186
Conner, Martin Sennet (Mike) 24, 29
Connor, Jay 202
Cornwell, Oliver Kelly (Ollie) 35, 38, 45, 46, 53, 73, 78, 112, 113, 190
Corrigan, Eugene F. (Gene) 90, 93, 95, 104, 110, 200, 214
Craven, Braxton 132
Craven, Ken 114
Crawford, Fred 174
Crompton, Geof 147
Crowell, John Franklin 174
Crozier, J. Richard 204
Crum, Dick 145, 188
Cummings, Jack 69
Cunningham, Bennie 172
Cunningham, Billy 94, 189

Darden, Colgate 44, 51, 52, 200
Daugherty, Duffy 57
Davis, Bob 199, 201
Davis, Charlie 205, 208
Davis, Craig 149
Davis, Nick 67
Davis, Walter 136, 139, 189
Dedmon, Lee 109
Dennard, Kenny 142, 149, 155
Denton, Randy 108
Derr, Paul 195
Dick, Larry 132, 143
Dietzel, Paul 85, 87, 96, 131, 139, 210, 212
Dillard, Harrison 59
Dobson, Frank 169
Dodd, Robert (Bobby) 44, 131, 159, 180
Donnan, Jim 90, 92
Dooley, Bill 114, 143, 145, 163, 188
Dooley, Vince 114
Doonan, Al 89
Dougherty, N.W. 29
Drisell, Charles (Lefty) 97, 183, 185
Dudley, William L. 12, 13, 14, 199
Duke, Benjamin 173
Duke, James Buchanan 173
Duke, Washington 173
Dunn, Mike 138
DuPre, Billy 97

Easterling, Don 195
Edens, Hollis 42, 43, 176
Edge, "Junior" 79
Edwards, Earle 57, 92, 112, 199, 193, 196
Edwards, Robert C. 83, 106, 110, 117, 132, 170
Eldridge, Pete 115, 116
Elias, Bill 199
Eliot, Charles William 4
Elkins, Wilson H. 184
Elmore, Len 184
Enberg, Dick 156
Enright, Rex 35, 42, 59, 66, 72, 209, 211
Eppley, Geary P. 35, 38, 40, 49, 184
Erikson, Charles P. (Chuck) 35, 36, 40, 42, 50, 95, 133, 141, 142, 190
Evans, Johnny 144, 194

Faber, John 104, 130, 184
Fadum, Ralph 86, 90, 110, 111, 112, 117, 120
Faloney, Bernie 183
Farrington, Max 38, 39
Feathers, Beattie 193
Feldman, Ellen 130
Fetzer, Bob 95, 142
Fike, Rupert 168
Fisher, Hilbert A. 35, 38, 195
Flax, Sam 158
Fletcher, Jay 108
Ford, Phil 127, 129, 136, 139, 140, 142, 146, 147, 148, 150, 151, 154, 189
Foster, Bill (Clemson) 169
Foster, Bill (Duke) 152, 156, 157, 175
Francis, Marvin A. (Skeeter) 96, 214
Freeman, E.V. 194
Friday, William C. 45, 64, 76, 80, 142, 190, 195
Fritts, Stan 121, 123, 124, 144
Fulcher, Bill 180
Fuller, Steve 144, 164, 169
Funkhouser, W.D. 29

Gabriel, Roman 98, 194
Galantai, Billy 73
Gallagher, Don 76
Gambrell, Billy 210, 212
Gammon, Von 13
Garcia, Randy 143
Garrett, Kenny 108
Garrison, Wilton 44
Gerard, Gerry 175